TONGERLONG

Henry Reynolds is one of Australia's most recognised historians. He grew up in Hobart and was educated at Hobart High School and the University of Tasmania. In 1965, he accepted a lectureship at the University College of Townsville (now James Cook University), which sparked an interest in the history of relations between settlers and Aboriginal people. In 2000, he took up a professorial fellowship at the University of Tasmania. His pioneering work has changed the way we see the intertwining of black and white history in Australia. His books with NewSouth include *The Other Side of the Frontier* (reissue); *What's Wrong with Anzac?* (as co-author); *Forgotten War*, which won the Victorian Premier's Award for Non-Fiction; *Unnecessary Wars*; *This Whispering in Our Hearts Revisited* and most recently *Truth-Telling: History, Sovereignty and the Uluru Statement*.

Nicholas Clements is an eighth generation Tasmanian who has spent most of his life in the Tamar Valley. In addition to being a family man and a keen rock climber, he is a part-time teacher of history, philosophy and psychology. He is also an adjunct researcher at the University of Tasmania, where he completed his PhD on the island's Aboriginal and early contact histories. His 2014 book, *The Black War: Fear, Sex and Resistance in Tasmania*, explored the motivations and experiences of both Aborigines and colonists during that conflict.

'Raw and engaging, Reynolds and Clements have rescued this forgotten hero from obscurity. Despite being stripped of their lore and having British law imposed upon them, Tongerlongeter and his allies fought fiercely for their country. I admire them greatly.'

Dianne Baldock, CEO of Circular Head Aboriginal Corporation

'Through meticulous research and imaginative reconstruction, Reynolds and Clements have given Tasmania a new hero – Tongerlongeter. Australians should revere him as much as their Anzac heroes – he defended his country to the death.'

Professor Peter Stanley, UNSW Canberra

'I felt proud reading the story of Tongerlongeter and his epic resistance who, in 19th century words, "held their ground bravely for 30 years against the invaders of their beautiful domains". Reynolds and Clements reveal the guardians of empire in turmoil. Did we know? We do now.'

John Pilger, journalist, writer and documentary filmmaker

'Henry Reynolds and Nicholas Clements have worked some powerful historical magic to conjure out of a dark and foggy Tasmanian past the image of a tall, handsome, noble warrior named Tongerlongeter ...'

Charles Wooley, *The Weekend Australian*

'This is a book about a war hero, his people, and his allies, men and women who fought the longest, in proportion the bloodiest, and among the most consequential wars in Australia's history. They fought with courage and skill until almost all of them were dead, and even then, the survivors did not surrender. They fought with honour for freedom and love of country.

Why have we never heard of them? Why can't we pronounce their names, let alone say them with respect?

A great reckoning must come in Australia. We must be clearer on who was patriot and who invader; who was defending land, Law and people and who cast that aside. We need to see that both sides lost, one all that life and liberty hold dear, the other the keys to living with this land.

This book does not remedy injustice, but it recognises it. It offers Tongerlongeter, his people and his allies respect, recognition and regret. May it be one of many such books.'

Emeritus Professor Bill Gammage, author of *The Biggest Estate on Earth: How Aborigines Made Australia*

For Kristy

TONGERLONGETER

FIRST NATIONS LEADER
& TASMANIAN WAR HERO

HENRY REYNOLDS &
NICHOLAS CLEMENTS

NEWSOUTH

A NewSouth book

Published by
NewSouth Publishing
University of New South Wales Press Ltd
University of New South Wales
Sydney NSW 2052
AUSTRALIA
https://unsw.press/

A catalogue record for this book is available from the National Library of Australia

ISBN: 9781742237770 (paperback)
            9781742238609 (ebook)
            9781742239521 (ePDF)

Design Josephine Pajor-Markus
Cover design Peter Long
Cover image Tukalunginta (Tongerlongeter), watercolour by Thomas Bock (1832). British Museum, London
Printer Griffin Press

Contents

Authors' note   viii

Introduction: Remembering their sacrifice   1

1   An extraordinary day   12

2   The explorers arrive   24

3   Confrontation at Risdon   35

4   Coming of age   52

5   Zombie invasion   76

6   A wayward brother   93

7   Retribution: 1824–27   110

8   Resistance: 1828–30   129

9   Striking terror: 1828–30   146

10   White devils   164

11   Things fall apart   182

12   Armistice   203

13   Exile   226

14   'Till all the black men are dead'   247

Conclusion: 'A brave and patriotic people'   266

Afterword   286

Acknowledgments   290

Notes   292

Index   337

Authors' note

The subject of this book, the warrior chief Tongerlongeter, is first named in the records four days before the end of the Black War – the bitter frontier conflict that consumed eastern Tasmania from 1823 to 1831. With the exception of his wayward kinsman Kickertopoller, who spent nearly four years living with a prominent Hobart family, no one fighting for Tongerlongeter's Oyster Bay nation or its ally, the Big River nation, was identified by name until the very end of the war. Even with the retrospective evidence of Tongerlongeter's involvement, piecing together his probable movements and thinking was a complicated exercise. In addition to clues in the written evidence, which included the broader ethnographic sources on how Tasmanian Aborigines (Tasmanians) thought and lived, Nick compiled a tally of some 900 incidents in which Tongerlongeter or his allies were likely involved. This fully referenced compendium, which can be accessed at <https://dx.doi.org/10.25959/hpxk-5f95> and lists every recorded attack on and by Oyster Bay – Big River people, helped us to identify and analyse patterns of resistance in south-east and central Tasmania. We have done our best to provide an accurate picture of Tongerlongeter's life, but in some respects, he remains as elusive to us as he did to the colonists.

We (Henry and Nick) are friends united in our passion for frontier history, and in our conviction that Tongerlongeter and others like him deserve to be commemorated. Neither of us was in a position to write this book alone. Henry, at eighty-two, has been researching and writing about Australian frontier history for more than half a century. His commanding perspective on how Tongerlongeter's story fits into the vast scope of Australian and imperial history, as well as his knowledge of the political landscape, made him the perfect person to bookend this great warrior's story. Nick, forty-four years Henry's junior and his PhD student between 2009 and 2012, has an extensive knowledge of the primary sources relating to the Black War. By dragnetting the colonial archive, Nick was able to tell the finer-grained story, while Henry was in the best position to reveal its broader significance. It could not have been a more harmonious or fruitful collaboration.

Although there are many gaps in the historical records relating to the Black War and its aftermath, particularly when it comes to the Aboriginal perspective, Tasmania's source material is remarkably abundant. A succession of British and French exploring expeditions to south-east Tasmania provided a rich record of pre-colonial life among Tongerlongeter's people and their neighbours. The colonial government kept expansive and well-organised records of the conflict, and the writings of numerous columnists, correspondents and diarists also survive. But by far the most valuable source is George Augustus Robinson, the missionary and government agent who spent ten years living with the Tasmanians. Robinson was by no means an objective witness, yet his voluminous journals and papers provide an unrivalled snapshot of Aboriginal experiences, beliefs and behaviours. What's more, Robinson developed a strong, mutually dependent relationship with Tongerlongeter, who appears often in his writings.

We have also done our best to take the historical investigation of frontier violence out of the abstract and into the messy reality of the 1820s and 1830s. When reasoning about events, every element, large and small, must be considered *in context*. A historian must have a detailed knowledge of the Tasmanian landscape and climate. They must also have the fullest picture of the situation that historical records can afford, being mindful of the prejudices, blind spots and motives of those involved. But even when drawing on all these strategies and sources, absolute certainty is rare. We have attempted to convey our degree of certainty by using qualified language. And while we have done our utmost to be rigorous and impartial, the nature of the evidence is such that we will inevitably have made some incorrect assumptions.

Some of the language used in colonial sources is considered inappropriate today, but we do not believe in shielding the reader, and have always remained true to the original wording. Some Aboriginal people prefer terms and spellings that differ from those we have used, but because of the lack of consensus here, we have chosen our terms with a range of considerations in mind. When in doubt, we have used those most common at the time. 'Native', while technically accurate, has attracted too many negative connotations over time. More recently, 'Aborigine' has come under similar scrutiny, but in Tasmania, where 'Indigenous' is unpopular, it remains the most appropriate term for a book like this. Even among historians, there is no agreement over some terms.

'The Black War', for instance, is problematic for several reasons, but ultimately less problematic and more widely known than the alternatives. While our terminology will not please every reader, our effort to combine accuracy and sensitivity has been made in good faith.

Early 19th century terminology can be confusing. We have clarified in the text where necessary, but a note on territories must be made here. 'Oyster Bay' is the large bay on the central east coast, but the 'Oyster Bay people/tribe/nation' was the name given to the alliance of bands which occupied a much broader slice of south-east Tasmania. Likewise, the 'Big River' (now the Ouse River) winds its way through just a fraction of the territory of the 'Big River people/tribe/nation', which envelops the Central Plateau and the river valleys to its south (see figure 11). These names evolved in the colonial press and have taken on a life of their own. There were probably Aboriginal names for these allied language groups, but no record of them survives. There is also confusion in the sources regarding the exact locations and status of homelands, as well as the nature of the relationships between and within bands and nations. The assumptions we have made align with those of most historians, but there is legitimate disagreement on some points.

Finally, it is our sincerest hope that all readers, but especially Aboriginal readers, find our research interesting and useful, for it is our fascination with Aboriginal cultures and histories that has driven us to write this and other books over the years. Admiration for people like Tongerlongeter transcends race, culture and creed – he is someone we can all look up to.

Introduction:
Remembering their sacrifice

Henry Reynolds

I began planning this introduction on 2 May 2022, three years and one week from when I started to write the introduction to the first edition. A fresh introduction to a new edition is obviously a good idea, but in this case it is essential given the changes that have taken place since 2019. The pandemic altered and circumscribed all our lives in a myriad of ways. Fires and floods dramatically intensified concern about damaging climate change. Other developments have more direct relevance for the substance of this book. As I write, a disastrous war is raging in Eastern Europe and rumours of a new Cold War proliferate. Australian leaders talk about preparing ourselves for coming conflict. But the past has haunted us as well. Racial tension in America gave impetus to the Black Lives Matter movement which had reverberations elsewhere in the world, including Australia. Slavery's dark legacy matters as well in many countries. In both America and Britain individuals and institutions wrestle with their respective country's deep involvement with, and manifest benefits bestowed by, the trade. Reputations are reconsidered;

monuments are removed. In the British Caribbean, demands for reparation grow louder and more insistent.

But the spreading tide of protest sweeps up the full legacy of European imperialism while running parallel with the even more momentous shift of economic and political power away from the north Atlantic to east and south Asia, to many countries once pinioned to European imperial overlords. Historical interpretation moves in harmony. The place of violence in both acquisition and preservation of empire is revisited. The central role of white racism undermines the myth of benign paternalism. Resistance to colonialism is rediscovered and celebrated. Forgotten warriors are brought back into national histories and accorded respect and honour. The resistance of small societies in places remote from the imperial capitals have now found a niche in the global saga of anti-colonialism.

It is our belief that Tongerlongeter fully deserves a place in this global story. Like many comparable figures in various parts of the world he has been retrieved from obscurity. We were keenly aware of this situation when we decided to tell the story of his life. He was virtually unknown even in Tasmania. This seemed an extraordinary situation. Local historians had been writing about the so-called Black War since the middle of the 19th century. At no stage had they shunned the subject or avoided the brutal reality of the British invasion. For their part, the local First Nation's community appeared to have forgotten Tongerlongeter, too. Some years ago, the Tasmanian Museum and Art Gallery set aside a large space for an exhibition about the war and worked closely with prominent members of the Aboriginal community. The display was widely and justifiably applauded. But there was no mention of Tongerlongeter nor a proper appreciation of the central role of the resistance by the Oyster Bay and Big River Nations.

Little appreciated in Tasmania – and until we first published his story in 2021 – Tongerlongeter was virtually unknown in the rest of Australia. The extraordinary saga of resistance by his warrior bands needs to be incorporated into our collective story of the frontier wars. But the story itself has been a highly contentious subject and for at least a generation one of the central fixtures of the ongoing culture wars. This should not be surprising. Australian historians have had difficulty with frontier conflict for a long time. They rarely dealt with it in the first half of the 20th century. Students reading the numerous general histories written in the 1950s and 1960s would have learnt very little on the subject. The abundant evidence in the colonial records – in books, official documents and newspapers – sat disregarded on shelves in libraries and archives. But what the great anthropologist WEH Stanner called the 'Great Australian Silence' in his 1968 Boyer Lectures was being challenged from a variety of directions.[1] Decolonisation in the wider world, the civil rights movement in the United States and growing assertiveness in Indigenous Australia was filling the soundscape with confronting voices. A new generation of historians responded with troubling stories. Everywhere they looked they came across evidence of conflict. They recorded forgotten incidents and unmistakable evidence of brutality and violence. They began the very difficult task of counting the death toll and identifying sites of mass killings. Eventually, the challenging, revisionist scholarship reached into every corner of the continent. Slowly, and often with reluctance, the nation came to accept the mounting evidence of conflict and the changes it forced on the overall image of our heritage. The once sunny story of peaceful pioneering could not survive.

While the new history of the frontier still arouses controversy, and indeed, residual hostility, it has come to influence the way the subject is taught in Australian schools, and pervades the work of novelists, poets, filmmakers, dramatists and visual artists. Yet big unresolved questions persist. Was frontier conflict warfare? If so, how does it compare to Australia's overseas wars? While they may appear to be simple questions, they require serious forensic examination. They also need to be approached from two directions – from the perspective of the colonists and then from that of the First Nations.

There was always plenty of evidence about frontier conflict in the public sphere of the separate colonies. No well-informed person would have been unaware of the manner in which the settlers gained control of country out on the frontiers. But whether it was war as recognised by European opinion or indeed by international law is a more complex question. At the very heart of the matter is the inescapable fact that the imperial government declared at the beginning of settlement in 1788 that the Aborigines had become British subjects, and this remained the case for all but a brief period between 1825 and 1837. The significance of this for

Tasmania will be considered shortly, but most Aborigines, for most of the time, were accorded the legal status of British subjects. Consequently, their violent resistance could be seen as criminal behaviour or as rebellion against the Crown, but it could not be regarded as warfare.

The second legal instrument employed by the imperial authorities was the declaration that the Aborigines did not exercise sovereignty over their home territories, nor did they have any legal claim over the land. This infamous doctrine of terra nullius applied all over the continent and remained embedded in Australian law until it was excised by the High Court in the *Mabo* case in 1992. The full implications of these pernicious legal ideas are not always appreciated. They had a powerful influence over the way frontier conflict was understood. For whatever conflict was about, it could not be about property or sovereignty; that is, about the ownership or control of territory, which have always been the great strategic issues at the heart of military conflict. So fighting on the frontier lacked the status of warfare as the Europeans understood it. It equated more to lesser forms of violence, akin to banditry, vendetta or common criminality, caused by such matters as theft, trespass, revenge or contested possession of women.

As in so many other areas, the *Mabo* case transformed our understanding of history. The High Court declared that Indigenous Australians were in possession of their traditional lands at the time of British settlement, and that their laws and customs could be recognised by the common law. In other words, they exercised a form of sovereignty over their own country. These principles applied all over the continent, from the Murray Islands in the far north to the southernmost point of Tasmania. The implications for history writing emerged slowly, but they were dramatic. Frontier conflict, wherever and whenever it occurred, had to be about the ownership and control of land. There was no other possible interpretation. The fighting, no matter how scattered or desultory, was warfare as it was understood in European jurisprudence. Given that it was practically universal and about the ownership and control of land over the whole continent, it had to be regarded as a war of the greatest consequence. Arguably, it was Australia's most significant war. It was fought on this country for this country. It was instrumental in a change in land ownership on a scale rarely equalled elsewhere in the world. Eventually, Australians will come to see that our own frontier wars mattered more to us than those issues in contention during the Great War of 1914–18 – the balance of power in Europe or the carving up of the Ottoman Empire.

But there was another historical change of the law that influenced the understanding of frontier conflict in Tasmania and New South Wales between 1825 and 1837. It mattered far more in Tasmania because it coincided with the intense frontier conflict between 1826 and 1831. As a result of fighting around Bathurst, in modern-day New South Wales, in 1824, the British government adopted a new policy to cope with Aboriginal resistance. It applied equally to Tasmania, and actually arrived as written instructions in Hobart before it reached Sydney. George Arthur, governor of Tasmania (then Van Diemen's Land) from 1824 to 1836, was obliged to put them into practice. He had no choice in the matter. The document contained provisions regarding 'the manner in which the Native Inhabitants' were to be treated when making 'hostile incursions for the purpose of plunder'. The Secretary of State for the Colonies, Lord Bathurst, instructed the two governors that they should

> understand it to be your duty, when such disturbances cannot be prevented or allayed by less vigorous measures, to oppose force by force, and to repel such Aggressions in the same manner as if they proceeded from subjects of an accredited State.[2]

The clear intention was to treat the Aborigines as if they were members of a foreign country. They were now to be considered enemies rather than rebellious subjects. Resulting conflict was not domestic insurgency – it was warfare.

There is abundant evidence that Arthur used Bathurst's instructions as a guide to the development of his Aboriginal policy. This is hardly surprising. He actually read the instructions to his officials and advisers on numerous occasions. This was the case when, in November 1828, he declared martial law in the central districts of the island. This was a quite radical decision. Martial law was rarely used in Britain itself, even when the country was at war. The colony's Solicitor-General, Alfred Stephen, explained that the effect of the proclamation introducing martial law was 'to place the aborigine, within the prescribed limits on a footing of open enemies of the King, in a state of actual warfare against him.'[3] Arthur referred to war again and again in his official correspondence, as did many settlers when they wrote to him and to the local newspapers. Both the quantity and the nature of the pertinent evidence puts the matter beyond doubt. Settler society in Tasmania in the 1820s was engaged in a war with the Aborigines of the interior, and in particular with the Oyster Bay – Big River nations, which bore the brunt of the fighting.

Although the colony's principal legal officer declared that the Aborigines were in a state of warfare against the King, they obviously had no idea who the King was and at best an uncertain understanding of where the white men had come from. But what about war? There is no simple answer. The way the various Aboriginal nations experienced invasion differed widely. Along the south-east coast, numerous European exploring expeditions dropped anchor in the sheltered bays between 1772 and 1802. Shore parties searched for water and collected plants, birds and animals. They had largely peaceful relations with the resident family groups.

We have no idea how widely news of these extraordinary events was carried to the other nations across the island. A generation of such visits had established a pattern of behaviour. The great ships sailed into view, stopped for a short while and then just as suddenly disappeared over the horizon. But everything changed and changed forever when three large parties of settlers arrived in a little over a year in 1803–04, two on the Derwent and one on the Tamar (see figure 12). The watching Aborigines may well have observed that the activities of these parties differed from what they had seen before. Still, the idea that the strangers had arrived for good may have needed some time to take root. The behaviour and intentions of the settlers must have been the subject of debate in the flickering light of innumerable camp fires.

The most common response was to watch the white men closely while avoiding close contact, even when parties of explorers and hunters ventured out into the hinterland. It was not hard to do. The strangers' progress across country was monitored; the landowners knew their country intimately, and in the early years they could invariably out-travel any party advancing on foot. There was sporadic small-scale conflict during the first twenty years of settlement. The large, more substantial confrontation at the Risdon settlement on the east bank of the Derwent in April 1804 is exceptional and will be discussed in chapter 3. Every now and then, Aborigines confronted individuals or small parties of Europeans who were wounded or killed as a result. Was this war though? It is more likely that Europeans were attacked because in some way or another they had transgressed the laws and customs of the lands on which they had intruded. They were punished accordingly, yet it was specific and individual, more what was in effect law enforcement than warfare.

What the Aborigines could not know was that the small struggling settlements were merely the beachheads for the massive inflow of free settlers and convicts, which followed the end of the Napoleonic Wars in 1815. The numbers alone must have astonished them. By 1820, the settlers began to pour out into the hinterlands of Hobart and Launceston with their convict servants and what must have seemed a countless number of sheep, which quickly spread across prime hunting grounds and critical river frontages. Avoidance became increasingly difficult. Traditional patterns of hunting, gathering and travel were disrupted. Conflict intensified; mutual hostility spiralled out of control.

This was particularly the case on the traditional lands of the Oyster Bay – Big River nations, which stretched in a broad band across the most desirable land on the island (see figure 12). Some time in the middle years of the 1820s, the transition was made from tribal justice to all-out war. Whether this was a conscious decision made at a particular time as a result of wide consultation, we will never know. But the objective had become intensely political. It was to drive the settlers and their animals off the ancestral hunting grounds. The resulting 'Black War', which engulfed much of central and eastern Tasmania between 1823 and 1831, was the most intense and lethal struggle in the long history of Australia's frontier conflict. The war parties led by the Oyster Bay chief Tongerlongeter and his allies were by far the most successful resistance force in the whole of Australia. They paid a terrible price. By the end of the war there were only twenty-six of their countrymen and -women alive, sixteen men, nine women and one child. Their nation would have numbered about 1000 when the British arrived on the island.

We are unable to date the precise beginning of the Black War, but we know exactly when and how it ended. On the last day of December 1831, the surviving twenty-six met Aboriginal members of George Augustus Robinson's 'friendly mission'. Robinson was a zealous missionary who saw himself as God's instrument in saving the 'benighted natives', but the real work of negotiating with the 'hostile tribes' was done by his Aboriginal guides. They were peaceful government envoys hoping to talk the warriors out of continued resistance. The two parties negotiated an armistice. It was not a capitulation. Robinson explained that the warrior band had accepted the offers of the government. They had agreed to go with Robinson's party to Hobart to meet the governor. That evening the two Aboriginal parties danced in turn. A week later, on the morning of 7 January, the whole party walked down the hill on Hobart's northern outskirts into Elizabeth Street and on to Government House, situated on a promontory overlooking the Derwent Estuary.

CHAPTER I

An extraordinary day

Henry Reynolds

Saturday 7 January 1832 was an extraordinary day in Hobart Town. It still looks that way 189 years later. That morning the *Hobart Town Courier* reported, 'with no small pleasure', the gratifying news that the Oyster Bay – Big River nations, 'the most sanguinary in the island', had surrendered themselves to the missionary George Augustus Robinson.[1] They were expected to arrive in town early in the morning. News obviously spread very quickly and by ten o'clock an expectant crowd had gathered at vantage points along Elizabeth Street, the presumed route the party would take down the gradual incline through the town to Government House. The two local papers gave contrasting reports of the event. The *Colonial Times* remarked that 'a more grotesque appearance we have seldom witnessed'. The *Courier*, reporting in its next issue a week later, observed that the party had walked very leisurely along the road accompanied by a large pack of dogs 'and were received by the inhabitants on their entry into town with the most lively curiosity and delight'. It was a mixed party, led by

Robinson and his son, his party of thirteen Aboriginal associates, and the twenty-six survivors of the war. The men had been given government-issue heavy cotton (or 'duck', as they were called) trousers, to wear before they progressed down Elizabeth Street. That concession notwithstanding, they did not come as prisoners or supplicants. The *Colonial Times* reported they were arrayed 'in battle order', each male carrying three spears in his left hand and one in his right, and as they continued advancing 'they shrieked their war song'.[2] As the procession approached Government House, Governor Arthur came out to meet them.

The delight of the crowd was unsurprising. It was a reasonable assumption that the Black War was now over, as indeed it was. Almost everyone had been touched by it in some way. In the previous eight years, Oyster Bay and Big River war parties had launched at least 711 attacks, killing or wounding 354 colonists. Well over 300 huts had been plundered or destroyed. Aboriginal nations in the north of the island also put up considerable resistance, but nothing comparable to what Tongerlongeter and his allies were able to effect.[3] Much of the violence had happened close to Hobart, not out on a distant frontier, and often no more than a few days' walk away. Most of these incidents were reported in the local newspapers and must have been the subject of many worried conversations. Anyone who had travelled into the rural districts had done so in a state of high anxiety. Robinson observed that the very name of the Oyster Bay – Big River nations was a source of terror among colonists.[4] Living in a small community, townspeople must have known some of the casualties. People who recovered from their wounds would have been seen about the streets. Veterans of the fighting must have enlivened many gatherings with stories that gained colour with the telling. Many of the men in the crowd would have been involved in the Black Line in October and November 1830, when almost 2200 convicts, settlers and soldiers tramped across the rugged, forested hills and valleys of the interior in a fruitless campaign to capture or kill Tongerlongeter and his warriors.[5] Women and children would have remembered how they had waited anxiously for as long as seven weeks to hear from their menfolk before they eventually returned home safely from the bush.

A big man draped in a cloak, his sad eyes unwavering beneath a heavy brow, Tongerlongeter must have been an imposing figure as he strode down Elizabeth Street for his meeting with the governor. The reaction of the crowd would surely have been one of surprise bordering on amazement that there were so few warriors left. The question that many spectators must have asked was how such a small band could have wreaked such havoc. It had been a reasonable expectation of both the government and the community that they were confronting a very much larger force sequestered in the trackless hills and mountains. It is also interesting that there were almost no calls for vengeance, no demands for prosecution or imprisonment. There is no evidence they were regarded as criminals. The contrast with the treatment of the bushranging gangs is instructive. Many people in the crowd that morning would have stood in a similar place when captured bushrangers had been brought in from the bush.

They came heavily chained. Their appointment was with the judge and the hangman, not with the governor.

The killing of two men in the north of the colony a few months earlier had triggered a debate over what to do with Aborigines who had blood on their hands. It elicited one of the most interesting discussions of the status of Aboriginal warriors. In a letter to a Launceston newspaper a correspondent 'J.E.' (almost certainly the surveyor James Erskine Calder) asked his readers:

Are these unhappy creatures the *subjects* of our king, in a state of rebellion? or are they an injured people, whom we have invaded and with whom we are at war? Are they within the reach of our laws; or are they to be judged by the law of nations? Are they to be viewed in the light of murderers, or as prisoners of war? Have they been guilty of any crime under the law of nations which is punishable by death, or have they only been carrying on a war *in their way?* Are they British subjects at all, or a foreign enemy who has never yet been subdued, and which resists our usurped authority and dominion? …

What we call their crime is what in a white man we should call patriotism. Where is the man amongst ourselves who would not resist an invading enemy; who would not avenge the murder of his parents, the ill-usage of his wife and daughters, and the spoliation of all his earthly goods, by a foreign enemy, if he had an opportunity? He who would not do so would be scouted, execrated, nay executed as a coward and a traitor; while

he who did would be immortalised as a patriot ... How
can we condemn as a crime in these savages what we
should esteem a virtue in ourselves?[6]

We can only speculate about what the twenty-six survivors thought of their journey from the Central Plateau to
meet the governor. They entered what for them was foreign
territory when they crossed the Derwent into the traditional
territory of the South-Eastern nation. The town itself, with a
population approaching 10 000, would have been a revelation.
They may now and then have watched what was happening
from their own country on the eastern shore of the Derwent,
but nothing would have prepared them for the innumerable
buildings of all shapes and sizes that had been constructed
during their lifetimes. They must have been astonished at the
great crowds of people who watched their progression down
Elizabeth Street. Their experience with Europeans had been
with the small groups who had pursued them or who lived
and worked on the rural properties.

There is no doubt they came willingly. They must have
longed for peace even more than the frontier settlers had.
They had been suddenly released from the vice-like grip of
unbearable anxiety, which had for years constricted their
lives. They had been hunted by British soldiers and the far
more lethal gangs of vigilantes. The Black Line (discussed in
detail in chapter 10) must have been a terrifying sight, with
large fires lit at night right across the homeland. While they
had characteristically avoided their pursuers during daylight

hours, they were always at risk of night attacks as they sat or slept by their camp fires. Troubled, broken sleep must have become chronic. And then there was the constant loss of their kin: men, women and children who were shot down, or who succumbed to the awesome rigours of the never-ending war of attrition. It would have been a reasonable assumption that there was no escape, that they would go on fighting until they too were hunted down. As it was, many of them had been injured, Tongerlongeter included. They showed their wounds to Robinson when he heard 'the vehement denunciations of the cruelties of the Europeans'. He later reported that all of the 'men, women and child had dreadful scars'.[7]

There is no detailed record of their meeting with George Arthur. With Robinson's envoys translating, it is very likely that Tongerlongeter repeated his people's acute grievances and outlined the suffering they had endured out in the bush. As a professional soldier, Arthur must have appreciated the tenacity and bravery of the men who had come to him seeking justice. He wrote to the Colonial Office in 1833 that he found it distressing to recall the 'injuries that the Government [was] unwillingly and unavoidably made the instrument of ... driving a simple but warlike and, as it now appears, noble-minded race from their hunting grounds'.[8] Having farewelled his visitors, who spent the night camping outside Robinson's house on the northern edge of the town, Arthur returned to his desk and wrote a hurried dispatch to the Colonial Office, 'detailing the general proceedings of the Government in this lamented and protracted warfare'. He explained that the most sanguinary of the Tribes under the [allied] chiefs 'Montpelliatier' and 'Tongerlongter,' who have always acted in unison, have at length been conciliated … and that 26 of them have, at their own desire, held a conference with me in Hobart Town, from whence with their own concurrence, as well for their own safety as for the security of the Settlers, they will be immediately embarked for Great Island where they will be treated with all kindness that humanity can dictate. I trust I may with confidence anticipate that there is now an end of the suffering of the Settlers from the bitter scourge from which the Colony has so severely suffered for many years. It is impossible not to reflect with sorrow upon the indiscriminate vengeance by which these savages have been influenced, but, as their wrongs have been many and great, His Majesty's Government will, I trust, regard them with the utmost compassion, and continue to extend both protection and kindness towards them in the asylum which has been provided for their habitation on Great Island.[9]

Arthur reflected on the consequences of the Black War, explaining that the 'continued hostility' of the natives had 'operated most injuriously in many ways'. Great expense had been incurred, dissatisfaction induced, improvements retarded, and immigration checked. He then referred to the new settlement underway in Western Australia and hoped that lessons learnt in Tasmania would be applied there. He proposed that official protectors be appointed to learn the local languages and institute a formal process for the purchase of Aboriginal land. These were policies by which, had they been in place in Tasmania, 'many deplorable consequences would have been averted'.[10]

It is significant that Arthur provided no detail about the negotiations with Tongerlongeter, because his dispatches were characteristically full of fine detail about the affairs of the colony. What promises were made that persuaded the warriors to travel to a distant island they had probably never seen before? The absolutely critical question is, was the exile to be temporary or permanent? It is extremely unlikely that they would have agreed to leave their homelands forever. We know what Robinson promised to prominent Aboriginal leaders. They would be able to return to their own country after a period on Flinders Island and there would be no attempt to subvert their cultural traditions.[11] His Aboriginal envoys, who did most of the actual negotiation, would have been fully aware of these promises, and they had without doubt been conveyed to Tongerlongeter and his comrades in arms. Arthur too was aware of the promises Robinson was making. He approved them. And in the meeting at Government House, Arthur almost certainly reaffirmed these promises. But did he intend to keep them? That we will never know.

His failure to mention the subject in his official correspondence suggests he thought it better to allow the promises to be abandoned. Clearly, had he put these promises in writing they would have carried far greater authority. They could have been taken up by the Colonial Office, which was developing growing humanitarian concern for the Empire's indigenous peoples. Arthur's dispatch gives the impression of a letter dashed off at the end of a very full day, yet the phrasing was very careful. He told the Colonial Office that the warriors had come in from the bush, 'at their own desire', and that the agreement to go to Flinders Island was, 'with their own concurrence'.

In this way, much of the actual story was skilfully elided. It allowed Arthur to leave out the promises that had consummated what was in essence a peace treaty. The warriors had met Robinson's party, which had been pursuing them for months. As later chapters will reveal, it was Robinson's initiative and it was clearly an official operation. The concurrence was the result of quite specific promises which they had every reason to believe would be honoured. But Arthur was in a difficult position. If it became known that there was a secret agreement to allow Tongerlongeter and his followers to return to the Tasmanian mainland, the settlers would have reacted with incessant hostility. And there is no doubt he believed, with good reason, that the settlers would resume their attacks and the surviving Aborigines would be shot down in the bush. In his mind, he may have believed he had betrayed their trust for their own good.

The warriors spent ten days in Hobart, initially at Robinson's house and then on a ship in the Derwent. We know almost nothing about what they did during that time. There were no reports in the local papers. Calder recalled years later that thousands of curious visitors walked up Elizabeth Street to look at them where they were camping in the open ground next to Robinson's house.[12] The small circle of journalists did not show much interest in them, unlike the town's professional painters, who grasped the opportunity to sketch both Robinson's envoys and Tongerlongeter's people. They appreciated the historical significance of the events that brought the war to an end. John Glover and Thomas Bock visited the two parties, probably when they were camped at Robinson's house.[13] Bock drew a highly competent pencil sketch of Tongerlongeter (see figure 2) and followed up with an oil painting now in the British Museum (see figure 1). Glover employed his sketches in his important painting of Hobart as seen from the eastern shore, where Aborigines are dancing on the shore and swimming in the Derwent. Hobart is bathed in light, the Aborigines are in the shade. We are not sure if Glover actually saw the two parties on the eastern shore of the Derwent and swimming in the river or whether they were placed there for symbolic effect, to illustrate the island's past and its future.

Local poets were inspired as well. 'Hobartia' declared:

> They came, sad remnant of a bygone race,
> Surviving mourners of a nation dead;
> Proscribed inheritors of rights which trace
> Their claims coeval with the world!
> They came like straggling leaves together blown,
> The last memorial of the foliage past.

A second poem, 'Lines Written on the Recent Visit of the Aborigines to Hobart Town', was similarly elegiac:

They are come in their pride, but no helmet is gleaming
On the dark-brow'd race of their native land;
No lances are glittering, nor bright banners streaming,
O'er the warriors brave of that gallant band.
They are come in their pride, but no war-cry is sounding,
With its woe-fraught note, over hill and plain;
For the hearts of those dark ones with gladness are
     bounding,
And bright songs of peace breathe loud in their strain.
They are come – they are come, and a boon they're
     imploring,
Oh! Turn not away from their soul-felt prayer,
But to high hopes of heaven this lost race restoring,
For yourselves gain mercy and pardon there.[14]

The interest of Hobart's painters and poets notwith-standing, the twenty-six survivors sailed down the Derwent without fanfare in a small crowded ship for the Furneaux Islands never to return. When he came to write his celebrated two-volume *History of Tasmania* twenty years later, John West took up the elegiac strain observing: 'It was, indeed, a mournful spectacle: the last Tasmanian quitting the shores of his ancestors! ... A change so rapid in the relations of a people to the soil, will scarcely find a parallel in this world's history'. The Chief Justice, John Pedder, opposed the removal altogether, believing that, 'it would be followed by rapid extinction. In denying to the aboriginal remnant an asylum within the country of their forefathers, we inflicted the last penalty which can fall on a race, whose lives the victors condescend to spare.'[15]

Tongerlongeter, the man who led Australia's most effective Aboriginal resistance campaign, died on Flinders Island off the north-east coast of mainland Tasmania. His was an extraordinary, tragic life. He witnessed the utter catastrophe that overwhelmed his people. As a child, he would have been brought up and educated in the ancient ways of his nation. He likely heard from his parents of the utterly inexplicable visit of the French expedition of Marion du Fresne in 1772 to the grand bay on the south-east coast that now bears the explorer's name. Along with his kin, he may have heard accounts of the numerous ships that had visited the lower reaches of the Derwent Estuary during his childhood. He was an adolescent when members of the French expedition of Nicolas Baudin came ashore on Maria Island in 1802 and may well have been there at the time. Even if he were elsewhere during that transient visit of eleven days, he would have heard many accounts of the way the white men behaved and listened as the older people grappled with the insoluble problems of where the strangers had come from and why they had suddenly appeared. He was probably in the Coal Valley two years later when his people came into conflict with the settlers' camp at Risdon on the east side of the Derwent, foreshadowing the brutal warfare that was to overwhelm years of his manhood and see the violent deaths of so many of his kin.

CHAPTER 2

The explorers arrive

Henry Reynolds

The sudden and totally unexpected arrival of European ships off the southern and eastern Australian coasts was an astonishing event. Around the tropical shores in the north they may have been preceded by the praus crossing the Arafura Sea from the Indonesian islands. Very few human beings have ever been confronted with such a dramatic life-changing series of events. The sight of the big ships in full sail offshore was extraordinary enough, and that was all that many coastal-dwelling bands initially saw. But for those living in locations that provided the ships with safe, sheltered anchorage and the promise of fresh water, what they witnessed was awesome in the full, original meaning of that word. Kickertopoller, the Oyster Bay man who became an envoy for George Augustus Robinson, told the missionary that he had been a child on Maria Island in 1802 when the two French ships of the Baudin expedition arrived offshore. The adults of his band 'could not conceive how the white men came here first'. When one morning they saw the ships at anchor off the island, 'they were all frightened and run away, that it looked like a small island and they could not tell what it was'.[1]

François Péron, the French naturalist who was on one of those ships, appreciated the dramatic impact his fellow crew members had on the local Aborigines when they came ashore. 'We were so novel to one another', he wrote:

> We are seeing [these] men at a time when all the faculties
> of their being are magnified. Our ships, the noise of
> our guns and their terrible effect, the colour of our skin,
> our clothing, our form, our gifts, everything we possess,
> everything that surrounds us, our gait, our actions, all are
> such marvels to them.[2]

Traditionally, Oyster Bay bands spent much of their time camped near the shoreline fringing more than half of Tasmania's east coast. The two earliest European expeditions sailed along those shores and briefly dropped anchor in much the same locality. Tasman's expedition of 1642 was the only Dutch exploring venture into southern Australian waters and there was no follow-up at all. The two ships skirted around the south coast and spent two days anchored in Blackman Bay, near today's Dunalley. Two heavily armed parties ventured onto the shore but did not make any contact with the Aborigines, Tasman recording in his journal that the 'natives of this country' did not show themselves 'though we suspect some of them were at no great distance and closely watching our proceedings'.[3] This was very likely the case, but whether any memory of Tasman and his men survived is impossible to say. There was no further European intrusion for 130 years.

In March 1772, two ships of the French expedition led by Marc-Joseph Marion du Fresne anchored in North Bay, about five kilometres from where Tasman had anchored 130 years earlier. A party went ashore and landed without any opposition. Members of the resident band appeared to be 'agreeable' to the landing. In his account of the expedition, Marion du Fresne's second-in-command, Julien-Marie Crozet, explained that they collected firewood and offered

> some dry lighted boughs and appeared to invite them to set fire to the pile. We did not understand what they meant by this ceremony, but we lighted the pile; the savages did not appear at all astonished at this, and they remained round us without making either friendly or hostile demonstrations. The women and children were with them.[4]

The French offered presents of the kind Europeans traditionally carried with them, but the recipients rejected everything 'with disdain', even iron, looking glasses, hand-kerchiefs and pieces of cloth. After an hour, Marion du Fresne himself landed in a second boat. The previous ceremony with the firewood and the lighted brand was repeated. But when it was lit a second time, the Oyster Bay party reacted with immediate hostility, retreated to a high dune and began pelting the Frenchmen with rocks. Marion du Fresne and an officer were hit. The French fired several shots and quickly retreated to their boats. A further landing around the bay provoked a shower of spears. This was met with a 'fusilade' that killed one and wounded several others, 'whereupon they immediately fled into the woods howling fearfully'.[5]

The bands living around and near Marion Bay on the south-east coast were the first Tasmanians to be confronted by visiting Europeans. They were the first to hear the sound of guns and to suffer their lethal impact. They would have told their distant kin about the extraordinary events they had experienced, and the news would have been discussed around camp fires far into the interior. This was the first time in Tasmania that there would have been a serious debate about the secret power of the white men's guns. It was no doubt repeated many times among the island's other nations. The problem everyone faced was to understand how the guns worked. They produced a bright flash as the powder ignited, and then a large bang and at some distance the targeted animal, bird or person was struck and often killed on the spot. The means of propulsion was not immediately apparent, but more mysterious was how it had happened, given that no one could see either the musket ball or the shot, which, on impact, became deeply embedded in the victim's body. The initial idea that magic of some sort was involved increased the sense of danger. Even when the British established their small settlements and guns were stolen and taken away, the mechanism was not immediately apparent.

While Tasman's 1642 visit had been an isolated event, du Fresne's was the forerunner of a dozen British and French exploring expeditions that called into the sheltered bays of southern Tasmania in the last quarter of the 18th century.

During the fifteen years between 1773 and 1788, expeditions led by Tobias Furneaux, James Cook and William Bligh spent time in Adventure Bay on Bruny Island. We have no idea if the Oyster Bay bands knew anything about their sojourns or had distant sight of their ships passing around their territory on the south-east coast. But in September 1789, Maria Island was visited briefly by a British ship on a private speculative voyage. Crew members were only on shore for a few days, and though they spent some time 'in endeavouring to inspire these poor people with confidence … they kept retreating very fast'. Seeing a fire in the distance, a party hurried forward attempting to secure a meeting, 'but the natives fled before our arrival'.[6] The assumption was that they had been alarmed at the sound of the guns that had been fired several times by parties seeking birds or animals for the pot or specimens to sell to collectors. Thirteen years later, Maria Island was visited by the much larger and keenly scientific French expedition led by Nicolas Baudin. The explorers had just come from the D'Entrecasteaux Channel near the southern tip of Tasmania, where they successfully made contact with the local bands.

The meeting of the Maria Island band and the French expeditioners produced some of the most important accounts of the Tasmanians just before the arrival of the British settlers on the south-western fringe of Oyster Bay territory eighteen months later. Péron was given the task by his commander, Baudin, of studying the Aborigines. He observed that:

Everything is curious in such a being, everything interesting: his antiquity, his origin, the changes in his affairs and his traditions in this regard, his language, his feelings, his ideas, his physical constitution, his increase in numbers, his infirmities, his longevity, his relationship to the climate, etc., etc.[7]

The Tasmanians were equally curious, though they were at an enormous conceptual disadvantage. Unlike the Frenchmen, who had travelled the world and read the accounts of previous explorers, the Aborigines on Maria Island were utterly baffled by the strangers. Even the most rudimentary questions were beyond their reach. They had no idea where the white men had come from, what they were doing, or what was the purpose of their sudden arrival. Péron observed that 'they do not know what our intentions may be towards them' or what perhaps is the object of our visit, 'and they could form no idea of these matters'. He continued:

They can only think that our intentions are hostile. Our presents, our kindness towards them, our protestations of friendship, all are suspect for them. They seek to interpret our looks. They observe us closely. Everything they see us do they suppose to be something mysterious, and always their suspicions of us are unfavourable. They redouble their vigilance against us, and they surround themselves with sentries in advanced positions who, from the top of hills and even in very tall trees, keep a watch on all that takes place in the vicinity.[8]

Péron was free of the normal condescension and even contempt for indigenous peoples in general, and for the Australians in particular, which can be found in much of the literature of the time. He was impressed by their vitality and the way their feelings were vividly expressed in their faces. While trying to collect a vocabulary by means of signs, he concluded that they seemed to be 'very intelligent and they easily grasped the meaning of all my gestures and seemed to understand both their object and their purpose'.[9] Baudin thought that the local men and women knew the effect of guns but were not so afraid as the people they had met on the shores of the D'Entrecasteaux Channel. He thought they had not been visited 'often by Europeans', and unlike the Bruny Islanders they had no European objects in their possession. They appeared to have no knowledge of iron and its usefulness. They did not attach 'the slightest importance' to the nails the Frenchmen wanted to give them and returned them 'as serving no useful purpose'. They showed no interest in gifts of biscuits or fresh bread, which they pretended to eat but threw away when their visitors weren't looking.[10]

Péron had no doubt about the essential humanity of the Tasmanians.[11] For their part, though, the Oyster Bay people they met on Maria Island were never sure the Frenchmen were human at all. They must have had endless debates on the subject and no doubt many theories were developed. We have no idea if they were ever able to discuss the problem with members of the bands around the D'Entrecasteaux Channel, who had much more experience with the Europeans. One clear possibility was that the white men came from the spirit world, that they weren't terrestrial beings at all. This was an assumption made all over Aboriginal Australia during the early years of contact.[12] The white men's clothes were an immediate source of curious enquiry. The visitors looked like people, but they were covered from head to foot with a bewildering array of articles of different shapes, sizes and colours, some of which had never been seen before. The problem was whether the clothes were covering or actually part of the visitors' bodies. Péron described what happened on their first meeting with an Aboriginal group of fourteen gathered around a big fire. Both parties 'took stock of one another for a little while', he wrote and then explained:

> We were so novel to one another! The natives wanted
> to examine the calves of our legs and our chests, and
> so far as these were concerned we allowed them to do
> everything they wished, oft repeated cries expressing
> the surprise which the whiteness of our skin seemed to
> arouse in them.[13]

There were other problems about the strangers that clearly created much uncertainty. Did they have normal sex lives? Were there any women among them? Did they perhaps keep them on the boats and not allow them on the shore? If they were all men, did they only have a single gender? If so, did they have sex at all and how did they reproduce themselves? In trying to solve these problems the first action was to open the men's shirts looking for breasts and then the much more obtrusive groping between trousered legs. Péron explained that, after the initial examination, their reluctant hosts 'soon wished to carry their researches further'. Wondering why, Péron thought: 'Perhaps they had doubts whether we were the same sort of being as themselves, perhaps they suspected we were of a different sex. However it may be, they showed an extreme desire to examine our genital organs'. It was an examination which was 'equally displeasing to us all'.[14] A midshipman observed that they 'never failed to feel in the trousers of those of us who had no beards'. To be left alone, it was necessary 'to show oneself without trousers'.[15]

Soon after, a party of Baudin's men were surrounded by a group of armed Aborigines who led away a no doubt alarmed fifteen-year-old boy. While he was not hurt in any way, one of the men reported that they 'caressed him and led him a short distance away'. They undressed him and carefully examined him while uttering 'great bursts of laughter'.[16] The Tasmanians were no closer to understanding why the white men had no women with them, or even if such creatures existed, when a few days later the French hauled up their anchors and disappeared over the horizon. As they sailed north along the Tasmanian coast, they met two ships coming south from Sydney on private fishing and sealing expeditions. The outside world was rapidly closing in on the unsuspecting Tasmanians. Meanwhile, the arrival of the French ships in Sydney led directly to Governor King's decision to send a small expedition to establish a permanent settlement on the Derwent. It arrived in Oyster Bay territory eighteen months after the French had left. This presented challenges far greater than the strange behaviour of Baudin and his crew.

Kickertopoller recalled in later life that the members of his band initially ran away when the French ships appeared, but as we have seen they eventually established amiable albeit edgy relations with the strangers. There was no such accommodation a short time before, when Péron and his friend Louis de Freycinet had sailed along the eastern shore of the Derwent, which was the western border of the Oyster Bay nation.

The Frenchmen had been with their shipmates in the D'Entrecasteaux Channel and had had numerous friendly contacts with the local bands. It was a different story on the shores of the Derwent, although they wished to 'have some communication with the natives'. Here and there they saw people on the shore, but as soon as the Frenchmen approached, they 'fled into the middle of the woods'. Freycinet hoped that with more circumspection and perseverance they would be able to 'overcome their terrors and remove their distrusts'. But it did not work out that way. The local bands responded by firing the country. Black columns of smoke arose in every direction, Péron commenting that 'everywhere we turned our eye, we beheld the forest on fire'. He concluded that 'even at this price' the local people wished 'to drive us from their shores'. They retreated to a high mountain, where the Frenchmen assumed many people had taken refuge. As Péron, Freycinet and five men 'all well-armed' walked forward, the 'spectacle was horrible'. The fires had burnt all the grass and most of the small trees and shrubs 'had experienced the same fate'. In some places, even tall trees had 'fallen to the earth by the violence of the flames, and vast fires raged among the rubbish'. When the French party eventually reached the top of the mountain, they found that 'the natives had fled, leaving their miserable huts'.[17] A fire of this intensity would have been an emphatic statement of hostility.

The Frenchmen gave up their attempt to communicate with the Oyster Bay bands and sailed south to join the mother ships. They came ashore and collected water with some difficulty in the creek running into Risdon Cove, on the Derwent's eastern bank, where a short time later the expedition under John Bowen was to plant the first British settlement in Tasmania.

CHAPTER 3

Confrontation at Risdon

Henry Reynolds

The astonishing news of the visit by the French ships to Maria Island in the summer of 1802 would have been conveyed throughout the territory of the Oyster Bay – Big River nations. Tongerlongeter, likely a boy of about twelve at the time, would either have seen the strangers himself or heard many stories about them during intense discussions among the adults of his own and neighbouring bands. News about the arrival of another party of strange white men on the eastern shore of the Derwent in early spring the following year would have eventually reached the east coast, and in all likelihood parties of senior men would have travelled along traditional paths to see for themselves.

Several European expeditions had sailed into the Derwent during the 1790s. John Hayes from the East India Company commanded two ships that spent six weeks there in April 1793. All records of the voyage were lost but it seems he had limited contact with the bands living on either side of the estuary. Five years later, in the summer of 1798, Bass and Flinders, while on their expedition to circumnavigate

35

Tasmania, spent a week over Christmas on the Derwent and made contact with a few individuals on the western shore. They anchored in Risdon Cove, filled their water barrels in the creek and recommended it as a suitable place for a settlement.

The advice was accepted when Governor King decided to establish a colony on the Derwent. The fact that Tasmania was an island implied that a French claim on it would have considerable legitimacy in international law. A small expedition was hurriedly assembled from Sydney's limited resources. By the middle of September 1803, two ships were anchored off Risdon Cove and the passengers and equipment were being unloaded. There were about eighty men, women and children. Convicts and soldiers made up more than half the complement, but there were also some free settlers and their families. Their arrival onshore was a prelude to a whirlwind of activity. Stores and equipment were brought ashore and secured, tents were set up, and long-suffering domestic animals were landed, including cattle, goats, pigs, sheep and a single horse. Within a day or two nearby trees were cut down and processed in a sawpit, and the blacksmith set up his forge. There was so much happening and so much noise. In November two more ships arrived with a further complement of convicts and their military guards. By the end of 1803 there were forty structures on the site.

In his first dispatch to Governor King, the camp commandant, Lieutenant John Bowen, reported that few of the local Aborigines had been seen and 'not apprehending they would be of any use to us I have not made any search after them, thinking myself well off if I never see them again.'[1] The white invaders may not have seen many Aborigines but they were no doubt constantly watched and every development scrutinised and discussed. Neighbouring bands would have sent parties to Risdon to see what was going on. What the British didn't appreciate was that a suitable place for their camp had been a favourite location for the local bands. The availability of fresh water in what was a relatively dry part of Tasmania was a telling factor, both for human consumption and as a resource attracting animals from the surrounding area. The open grassland that gave promise of pasture for the domestic animals and space for crops had no doubt been cleared of undergrowth by regular and systematic burning. So even when small parties began travelling out from the fledgling settlement they were rarely alone. Hunters trained from childhood could travel quietly and quickly in the wake of slow-moving and noisy white men without being seen.

But regular scrutiny could not answer the fundamental question. Had the behaviour of the Europeans changed dramatically? Were they not going to pack up and sail away over the horizon as they had been doing in southern Tasmania for thirty years? Telling differences may have quickly been apparent. The party at Risdon included women, children and numerous exotic animals, which quickly moved onto the land rather than returning to the ships every night as previous parties of visitors had done. And the two ships that had brought the intruders and all their possessions sailed away a few weeks after the arrival. The newcomers were clearly behaving differently, but that was not necessarily proof that they were going to stay for good. The transition from visitors to invaders was a conceptual leap. The Oyster Bay – Big River people had, like the other Tasmanian nations, maintained their independence and sense of distinctive identity across hundreds of generations. Belonging to country was such an overpowering idea that it was almost incomprehensible that complete strangers could suddenly arrive and overturn the way their world was organised. And big questions could not be easily answered. Where had they come from? What were they doing? And even more portentous, why had they turned up out of nowhere?

The situation spun further out of control later in the summer of 1803–04 with the arrival early in February of two more ships, which anchored briefly off the eastern shore of the Derwent and then sailed across to Sullivans Cove on the western shore. On board were more than 250 newcomers. These included convicts, soldiers, free settlers and their families, and the colony's first governor, Colonel David Collins. They brought with them an even greater variety of equipment and other possessions. The new settlement on the site of Hobart superseded Bowen's camp at Risdon, but both were maintained for the time being. The Oyster Bay bands must have been immediately aware of the new settlement. The arrival of the second ship on 11 February was marked by an eleven-gun salute. The utterly unprecedented sound would have reverberated all over the Derwent Valley. They would also have watched the coming and going of small boats between the two camps and scanned the developments that were visible from the eastern shore.

The soldiers, officials and free colonists in both settlements were free to wander where they pleased, and many
of them owned guns. Parties ventured into the surrounding
country hunting and exploring or, as Hobart's pioneering
clergyman Robert Knopwood put it, 'shooting, hunting and
excursioning'.[2] Risdon's official surveyor, James Meehan, led
a series of exploration parties on six expeditions over a wide
area between 7 November 1803 and 7 February 1804. He
had crossed the Derwent and walked all over the future site
of Hobart a few weeks before the unexpected arrival of the
Collins party. It is likely that members of local bands watched
the parties as they crossed their territory. They would have
had no idea what they were doing. The strangers spent little
time hunting, and the surveying they performed would have
appeared to be a meaningless pastime.

While walking north from the upper Derwent in early
February 1804, Meehan came into conflict with what was
probably a Big River hunting party. The hunters may not
have had close contact with the white men before, though
they certainly would have heard about them. Meehan
shot at them twice. The first time was because they pulled
out one of the surveying markers. 'Am obliged to Fire on
them', he wrote in his journal. In that one brief sentence,
he illustrated that a significant change had taken place in
the attitude of the Europeans. Apart from the clash that
had occurred in 1772 at North Bay, none of the members
of visiting expeditions are known to have fired at the
Tasmanians, despite occasional danger and provocation.
But Meehan came from New South Wales. He had been

out on the frontier and had necessarily adopted the harsher and more aggressive attitudes that had already emerged in the new colony. The same was certainly the case with the soldiers of the New South Wales Corps who protected the Risdon settlement.

At the time that Meehan was travelling around Oyster Bay territory, his New South Wales colleague, the botanist George Caley, was writing a report to his patron Sir Joseph Banks on the state of the colony. He observed that the peace of the community had been 'much disturbed at times'. The greatest alarm 'was to be apprehended from the natives', who were involved in a 'sort of war'. At Risdon the spirit of amicable interaction that had characterised the relationship with visiting explorers had been supplanted by rancour, dread and deadly hostility.[3]

There was a serious confrontation between the Aborigines and the soldiers at Risdon on 3 May 1804. It has featured in Tasmanian histories ever since. It was controversial at the time and continues to be so. This is partly due to the fact that we have very little direct evidence about exactly what happened, which allows contrasting and often conflicting interpretations to proliferate. Perhaps the most telling piece of evidence was provided by Robert Knopwood, who noted in his diary on the day in question: 'At 2pm we heard the report of cannon once from Risdon'. Governor Collins sent a message to ascertain the cause. That evening Knopwood received a letter from his friend Jacob Mountgarrett, the surgeon and magistrate at Risdon:

Dear Sir,

I beg to refer you to Mr. Moore[4] for the particulars of
an attack the natives made on the camp today, and I
have every reason to think it was premeditated, as their
number far exceeded any that we have heard of. As you
express a wish to be acquainted with some of the natives,
if you dine with me tomorrow you will oblige me by
christening a fine native boy who I have. Unfortunately,
poor boy, his father and mother were both killed. He is
about two years old. I have likewise the body of a man
that was killed …[5]

At the foot of the page Mountgarrett added: 'The number of
the natives I think was not less than 5 or 6 hundred.'

Knopwood's entry for the day continued: 'At 8, Lt Moore
came to my marquee and stayd sometime; he informed me of
the natives being very numerous, and that they wounded one
of the settlers, Burke, and was going to burn his house down
and ill treat his wife etc. etc.'[6]

Apart from the information provided by Knopwood,
there are only two other accounts of what happened on that
day. The first was a brief and inadequate official report Moore
wrote for Governor Collins three days later.[7] The second was
provided by Edward White, an assigned servant at Risdon. It
was twenty-six years after the event and provided under oath
to the official Aborigines Committee on 16 March 1830.[8]
Both accounts have their limitations, and they provide us
with conflicting evidence. We know nothing about the events

of that day from the point of view of the Oyster Bay – Big River people. The limitation of the evidence has meant that many interpretations of varying cogency have been published over the years. Rather than endeavour to reach a consensus of previous views, I will outline what I think is the most probable, if tentative and entirely personal, interpretation of the events.

To begin with, how many Aborigines came down the valley in the middle of the morning? Mountgarrett estimated there were five or six hundred, and certainly their number 'farr [sic] exceeded any that we have ever heard of'. White told the official committee there were 300 of them. Clearly, no one could be sure how many men, women and children were involved. But Mountgarrett was right about the numbers being unprecedented. There were several later reports of very large numbers gathering a short distance east of Risdon in the Coal Valley. There are at least two reasons to suspect it was an annual event. The valley was largely cleared of vegetation as a result of 'firestick farming' over many generations, so was an ideal place for hunting. More to the point was that, in what was one of the driest parts of Tasmania, the Coal Valley was an invaluable and probably never-failing source of fresh water. The second consideration is that early May was likely the time when the Big River bands made their annual migration from the wintry Central Plateau to the milder east coast. The gatherings would have been highly significant events on the seasonal calendar. Small bands coalesced, refreshing friendships, exchanging gossip, negotiating marriages and settling old disputes. Many nights would have been spent dancing. They met their contemporaries from all over the widespread lands of the nation and no doubt looked admiringly at possible future marriage partners. But in 1804 there must have been much talk about the white interlopers, who would have been avoided as the bands converged on the Coal Valley. There would have been much pooling of knowledge of the strangers and endless discussions about what their arrival foreshadowed.

Such large gatherings were only possible when there was enough food, and all over Australia they were confined to certain locations at propitious times. For the bands gathered in the Coal Valley this meant hunting on a large scale. Even then, the inability to preserve meat meant that the large congress might only last for a few days. It required a 'drive', when as many people as possible were spread out in a long line to create noise to drive as many animals as possible towards the hunters. Clearly the strategy at Risdon was to drive the animals down towards the Derwent where they could be cornered. Edward White understood what was happening, telling the gentlemen on the Aborigines Committee that the 'Natives come down in a circular form, and a flock of kangaroos hemmed in between them; there were men women and children'. But he was wrong when he assumed 'they did not know there was a white man in the country when they came down to Risdon'.[9] Evidently the participants in the drive believed that they would not be attacked or molested by the white men, otherwise they would not have proceeded with women and children in train in such an open manner. They were obviously confident about their safety.

There is no reason to suppose that the small European community understood why such a large number of Aborigines had suddenly appeared in utterly unprecedented numbers. It is unsurprising that they concluded they were in danger. Coming from New South Wales, where frontier violence was already common, this was a reasonable assumption. Moore reported that 'their appearance and their numbers I thought very far from friendly'. He also asserted that Burke, one of the settlers, had been attacked. But White was adamant that this was not true, explaining that 'the natives were never within half a quarter of a mile of Burke's house', and that they 'did not attack the soldiers; they would not have molested them'.[10]

The first confrontation took place as members of the hunting party approached the settlement. This was when the three people mentioned by Mountgarrett were shot. They were almost certainly taken by surprise, particularly the man and woman who had their two-year-old son with them. They may have been standing still when they were targeted. It is obvious they were not intending to attack the Europeans. They were needlessly killed, and it was probably just fortuitous that the child was not shot. It is the most telling piece of evidence illustrating the brutal aggression of the ordinary soldiers of the New South Wales Corps, well schooled in colonial violence.

How many more died in this first encounter? Perhaps it was fewer than we might suppose, even if the intention was to kill more. At the sound of the first gunshots, the hunters would have taken evasive action. They would not have stood still while the soldiers took aim or even had to reload. Shooting an adversary who was rapidly moving away was very difficult with an inaccurate muzzle-loading musket, and once the Aborigines started running, there was no way soldiers with heavy guns and ill-fitting shoes could get close enough for an effective shot. Consequently, there was likely much more shooting than there were corresponding casualties. There is abundant evidence from the time of the first exploring expeditions that the Tasmanians could travel across country with amazing rapidity and were able to hide in ways that perplexed their pursuers. So the idea that the soldiers could effectively pursue the hunters back up the valley has little to recommend it.

The hunt obviously came to a sudden end, but whatever happened then? It is reasonable to suppose that the women, children and old people retreated over Grasstree Hill and down into the Coal Valley. An adolescent Tongerlongeter was probably with them. White said the shooting started at eleven o'clock, so the valley behind the settlement would have been clear by about half past eleven or soon after. Yet at two o'clock we know the cannon was fired. Moore reported a 'great party was in camp', hence the firing of the cannon. So what was the great party doing? Moore's account is quite confusing, because it gives no sense of the passing of those crucial three hours. He did, however, add one intriguing detail, almost as an afterthought, that 'during the Time they were in Camp a number of old men were perceived at the foot of the Hill near the Valley employed making spears.'[11]

What are we to make of this? The presumption must be that significant numbers of warriors were still around the campsite in the bottom of the valley because they were planning to attack the Europeans. What other explanation is plausible? The intention may have been to exact revenge proportionate to the numbers of their countrymen who had been killed. Perhaps a grander plan was being considered. The very large number of men of fighting age may have suggested the possibility of driving the invaders away. Like their enemies, they would have been keenly aware that this was a rare moment when the numbers favoured the original inhabitants and they could consider a coordinated assault. It is reasonable to presume that there must have been what was, in effect, a war council of band leaders from all over the national territory, deciding on tactics even down to dispatching older men to make more spears in an environment where they would have been in danger. At this early stage of contact, the limitations of European guns may not have been apparent. Their range and accuracy was presumably still a mystery. It clearly took both morale and courage to remain in the danger zone.

Members of the large party would not have been drawn up together like a detachment of European infantry but, rather, scattered in all directions, stalking the white men like hunters and keeping out of sight as much as cover would allow. The objective would have been to creep up closely enough to be within spear-throwing range. Moore and his soldiers must have been intensely frustrated, because there were probably no easy targets for their muskets, which undoubtedly would have been primed and ready for use. They would have felt threatened. Was this a reasonable fear? It surely was. We must remember that while all the members of the besieging party were warriors, there were only twenty-four soldiers in the camp. If it had come to close hand-to-hand fighting, it is likely the advantage would have been held by the warriors, who were bigger, stronger and fitter than the British defenders.

And so Moore and Magistrate Mountgarrett decided to use the cannon, their ultimate weapon. In hindsight, it was a reasonable decision by the two men responsible for the safety of the hundred or so people in the camp.[12] There seems no reason at all to suppose the cannon was not loaded, as some recent commentators have suggested. The cannon's effect is impossible to determine beyond the fact that Moore reported it led to the warriors dispersing. Were there many casualties? It is important to establish that when the cannon was fired the women and children who had been part of the drive in the morning were almost certainly far away. And there is the question of how effective the cannon would have been in the circumstances. Designed to fire on closely ranged companies of infantry or the crowded quarterdecks on sailing ships, it sprayed small projectiles in all directions like an oversized shotgun. On that day, the problem would have been where to point the gun and who to aim it at. With warriors coming from everywhere, there was no obvious target. So it is very likely that some warriors were hit and certainly wounded, but the firing, while achieving its objective, may not have killed as many warriors as most writers then and since have supposed. It may well be, however, that firing the cannon saved the camp from being overrun.

This assessment runs counter to a great deal of the writing about what is commonly called the Risdon massacre.

Two deeply entrenched, albeit contradictory assumptions have, hitherto, kept it out of interpretive reach. One is that the Aborigines were constitutionally unable to resist the European invaders effectively. To put it crudely, they were thought to lack both the guts and the gumption. To generations of Australians who had grown up assuming the Tasmanians were the most primitive people on the planet, the notion of their mounting a well-organised attack on a European camp seemed fanciful. The idea that it might have been successful was even more ridiculous. Evidence beckoning in this direction was simply overlooked. Australian historians contrasted the Aborigines' skills with the martial capacity of Māori, Bantus and Amerindians, and didn't choose to see that all over Australia, Aboriginal nations resisted their radical dispossession in ways consonant with their economic means and social structure. And that is why the brief seasonal gathering of widely scattered bands allowed the Oyster Bay – Big River warriors to mount a challenge the scale of which was quite unusual in Australian history. What occurred in the ensuing thirty years provides the strongest affirmation of this interpretation of the events on that fateful day at Risdon. The men of Tongerlongeter's generation fought the settlers and their military forces with a vigour, intelligence and courage that put the question of their status as warriors beyond doubt.

The belief in Aboriginal inadequacy arose seamlessly from an intellectual milieu obsessed with the twin beliefs of racial hierarchy and social evolution. These ideas were profoundly challenged in the second half of the 20th century but linger on in dark atavistic corners. Nevertheless, there are contemporary ideas that paradoxically have a similar effect. This can be seen in relation to the confrontation at Risdon. A common view is that the Aborigines were victims rather than combatants. Much is made of the firing of the cannon, which it is suggested was unleashed on the hunting party of men, women and children, leaving large numbers killed. The emphasis tips away from Aboriginal resistance to European brutality. It evokes pity and compassion for the victims, not respect for their courage and resourcefulness. But it persists because it is politically potent, evoking white guilt in place of a more complex, nuanced story – one about combat rather than genocidal massacre. Frightened, anxious soldiers are harder to condemn than casual murderers.

Considering the troubling events from the other side of the Derwent, David Collins was concerned about the likely future consequences. Having earlier been in New South Wales for eight years and spent time studying the Aborigines in the Sydney area, his views carried considerable authority. In a dispatch to Governor King written later in May, he warned that he well knew that 'these indiscriminating Savages will Consider every White Man as their Enemy, and will if they have Opportunity revenge the Death of their Companions'. He reported that a few days after the confrontation a group of men gathering oyster shells from the eastern shore was attacked by a 'numerous Party of Natives and beat off with Stones and Clubs'.[13] But Collins could not have known the significance of the Risdon confrontation. He could not have known it would live on in local memory – that it would not be engulfed in Australia's cult of forgetfulness about frontier conflict.

Many writers discussed its long-term impact during the 19th century. In his pioneering 1819 book, William Charles Wentworth asserted that the Tasmanians 'maintain the most rancorous and inflexible hostility towards the colonists'. But it was not the result of 'the ferocious nature of these savages', rather it was the result of the 'unpardonable conduct of our country men' and the 'murderous discharge' unleashed at Risdon. Since then, all communication with them had ceased, and 'the spirit of animosity and revenge' had been 'fostered and aggravated to the highest pitch'.[14] Wentworth visited Hobart on his voyage back to Britain in 1816, and probably picked up stories about the event while talking to locals. Settler GT Lloyd, who arrived in Tasmania four years later, believed that because of Risdon, 'that cruel and impolitic act, the link of friendship was rashly severed, never again to be re-united'.[15] John Pascoe Fawkner who, as an eleven-year-old boy, was in the colony at the time of the Risdon confrontation, recalled in later life that, from then on, 'it was war between the races and no quarter'.[16] In their carefully considered report of 1830, the Aborigines Committee concluded that: 'Whether or no the resentment occasioned by this encounter has been ever since maintained, and has continued to influence the Natives in their feelings towards the white population, it is impossible with perfect certainty to determine'.[17]

By 1830, Risdon's influence on Aboriginal violence was of largely academic interest, as the colony was then engaged in an intense war with Tongerlongeter and his defiant warriors. But the impact of the Risdon confrontation remains an interesting and important question. We have no idea if Aboriginal bands in other parts of the island knew what had happened on that day or what they heard and how much later. It seems most unlikely that any information would have dramatically changed their own attitudes to the white men. Despite the presence of a common enemy, the traditional enemies of the Oyster Bay – Big River nations probably felt little solidarity with them. But the fact that so many bands had congregated together at Risdon magnified its significance. It was not like other clashes with the invaders, which were confined to small groups and news of which may have spread only slowly to other bands. Hundreds of people shared that experience and took their sense of outrage back into every corner of their nation's heartland.

CHAPTER 4

Coming of age

Nicholas Clements

Tongerlongeter was just an adolescent when his people were ejected from their country at Risdon in 1804. While the strangers' creeping presence must have weighed heavily on everyone's minds, his childhood was in large part a traditional one. Tongerlongeter's mother, like a thousand generations of women before her, would have given birth on the move, probably catching up to her kinfolk before nightfall, her newborn wrapped in a fur.[1] The year was around 1790. Two years later, in a different part of south-east Tasmania, the French biologist Jacques Labillardière was recording the way mothers interacted with their children, and noted how they 'lavished on them the marks of the greatest affection.'[2] From this and various other sources, it seems that stable, loving childhoods were the norm in Tasmania.[3] Given the calibre of the man Tongerlongeter became, we can assume his childhood was no exception.

From a very early age, Tongerlongeter would have learnt that every aspect of his life was inextricably bound up with his kin. They ate together, slept together, travelled together, laughed together, fought together. Individualism was not just foreign – it was incomprehensible. His boyhood would have been analogous to an endless school excursion. Surrounded by playmates, his lessons consisted of watching, listening and trying. Just like school today, there were times to work and times to play, times to be silly and times to be serious. There was crying and joking, punishment and praise. But here the analogy peters out. There were no school bells, uniforms or classrooms. School was not a building where young people went five days a week to be instructed by strangers. In a society where education was for life rather than careers, such contrivances were never necessary. While not without its hardships, both cultural and environmental, Tongerlongeter's youth would have been healthier and more loving than that experienced by the average English child of the time.[4]

Tongerlongeter would have noted early on who earned the admiration of his kinfolk and who didn't. Learning from respected individuals was crucial, for in a society unfamiliar with material wealth, one's social standing was everything. There were no hereditary titles or class structures; the respect of one's peers depended entirely upon character and skill. The character traits one was supposed to display, and the roles they fulfilled, were largely determined by gender. Men did the hunting and fighting, while women dived for shellfish, climbed trees for possums, collected plant foods, cooked, built huts and fires, and cared for small children. As he learnt what it meant to be a man, Tongerlongeter would have observed the patriarchal division of labour and how the most wearisome work fell to women, yet he would also have noted that men were generally protective and kind towards women.[5] Above all, Tongerlongeter's youth schooled him in the interdependence of men and women in all of life's essential projects.

Pre-colonial Aboriginal society, unburdened as it was by industrialisation, materialism and stifling etiquette, has often been romanticised. And this is not without some justification. It is certainly easy to envy a people with such rich social and environmental connections. But up close, human beings and human cultures are always messier than they first appear. Tongerlongeter wasn't perfect and nor was his society. Like the rest of us, Tasmanians experienced the full gamut of human failings. Jealousy, anger, superstition, vengefulness, disloyalty and domestic violence were each noted by observers at various points.[6] But the surprising thing about this list is how short it is. Indeed, the tightly woven cultural fabric of tribal life made for an impressively well-functioning society. It had a sophisticated web of obligations, customs, prohibitions and spiritual imperatives. These same webs protected the vulnerable, be they children, the elderly, the sick or the disabled.[7] They also laid out formulas for resolving disputes and navigating romantic relationships.[8] Such cultural protocols provided every member of society with a blueprint for how to live. And nothing speaks for the effectiveness of this culture more than its incredible longevity. Aboriginal Tasmanians have been on the island for at least 40 000 years.[9] They have survived multiple glaciations and the longest geographic isolation in human history. And they are still here.

It is no coincidence that the culture of such an enduring society was preoccupied above all with community. The smallest unit of Tasmanian society was the hearth group – four to eight closely related people who shared a fire.[10] Hearth groups were semi-autonomous and often operated parallel to but independent of their band. East coast bands appear to have comprised around a dozen hearth groups, totalling up to eighty people. Tongerlongeter's band, the Poredareme, had its homeland centred on the region between the Little Swanport and Prosser rivers (see figure 11). The evidence delineating band territories is incomplete and messy, but the Poredareme's seems to have stretched north as far as Oyster Bay and as far south as the Tasman Peninsula, while it extended inland almost as far as Oatlands and the Coal Valley.[11] Exactly what significance this place held for the Poredareme, and what their obligations to it were, are not explicitly recorded. They even shared some of it with their neighbours, the Laremairremener.[12] What is indisputable, though, is that these were a people doggedly attached to their country.

The Poredareme were not alone in their corner of Tasmania. They belonged to a larger alliance comprised of probably twenty bands. This loose confederation, known to the whites as the Oyster Bay – Big River tribes or nations, occupied the country north of the Derwent River and south of Campbell Town. In the summer, many Oyster Bay and Big River bands ascended onto the Central Plateau. Occasionally, they would even venture north of the plateau to fight enemies or to collect ochre, a pigmented clay coveted for its insulating properties when mixed with animal fat and smeared on the body, but also for its ritual and aesthetic value.[13] Culturally and linguistically, the Oyster Bay and Big River nations were one people, distinct from surrounding nations.[14] This did not mean they were always on friendly terms, but it did provide a foundation upon which to build strategic alliances. Good relations were also important because the economies and customs of eastern bands called for regular movement through the country of surrounding bands.

The exact patterns in which the Poredareme and their allies moved are unclear. The surviving evidence, limited as it is, provides us with only a handful of certainties. Tongerlongeter's people were regularly absent from their country. Likewise, allies passed through Poredareme country, and enemies occasionally invaded. Over the course of a year, bands like the Poredareme might travel well over a thousand kilometres, following designated routes through the country of their allies. As it was with most eastern bands before the Black War, the Poredareme generally spent winters by the coast and the warmer months inland. Animated by the lure of better weather, as well as cultural obligations and rendezvous with friends, Oyster Bay and Big River bands typically moved every day or two, except in the winter or when special places or events attracted longer stays.[15] But the main reason for this incessant movement was food.

As hunting and foraging peoples, the Tasmanians knew not to over-exploit any one area. This was not a matter of just passively moving on every day. Through much of the year, when conditions were right, bands such as the Poredareme engaged in strategic burning, or 'firestick farming'. The impressive scale and sophistication of this practice has only recently been appreciated. An intimate knowledge of weather and fire ecology allowed bands to burn precise areas at controlled temperatures inorder to produce the right food and cover for specific game animals. The next time they or their friends traversed that country, the desired animals would, it was hoped, be lunching on the new growth. What's more, in conjunction with these land-management burns, men would hunt the fleeing game by placing themselves in the path of their escape.[16] Yet another benefit of burning was the reduction of undergrowth, which allowed easier movement. Millennia of firestick farming fundamentally reshaped the Tasmanian landscape into a vast mosaic of microhabitats crafted to serve the needs of hungry travellers.[17]

Few Europeans observed the full daily routine of the Tasmanians before it was thrown into chaos. Still, with careful deductive reasoning, a typical day in Tongerlongeter's childhood can be reconstructed with some confidence. Most of his people had nothing but grease and ochre to keep warm, so the sun had to do its work before they would leave their fires. If the weather were foul, the majority might remain in camp all day, but generally everyone was mobile by midmorning.[18] Departures were typically staggered, with the men leaving first to hunt. Thereafter, the women, children and elderly gradually broke camp, foraging as they went for plant foods and smaller animals.[19] Food was the Poredareme's main but by no means sole imperative. Straight stands of tea-tree for spear-making, cider gums for brewing alcohol, and quarries for mining ochre or stone tools were also important.[20] In gullies or forests they stuck to well-worn paths, while in open country their routes varied.[21] Years later, when he was being guided through Oyster Bay – Big River country, George Augustus Robinson observed that Aborigines travelled in single file and regularly 'divided themselves so as to hunt as they went along'.[22]

As the crow flies, a day's travel generally amounted to only a few kilometres, though with hunting and foraging excursions along the way, the Poredareme could cover considerable ground.[23] Having spoken to numerous contemporaries acquainted with the Aborigines, the early historian John West wrote: 'Their locomotion was predetermined, and their encampments regularly chosen; generally on the banks of a river or a lagoon. Each family had its fire; hunted separately; and erected a hut for its own accommodation'.[24] The first members of the band would generally arrive at camp around midday. Fire and shelter were their first priorities. In wet or cold conditions, the women were capable of erecting impressively large shelters, though if a simple windbreak would suffice, they rarely indulged in anything more luxurious.[25] When the hunters returned, the band ate lunch together.[26] Afternoons were spent on anything from spear-making and hair care to play-fighting and conversation. As the day faded, families usually retired to their separate fires. On more nights than not, Tongerlongeter witnessed singing, dancing and storytelling – some of it of great cultural or spiritual import, much of it just for fun.

Social and spiritual obligations could take the

Poredareme far from their homeland. They would sometimes cross paths with neighbours; they also went stretches
without seeing anyone. More substantial gatherings, such
as the one at Risdon in 1804, were held just a few times a
year.[27] These 'corroborees' served an array of social, spiritual,
economic and political functions. As a youth, Tongerlongeter
would have anticipated them with great excitement. They
were occasions to make friends, flirt with girls, take part in
grand hunts, and marvel at the elaborate ceremonies that
kept his people's world in balance.

Major ceremonies often took place during a full moon.[28]
The moon was central to the Tasmanians' mythology. They
chiselled its form into stone, depicted it in charcoal on
the walls of their huts, and even carved it into their own
bodies, producing raised circular scars.[29] The intricacies of
their lunar beliefs are not recorded, but Tongerlongeter's
people were clearly awed by the luminous orb that swelled
and retreated each month. 'I rather think they adored the
moon', wrote the early Oyster Bay settler John Lyne. In his
reminiscences, Lyne recalled 'a tribe camped on the face of
a hill about two miles [three kilometres] away in front of
our house at the time when the moon was full and we could
see capering [lively dancing] before a large fire'.[30] Likewise,
another Oyster Bay settler noted: 'At the full of every moon
it would seem each distinct Tribe assembles to gather in a
general corrobboree by moonlight'.[31]

The moon was important, not least because it repressed
the darkness, for it was in the darkness that evil spirits were
believed to lurk. As a boy living close to a popular tribal

meeting place at Pitt Water near Sorell, George Lloyd recalled mingling with Oyster Bay people in the early 1820s. On one occasion, he claimed he was permitted to view a lunar ceremony. His account is no less interesting for its condescension:

> Amongst the neighbouring tribes of Aborigines it is customary to meet at some time-honoured trysting-place at every full moon, a period regarded by them with most profound reverence. Indeed, judging from their extraordinary gestures in the dance, the upturned eye and outstretched arm – apparently in a supplicating spirit – I have often been disposed to conclude that the poor savages were invoking the mercy and protection of that planet as their 'guardian deity'.[32]

As Lloyd and others noted, though, while the Tasmanians were guarded about certain ceremonies, we can confidently say that they were the most important events on the cultural calendar.[33]

Major ceremonies could go late into the night. Participation was often ecstatic and exhausting. In one case, Lloyd writes, 'the savage reunion kept up until one and two o'clock in the morning'. The next morning, 'the head warrior' (possibly Tongerlongeter) directed 'men, women, and children' to wade into the shallow bay to hunt the stingrays

> with their long heavy sticks furiously beating the water, accompanied with frantic yells and other unearthly

sounds ... discovering their devoted prey, they cast
the deadly weapon ... having satisfied their warrior-
propensities by destroying numbers of those dangerous
creatures, the hunters would retire to their camp-fires
and regale themselves upon the usual coast-fare, oysters
and steaming opossum.[34]

They did not eat these 'ray-fish', which suggests the hunt was
purely ritualistic.

Lloyd's account is most likely connected to the 'Oyster
Bay legend' recounted in the 1840s by Kallerromter, the last
known Poredareme warrior. He told of how his ancestors,
who 'had no fire', were visited by two mysterious men. These
strangers

slept at the foot of a hill – a hill in my own country.
On the summit of a hill they were seen by my fathers,
my countrymen, on the top of the hill they were seen
standing: they threw fire like a star – it fell amongst the
black men, my countrymen. They were frightened –
they fled away, all of them; after a while they returned,
they hastened and made a fire – a fire with wood; no
more was fire lost in our land. The two black fellows are
in the clouds; in the clear night you see them like two
stars. These are they who brought fire to my fathers.
The two black men staid a while in the land of my
fathers. Two women (Lowanna) were bathing ... A
sting-ray lay concealed in the hollow of a rock ... The
sting-ray was large, he had a very long spear; from his

hole he spied the women, he saw them dive: he pierced
them with his spear, he killed them … he came close
into shore, he lay in still water, near the sandy beach;
with him were the women, they were fast on his spear –
they were dead! The two black men fought the sting-
ray; they slew him with their spears … The two black
men made a fire … On either side they laid a woman …
The black men sought some ants, some large blue ants
(pugganyeptietta); they placed them on the bosoms
(paruggapoingta) of the women. Severely, intensely
were they bitten. The women revived – they lived once
more. Soon there came a fog … the two black men went
away, the women disappeared: they passed through
the fog, the thick dark fog! Their place is in the clouds.
Two stars you see in the clear cold night; two black men
are there – the women are with them: they are stars
above![35]

The stingray story is structurally similar to other
Tasmanian myths, in which the spiritual connections to
country and to celestial bodies are powerful themes. This
is consistent with hunting and foraging societies the world
over. For such people, understanding and protecting their
environment is a matter of life and death. To someone like
Tongerlongeter, country was more than land. It was alive
with spirits and pregnant with the history of his people. The
stars too played a major role in Tasmanian mythology. 'They
spoke on the subject of the stars with great zest', Robinson
noted.[36] He also observed how they 'described constellations

in the heavens as resembling men and women, men fighting, animals, and limbs of men.'[37] Incidentally, he even noted that 'They call the black spot in the Milky Way or Orion's Belt a stingaree and say the blackfellows are spearing it.'[38]

Between the earth and the stars was a rich spiritual landscape. The Tasmanians were animists, which is to say they saw not only humans as animated by spirits, but also the natural world. As Tongerlongeter and his people moved through the landscape, the spirit world was no less important than the climate or the terrain. Everything was determined by beings unseen. The right behaviours and rituals were essential. In the east, for instance, men sang a particular song while straightening spears,[39] as did women before fishing or before their menfolk went into battle.[40] They believed kangaroos could not be hit with an old waddy (throwing club),[41] and that certain clever men could stop the wind by confronting it with a firebrand.[42] These are but a few of the ritualised ways the Poredareme and their neighbours interacted with the spirit world in the hope of tempering nature and protecting themselves from misfortune.[43]

In 1829, Gilbert Robertson, the leader of a 'roving party' employed by the government to capture Aborigines, recorded in his journal an encounter between an owl and his two Poredareme guides. The owl,

> having perched upon a tree near to our break wind began
> to hoot his evening note – the two blacks attached to
> the party started up and began an earnest conversation
> principally addressed to the Bird who occasionally

hooted his responses, on hearing which they shouted with the most extravagant demonstration of joy[;] when this whimsical Conversation had ceased Tom [one of the guides] explained to us that the Bird (which he called *Cocolo diana*) was capable of giving any information he required.[44]

Like Robertson, we can only speculate about the belief system underpinning this interaction. Clearly, though, animals were not mere prey. There were numerous taboos on killing and eating certain animals.[45] These varied depending on the band and the context. For instance, James Backhouse, one of two Quaker missionaries who spent considerable time with the exiled survivors in the 1830s, wrote: 'Some of these people only eat the male [wallabies], others only the females … [and] hunger will not drive them to deviate from it'.[46]

And taboos were not limited to animals. Tasmanians were also loath to mention the names of the dead or venture near their remains.[47] Indeed, the dead were a significant preoccupation. Funerary practices varied from nation to nation, and their meanings remain a mystery.[48] Tongerlongeter and his allies appear to have used at least three methods – cremation, burial, and interment in hollow trees. The latter, apparently reserved for men who fell in combat, involved skewering the body with spears to suspend it upright in its wooden tomb.[49] Tongerlongeter's people believed their personal spirits, which abided in their breasts, were not extinguished by bodily death.[50] Yet their understanding of the afterlife bore no resemblance to the heaven and hell of

Christian theology. The Tasmanians were not concerned about being judged in the afterlife; they were worried about what the spirits of the dead might do to them in *this* life. Joseph Milligan, commandant of the Flinders Island Aborigines Establishment in the 1840s and 1850s, learnt that, even after years of exile, 'The Aborigines were extremely superstitious believing implicitly in the return of the spirits of their departed friends and relations to bless or injure them.'[51] This worldview was the lens through which every aspect of life was refracted, and it is the lens through which we must view Tongerlongeter's story.

In 1831, as Robinson impatiently urged his Aboriginal envoys to track down Tongerlongeter's band of resistance fighters, he found his quest dictated more by the spirit world than by any earthly concerns. His envoys spent much of their energy trying to avoid the wrath of hostile spirits and solicit the aid of friendly ones.[52] At play was an ongoing cosmic battle between the living and the dead, and if not dealt with carefully, the departed could create all manner of strife.

There were both protective and malicious spirits inhabiting the country of each band.[53] According to one of Robinson's Aboriginal informants, Markaneyerlorepanener was the name of the evil spirit haunting the Oyster Bay area.[54] George Walker, the Quaker missionary who accompanied Backhouse to Flinders Island after the war, observed: 'All diseases and casualties are attributed to the agency of this malevolent power, who also is thought to preside over the elements, especially in the phenomena of thunder and lightning, of which they are accordingly much afraid.'[55]

Night-time was the worst, as the darkness gave cover to all manner of evil. Jorgen Jorgenson, another roving party leader who spent considerable time conversing with his Aboriginal guides, noted that they had 'a great dread of a malevolent power ... They say when it is daylight they have no fear of the "Devil" – he only annoys and torments them at dark'.[56] Similarly, a Bruny Island man told Robinson that this evil spirit 'is like a black man only very big and ugly, and that he travels like the wind, that he comes and watches the natives all night and before daylight comes he goes away like swift wind'.[57] Only when the moon was bright and the sky clear would Tasmanians willingly venture beyond the glow of their fires.[58] 'The superstitious terror of the black', wrote John West, 'prevented his wandering from the camp, lest the evil spirit that haunted the darkness should carry him away'.[59] If in desperation they were forced to move in the dark, the experience left them literally trembling with fear.[60] This abiding dread of evil spirits was central to the worldview of the Oyster Bay – Big River people. As Tongerlongeter grew into a man, he became steeped in the mythology that underpinned this belief in 'devils', as they referred to them in English. If he was like his peers, he also began drawing a connection between these malevolent ancestor spirits and the mysterious white men inching closer and closer to his country.

Upon becoming a man, Tongerlongeter was inducted into the myriad secrets undergirding his people's worldview.[61] History, religion, rites, ceremonies – millennia of accumulated knowledge – would ultimately be committed to memory in the form of songs, dances and stories.[62] Tribal symbols, now of uncertain significance, were cut deeply into his flesh, the wounds packed with ash so that the healing slowed and the scarring bulged and glistened.[63] Like any young man, he would have felt the weight of his newfound knowledge and status. But Tongerlongeter was no ordinary young man. While puberty had given him impressive height and a commanding presence, it was his intelligence and resolve that distinguished him most, first as a Poredareme warrior and eventually as the island's pre-eminent resistance leader.

Tongerlongeter would have married well before he made his name in war against the white men. 'When [he] arrived at the years of maturity', Robinson wrote, a man's primary object is to find 'a wife who can provide'.[64] Tongerlongeter eventually married the Big River woman Droomteemetyer, but this took place in the final years of the Black War. His previous wife, whose name is not recorded, was abducted by white men sometime before this.[65] But even this woman was probably not his first wife. Because white men targeted women and girls, very few survived into the second half of the war. Those who did were often widowed, though it was never long before they were remarried to a high-status man.[66] Given how common death and remarriage were during this period, Tongerlongeter may have had several wives from the time he came of age until the time he married Droomteemetyer. This latter relationship was born in extremis, and the couple probably had nothing like a typical courtship. His first marriage, however, would have been more traditional. Once wed, Tongerlongeter was expected to hunt for and protect his wife.[67] The couple probably had children, but if so, they likely died in the war too.

Tongerlongeter's principal task as a man was hunting. It was often difficult and could consume several hours of every day. The weapons he used were the same as those used in warfare, namely the spear and the waddy. The former, fashioned with stone tools and then straightened and hardened in the fire, was the hunter's primary weapon.[68] Trained from their earliest years,[69] Tasmanian men wielded their spears with incredible skill.[70] George Walker observed: 'The aboriginal natives are very dexterous in the use of these weapons, which are of wood, from nine to twelve feet in length. They throw them with such force and skill, at from fifty to one hundred yards [forty-five to ninety metres], as rarely to fail in transfixing the object of their aim'.[71] While travelling with Aborigines, Robinson noted that they regularly 'amused themselves at night in spearing trees. In this way the men exercise themselves'.[72] Like every European who witnessed their skills, Robinson was amazed at the distance and accuracy men like Tongerlongeter could achieve with these simple javelins. They were just as deadly with a waddy, which was thrown in a spinning motion. As one observer noted, 'they are trained up from infancy to throw [waddies] with surprising dexterity and precision'.[73] These heavy sticks, bulbous on one end, were also used as clubs to dispatch wounded game.[74] At nearer distances, they also knocked down small game with stones, which they threw with an accuracy that left white observers astounded.[75]

Tasmanian men were, to quote Robinson, 'passionately fond of hunting'.[76] Even when they were not engaged in the chase, they sang, danced and told stories about hunting exploits.[77] Lloyd's description of a hunt gives some sense of why it was so alluring:

> On sighting their prey, the most skilful hunter instantly
> dropped to the earth, and creeping alternately on
> hands, knees, and stomach, behind trees and stumps
> ... insinuating his supple body through the high grass,
> like a wily snake, until he had successfully arrived
> within thirty or forty yards [twenty-five or thirty-five
> metres] of the unwary victim [when] he would carefully
> raise himself up behind the trunk of a tree ... [before
> sprinting] towards his prey with the agility of a panther,
> and hurling the spear.[78]

Success was far from assured, but experienced hunters had a deep bag of tricks that tipped the odds in their favour. Most hunts were elaborate team efforts. Just as fire could be used to herd game into an ambush, so too a line of men could 'beat the bush' to create the same effect.[79] For the best chance at hitting the fleeing game, hunters might build an artificial bottleneck out of branches, or simply herd their quarry into a gully or towards a cliff edge.[80] Kangaroo, wallaby and wombat were the main fare, while an array of smaller or scarcer game added variety and challenge. Emus were especially prized, though these sprightly birds were difficult to bring down.[81]

Before Tongerlongeter's world was destroyed by the white invaders, it was in some respects improved by them. Dogs imported from the British Isles were rapidly adopted by the Poredareme and their neighbours in the years following the initial invasion. Stolen from the strangers or exchanged for sex, their impact was immediate.[82] The most common hunting dogs were Irish deerhounds and greyhounds. These powerful, athletic animals could bring down a kangaroo on their own, especially when hunting in a pack. Tongerlongeter came of age just as this revolution in hunting was taking place. Strategies changed and hunting times were reduced. The old ways were not lost but rather complemented by the new, four-legged technology. What's more, dogs became beloved companions and sources of warmth at night.[83] In time, they would also become life-saving allies against the white man and his incessant nocturnal assaults.

The white strangers were not Tongerlongeter's only enemy. Since time immemorial, the Poredareme had had to guard against more familiar foes, and they against them. As in tribal societies the world over, suspicion of outgroups was as natural as breathing. Records of intertribal violence necessarily coincide with European encroachment, which likely exacerbated the phenomenon, yet there are strong reasons to believe it pre-dated this. For one, Tasmania's various bands and confederacies had not united, despite some 14 000 years of isolation from mainland Australia.[84] Quite the opposite. The island was so fractious that no common language or culture had ever taken root. While the regularity and intensity of violence varied, and particular relationships might warm or cool depending on circumstances, war was never far from people's minds.

The most serious intertribal violence occurred between enemies from different language groups. The reasons for these conflicts varied. There is even evidence of seasonally arranged battles that may have stemmed as much from tradition as from any specific grievance.[85] Conflicts between Oyster Bay and Big River bands, on the other hand, seem for the most part to have been settled ritualistically. While one or two men might be injured or killed in such resolutions, the violence was contained, and a sense of justice preserved.[86] But the white invasion would test this balance. As women became scarcer and bands were pushed off their country, tensions could escalate, even between traditional allies.[87] The best-documented case, which probably occurred in the mid-1820s, was recounted by Robinson's Poredareme guide. His people, presumably led by Tongerlongeter, had given beads to the Luggermairrerner (a Big River band) in exchange for red ochre. When the pigment was not forthcoming, a 'war' ensued in which Poredareme and two allied bands fought the Luggermairrerner in a series of engagements. The Luggermairrerner initially 'killed several of their women and took some away'. In a subsequent battle, the Poredareme and their allies were victorious. However, this was not the end of the matter. The Luggermairrerner attacked again with a 'shower of spears' but were unable to rout the Poredareme. Afterwards, Tongerlongeter's warriors 'tracked them and fought with them and beat them off'.[88]

Disputes over women were at the heart of most of the

recorded intertribal violence in Tasmania, though it may not always have been that way. As subsequent chapters will attest, the scarcity of women and girls, due to their murder and abduction by white men, left many bands bereft of females. Because of women's importance to every realm of tribal life, the surviving men were desperate to replace them. This led inevitably to competition and violence.[89] Nevertheless, some amount of raiding for and fighting over women undoubtedly occurred before the arrival of Europeans.

While marriages were usually between men and women from different bands, the brides were not always consenting. Integrating females from enemy nations was an important source of genetic and linguistic diversity, though it could also stoke conflict.[90] The abduction of even one member of a tight-knit band elicited immense sorrow and anger. Such an affront could not go unpunished, and the result was sometimes a cascade of violence. An incident related to Robinson by the Bruny Island man Woorrady is telling. Woorrady's brother had abducted his wife from an enemy band, the Melukehedee. Despite their turbulent beginning, he was besotted with his new spouse. The feeling, however, was not mutual, and the reluctant bride soon absconded back to her people. Woorrady's brother, 'a big man and a warrior', went alone in pursuit of her. As Woorrady told it:

> He followed her to her own country and at last saw the object of his search with two men of her nation and some women. He halted a short distance from them and began preparing his spears, when he advanced and

fought with the two men. At length one [of the men] run away as if vanquished, but this was only a ruse and he came round the bush and attacked in the rear and speared him in the back. They then closed upon him and the women, particularly his wife, were most conspicuous in their savage cruelty towards him; she beat him on the head with a large tine. They killed him.

When they discovered what had happened, Woorrady's band sought revenge. The next time the Melukehedee 'came to the Huon River for eggs. The natives then fell upon them and killed a great number. WOORRADY killed his brother's wife after first violating her.'[91] As with animosities between the Poredareme and their enemies, it is impossible to know when or how such tensions first arose. Those involved may have had no idea either. The tit-for-tat had probably gone on for generations.[92]

All of this produced a culture preoccupied with warrior virtues. From a young age, boys honed their martial skills and warrior's mentality. As adults, mock battles were a source of entertainment and training.[93] A man's courage in battle formed the bedrock of his reputation, both among his own people and throughout the island.[94] Even more than hunting, warfare was celebrated in popular culture. It was depicted in charcoal dioramas on the walls of huts, such as the one discovered by the surveyor James Calder, which he described as 'a battle piece, a native fight – men dying and flying all over it.'[95] Victories became the subject of impassioned retellings.[96] Woorrady, for instance, regaled Robinson's party every other night with 'the exploits of his and neighbouring nations in hunting and their predatory wars.'[97] Another of Robinson's envoys delighted 'the other natives by telling them stories every night ... by singing them, each verse ending in a chorus, and consist of long journeys or travels with their various adventures, exploits of amorous adventures, [and] exploits in war, &c.'[98]

Tasmanians also paid homage to martial skill in their dances.[99] In one such 'War Dance', 'The motion of the body is the shifting attitude to avoid the spear in fighting; sometimes they call out "the spear is coming"'.[100] Given the centrality of war to the worlds of men like Tongerlongeter, it is not surprising that European colonists – most of whom had no military training and few bush skills – found them worthy adversaries.

As important as each warrior's skills were, a war party's strength rested on its ability to execute coordinated manoeuvres. This was especially true for the guerrilla-style attacks routinely made against the huts of the white invaders. The challenges Tongerlongeter faced in organising and leading a tactical response to such a novel and powerful enemy were tremendous. Numerous factors needed to be considered in order to execute an attack on a hut. These included objectives, reconnaissance, ritual preparation, weaponry, wind speed and direction, guard dogs, the strength of and distance to neighbouring whites, retreating and regrouping, topography and cover, surprise and misdirection, ensuring clear lines of communication, and assigning roles to upwards of twenty warriors in order to exploit their individual strengths and mitigate their weaknesses.[101] Then there was the burden of knowing that the lives of family members and lifelong friends hung on such decisions. While Tongerlongeter was celebrated for his victories, the deaths of his comrades undoubtedly weighed on his conscience. Their bodies had to be retrieved and rites conducted. In camp at night, his ears would ring with the wailing of the families, and all of this had to be borne with an iron resolve because the next day would be the same.

In less turbulent times, Tasmanian chiefs were 'merely heads of families of extraordinary prowess',[102] but in times of war, bands embraced strong, centralised leadership.[103] The criteria for leadership were meritocratic. Any aspiring leader had to prove himself as a man of ability and integrity. According to one observer: 'Each tribe, or portion of a tribe, is under a chief, who does not appear to be hereditary, but to attain his rank from his daring in war'.[104] And these warrior chiefs appear to have wielded considerable power. '[T]he chief of a nation has great power', claimed one Poredareme man. 'He is absolute, he can put to death whom he chooses, and can take away any of the young women of the tribe'.[105] During the Black War, these 'big men', as Robinson called them, were the backbone of Aboriginal resistance in Tasmania, and Tongerlongeter was the most effective and iconic of them all.[106]

CHAPTER 5

Zombie invasion

Nicholas Clements

The landing of an alien spacecraft is a common analogy used to illustrate what the arrival of Europeans must have been like for the bewildered Tasmanians. Just as a visitation by little green men would be a cataclysmic event if it happened today, so too the ships and gadgets of the pale-faced visitors left Tongerlongeter and his people reeling with wonder and trepidation. But the alien landing analogy doesn't hold up. Even if such a staggering event were to take place today, we are all familiar with the concept of aliens and of the cult mythology surrounding their alleged visits. Tongerlongeter and his fellow Tasmanians, by contrast, had not even considered that foreign lands and peoples might exist. The race was now on to discover who or what these beings were.

It was not possible to simply ask them. Until this point in history, there had never been a meeting between such radically different peoples. Not surprisingly, early encounters were characterised by confusion, indignation, amusement and frustration. Other than their odd manner and appearance, it was the newcomers' baffling technology that most distinguished them. Tasmanians had the simplest toolkit of any modern humans, while the European explorers they encountered, with their sophisticated ships and scientific instruments, were to the late 18th century what the Apollo astronauts were to the mid-20th. As one historian put it: 'People who could not boil water were confronted by the nation who had just contrived the steam engine'.[1] Culturally and economically, the distance between the two peoples was even wider. A Frenchman and an Englishman, even if they didn't speak the other's language, could achieve basic communication because of their many shared beliefs, expectations and aspirations. But when either tried to communicate with the Tasmanians, there was scarcely enough common ground to get started.

Naturally, Tongerlongeter sought to fit the newcomers into his existing worldview. Since his people had no precedent for such visitations, they turned to the spirit world for answers. Tasmanians believed the spirits of their deceased ancestors departed to a distant island.[2] Indeed, this appears to have been an exceptionally old belief system, as it was also common among Victorian Aborigines, from whom the Tasmanians had been separated for some 14 millenia.[3] These spirits were sometimes known to return and cause mischief among the living, but could it be that they were now coming back in embodied droves? There were certainly details that didn't fit – the physical changes, the strange animals and tools, the queer behaviour – and yet it must have been the best explanation on offer, as bands around the island all seemed to converge on the same conclusion – the white men were not men at all. Rather, they were ancestor spirits returned from the isle of the dead and somehow changed into sickly effigies of their former selves.

Deathly pale and draped in bizarre coverings, the white visitors looked if not dead, then at least cursed by some ghastly affliction. The leap to seeing them as malign spirits returned from the dead was not a big one. It may even have occurred to them at the very first moment of contact. Robinson's Bruny Island confidant, Woorrady, told him that 'when they saw the first ship coming at sea they were frightened, and said it was WRAGEOWRAPPER'.[4] Among the Bruny Islanders, Wrageowrapper was the word for evil spirit.[5] Remarkably, the Tasmanians' spiritual assumptions about the white men persisted throughout the period of early contact and into the war. Even in exile, the missionary James Backhouse found: 'One of their names for a white man signifies a white devil, or spirit; this has probably arisen from their mistaking white men at first for spiritual beings'. It was an observation confirmed by several others on Flinders Island.[6]

According to Backhouse, the exiled Tasmanians 'also say they suppose that when they die, they shall go to some of the islands in the Straits, and jump up [transform into] white men'.[7] His friend George Walker went into more detail: 'It is professed to be believed by some of them that they are transformed after death into white men, and that they return under this renewed form to an island in the Straits ... they connect it with some vague idea respecting the deceased visiting England', which of course was what the white strangers called the mysterious island from which they came.[8] Robinson was told the same story by bands throughout the island,[9] but the most compelling evidence for this belief comes from a rare fragment actually written by an Aboriginal Tasmanian. Walter George Arthur was born in the north-east around 1820. While his tribal name was not recorded, we know he was captured in April 1828 and acquired some basic literacy during his time at the King's Orphan School near Hobart. Sometime after rejoining what was left of his people on Flinders Island, Walter scrawled the following: 'White people coming in the country first and black people see them ... black people died then arose from the dead [and] became white men'. His final sentence trails off: 'But when I see in my country coming about ...'[10] Given how ubiquitous and stable such beliefs appear to have been, we can assume Tongerlongeter also viewed the arrival of the white strangers as, to put it in terms we might better appreciate today, something akin to an ancestral zombie invasion – one that eventually became apocalyptic.

The return of their deceased kin was extraordinary enough, but newly embodied, they now possessed the most inexplicable things, from otherworldly foods to outlandish creatures, some of which they actually sat atop of, allowing them to move at incredible speed. Most perplexing of all, though, were guns. Initially, Tasmanians didn't even run from these strange sticks, though they soon learnt to appreciate their destructive capability.[11] But what *were* guns, and what was the source of their great power? Robinson found that, in the beginning, they believed 'white men had weapons that vomited forth thunder and lightning', and even late in the war he still felt that 'these people attribute magic qualities to firearms'.[12] It is difficult to know when or even if Aborigines were disabused of such notions, though they soon learnt that these 'thunder sticks' had weaknesses they could exploit. In 1826, the *Colonial Times* reported: 'we find by every day's experience, that the natives are no longer afraid of a white man – that they know, [once] a gun is fired off, it is useless'.[13] That same year, the paper observed, 'when a person happens unfortunately to get surrounded by a tribe, they will rush in upon him the moment after he discharges his musket, fully aware that, before he can again load and prime his gun, they can close upon him, and thereby put him to death'.[14] Any Aborigine who survived until the mid-1820s had figured this out.[15]

But all this was in the future. In the years immediately following the arrival of the British in 1803, there was little contact between the newcomers and the local Aborigines. Undoubtedly, though, the latter were acutely aware of the former. Woorrady told Robinson:

> when the first people settled they cut down the trees,
> built houses, dug the ground and planted; that by and
> by more ships came, then at last plenty of ships; that the
> natives went to the mountains, went and looked at what
> the white people did, went and told other natives and
> they came and looked also.[16]

It was some time before the new arrivals ventured far beyond the Derwent Valley. The first were hunting parties, mostly convicts charged with supplying the ill-equipped and at times almost starving settlement with meat and furs.[17] By 1810, these hunters were penetrating deep into the Tasmanian interior, where encounters with Aborigines were more likely.[18] The governor's decision to arm groups of felons and send them out unescorted and with valuable hunting dogs was, to say the least, a gamble. A significant portion of those men 'went bush' and became Tasmania's first bushranging gangs. To give a sense of how pervasive this practice was, of the 292 convicts aboard the first shipment of felons to Tasmania, sixty-eight went bush, some more than once.[19]

After Risdon, it was hunters and outlaws who had the first significant encounters with Aborigines. While some of these interactions may have been mutually beneficial, or at least non-violent, hostility was the norm. Based on a range of evidence, including a series of edicts issued by the colony's first three governors,[20] it is clear that the conduct of these men towards Aborigines was anything but humane.[21] For at least the first decade, however, even formidable gangs of bushrangers found themselves outnumbered and outmatched by local bands. Aborigines regularly ejected such intruders.[22] As the diary of the colony's first chaplain, Robert Knopwood, attests, the Aborigines kept the diminutive white population on almost constant guard, and parties venturing beyond the settlements well understood that they were taking their lives in their hands.[23] For their part, while they sometimes resorted to lethal violence, local bands were remarkably restrained. It was, they could see, unwise to arouse the full wrath of the otherworldly strangers.

During the colony's first decade, the east coast was too

distant for the hunters supplying the Derwent settlements, but bushrangers did occasionally make it that far. In 1805, for instance, a group of escapees managed to reach Tongerlongeter's country in a stolen boat, 'where one of them was killed by the Natives whilst hunting'.[24] Between 1806 and 1808, the notorious bushrangers Richard Lemon and John Brown also spent time in the Oyster Bay area. It is unknown whether any Poredareme were among their victims, but while at large, the duo reportedly killed two men and a woman. Acting alone, Lemon claimed to have also tortured and killed two women; shooting and wounding four others.[25] And Lemon and Brown were not the only marauding sadists during this time. In his testimony to the Aborigines Committee, a panel of officials convened in 1830 to investigate the origins of the Black War, James Hobbs recounted the story of one of his whaleboat crewmen, James Carrotts. Carrotts, an ex-bushranger pardoned in 1813, told Hobbs 'he had once cut off a Native man's head at Oyster Bay, and made his wife hang it round her neck, and carry it as a plaything; from Carrotts' manner he credited the story'.[26] It is hard to know what to make of such claims, particularly in the pre-war period when most bands would have been more than a match for such men, yet the evidence that some bushrangers raped and murdered Aborigines is strong.

Bushrangers were not the only early trespassers on Poredareme country. Ships would have been visible to them at least once or twice a year from 1802 onwards. Some were just sheltering, but most were hunting seals or whales. These 'sealers', as all such men were called, came from the same social class as the convicts. Many were or had been under sentence, and just like a convict's, a sealer's life was typically one of deprivation and violence. Not surprisingly, they developed a well-earned reputation for lawlessness and cruelty.[27] Some ships came for just a few days, while others dropped crews off near remote seal colonies to club and process as many of the animals as possible before being picked up again several months later. Most sealing outfits focused their efforts in Bass Strait, but for those sailing via Hobart, the waters between Maria Island and Oyster Bay were home to the most prolific seal colony in south-east Tasmania, as well as considerable numbers of whales.[28]

At least three whaling vessels were operating off the coast of Tongerlongeter's country in 1803.[29] The first recorded sealing operation in the area began in 1805. In March of that year, Knopwood noted that the schooner *Nancy* had sailed past Oyster Bay, where its crew spied and rescued '8 men that belonged to the *Sophia* that were sealing there. The natives had set fire to their house and robbed them of their provisions. Had not the *Nancy* came they must have perished. The natives destroyd about 2000 skins'. The terrified men, Knopwood discovered, had been there since January.[30] The local Aborigines were sending a clear message. Sealers eventually became notorious for abducting Aboriginal women but, had this been the motive for the attack, it is unlikely any would have survived to tell the tale. By plundering or burning their every possession, the warriors were probably just issuing an eviction notice.

In 1805, Tongerlongeter was only around fifteen and may not have been involved in these attacks. But his day was coming. As long as there were seals, there would be sealers. In 1815, the merchant trader William Stewart reported on the sealers' practice of 'hunting and foraging' for Aboriginal women. Once in captivity, the sealers

> transfer and dispose of [the women] from one to another as their own property; very few of whom ever see their Native Home again … and, if they do not comply with their desires or orders in hunting, etc., they by way of punishment half hang them, cut their heads with Clubs in a Shocking Manner, or flog them most unmercifully with Cats made of Kangaroo Sinews; several of them have from two to six women, who they claim as their own private property in this Manner.[31]

Only a minority of the women and girls abducted by sealers were alive when government agents set about liberating them in the early 1830s.[32] Among those who both survived and had their place of origin recorded, sixteen were from Oyster Bay or Big River bands.[33] While north-east Tasmania was hit worst by sealers, the Poredareme were not exempt from this scourge.

An Aboriginal woman's prospects, once she fell into the hands of sealers, were bleak.[34] The stories of four Oyster Bay women illustrate just how bleak. Looerryminer's case was typical. On Flinders Island, she told Backhouse how 'the sealers rowed away with her' and she was shipped into slavery in Bass Strait. Looerryminer went on to describe 'the manner in which these men flogged the women who did not pluck Mutton-birds, or do other work to their satisfaction. She spread her hands to the wall, to shew the manner in which they were tied up, said a rope was used to flog them with, and cried out with a failing voice till she sank upon the ground, as if exhausted.'[35] Looerryminer's fate was shared by two Poredareme sisters, Tekartee and Tanlebonyer. Just before her death in 1831, Tekartee told Robinson 'that one of the sealers named Hervey stole her away when a little girl' and that 'the sealers flog the women.'[36] Hervey later sold Tekartee to a fellow sealer 'for some seal skins.'[37] Her sister, Tanlebonyer, was abducted by a sealer named John Brown, who prostituted her to other sealers for the price of one seal skin or one kangaroo skin per night.[38]

Mathabelianna's case was different but no less heart-breaking. The circumstances of how she ended up on George Meredith junior's sealing vessel are not known. Meredith was the eldest son and namesake of the east coast's earliest and wealthiest settler. Father and son established a sealing and whaling base at Oyster Bay in 1824, which Meredith junior operated.[39] Some years later, Meredith, John Brown and several other sealers embarked on a slaving expedition to Point Nepean, Victoria. They took Mathabelianna with them, forcing her to 'entice' women and girls from a curious local band to where they could be seized and bound by Meredith and his crew. Meredith then took his captives to the Furneaux Islands in Bass Strait, where he sold the lot for £7 each, Mathabelianna included.[40] It was a lucrative but deadly trade. Meredith was speared to death on a subsequent expedition, something Robinson considered a 'just retribution', as 'Many aggressions had been committed by the Merediths on the natives at Oyster Bay'.[41]

Tongerlongeter and his neighbours on the east coast were far from passive in the face of incursions by sealers. In November 1818, the *Hobart Town Gazette* reported on the harrowing journey of five men who had sailed to Oyster Bay to hunt 'kangaroo, seal, and swan':

Their labours were attended with more than usual success; having at this place procured 300lbs. [135 kilograms] of swan feathers, 60 swan skins, 100 kangaroo skins, and 34 live swans; and … 150 seal skins. Their labours being thus successfully terminated, they were inclined to return home; and in order to arrange for that purpose, on the 13th instant they put into Grindstone Bay [in Poredareme country] … where from contrary winds they were detained three days. During their stay at this place, they went a second time to Big Swan Port [Oyster Bay], for the purpose of increasing their number of seal skins, leaving behind John Kemp in care of the live swans, 4 kangaroo dogs, 3 muskets, some ammunition, sealing knives, and the various skins, &c. they had procured. After having obtained more seal skins, they returned the same day to Grindstone Bay; and when near the shore, the first object which attracted their sight was the corpse of their unfortunate companion Kemp lying at the water's edge, cut and mangled in a manner too shocking to relate. Foley instantly jumped out of the boat and had only time to perceive that the greater part of the articles left with the deceased were destroyed or taken away, when the natives, who were in ambuscade, suddenly appeared on the beach, armed with spears.[42]

Clearly, these men were not the only visitors to Poredareme country in this early period. The article ends by noting: 'We are credibly informed by a person who has often visited Oyster Bay, that it is a favourite resort of the natives, no less than 500 having been seen assembled there at once'. Moreover, several months later,

> A man returned from Oyster Bay on Monday, who had been speared by the Natives supposed to be the same by whom John Kemp was killed some time ago. The tribe who frequents Oyster Bay should be particularly guarded against, as they seem to have such a strong and rooted animosity towards the white people.[43]

For the first decade and a half after the white men settled, their number grew slowly and their expansion out from the Derwent was limited. In 1810, their southern population numbered barely a thousand, and by 1814 it had increased to just 1444. But by 1823, the total number of strangers on the island had swelled to over 10000 – the majority convicts.[44] That year, nearly 180000 hectares of land were granted to arriving immigrants and felons who had served out their sentence. The trickle of invaders had become a flood, flowing swiftly and inexorably up the fertile valleys that were home to many of Tongerlongeter's allies.[45] While Tongerlongeter would certainly have encountered white men during his band's seasonal peregrinations, the strangers rarely visited his homeland before 1821. During that year, though, six families settled at Oyster Bay on grants totalling 3197 hectares. By the time of the census in 1823, thirty-eight settlers and thirty-one convicts, together with more than 4000 sheep and cattle, were already living on or near Poredareme country.[46] That same year, the line of farms extending north from Hobart linked up with those sprawling southward from Launceston. It was a hairline crack in Tongerlongeter's world that would soon become a critical rupture.

Before the mid-1820s, most Oyster Bay and Big River bands took a cautious approach to the invaders in their midst.[47] As affronted as they were by the violence they experienced at the hands of white men, and by their unwanted presence, they were also wary of their power. It seems most bands tried to avoid all-out war for as long as possible. There is even some evidence of non-violent interactions occurring on the fringes of settlement. In the early 1820s, for instance, Gilbert Robertson reported a visit by '87 of the Natives on one occasion at his own house at the Coal River; they behaved themselves very peaceably; there were men, women and children'.[48] This amicability might in part be explained by Robertson's overt sympathy for the Aborigines, and as we will see, because he too was black. Some settlers later claimed that during this same period they offered food and friendship to Aborigines who approached them. Interestingly, though, there are next to no contemporaneous accounts of this.[49]

The evidence comes almost exclusively from testimonies given to the Aborigines Committee in 1830. While these testimonies should certainly not be dismissed, and some settlers surely made such overtures, the 'respectable' men who were questioned by the committee were plainly trying to distance themselves from the violence then engulfing the island. Having done all they could to befriend 'these poor uncultivated beings', they laid the blame for the war squarely at the feet of the convicts, who as a matter of course, they declared, 'shoot and hunt the Natives'.[50]

The small but significant number of Tasmanians who learnt something of the white man's language is further evidence of non-violent contact before the war. This was due less to direct interaction between bands and settlers than to individual and small groups of Aborigines spending time on the fringes of white society.[51] There were various reasons they did this. Individuals whose country had already been usurped or their bands decimated had few options but to join refugee camps on the fringes of colonial towns. Likewise, many children were stolen from local bands in the pre-war years.[52] 'In 1817', one historian noted, 'there were at least fifty Aboriginal children living with settlers', and that these were 'almost certainly refugees from armed conflict'.[53] Many of these children ended up in a state of vagrancy with a strong taste for, if not a dependence on, the white man's goods. The most sought-after items were flour, sugar, potatoes, tea, alcohol and tobacco. To acquire such items, some were willing to beg, steal, or prostitute themselves.[54] Surviving references are all alike; as one observer put it, 'they are in every respect the most destitute and wretched portion of the human family'.[55]

As early as April 1818, a local newspaper noted that 'notwith-standing the hostility which has so long prevailed in the breasts of the Natives of this island towards Europeans … Several of them are to be seen about this town and its neighbourhood, who obtain subsistence from the charitable and well-disposed'.[56] Three months later, it observed that the Aborigines 'constantly avoid the settlements, into which a few women have very lately introduced themselves in a state of famine'.[57] And then, in November, two Aborigines who had lived about Hobart for some time 'were charged with robbing Robin Gavin of several articles, and James Goodwin of a musket at Coal River; after which they escaped to the woods, and were there apprehended, both armed'.[58] The circumstances of these destitute 'fringe dwellers' were clearly dire, because in December a correspondent to the *Hobart Town Gazette* decried 'That most shameful, cruel, and barbarous custom of encouraging the Black people to murder or mangle one another for the sport of the learned, the polite, and the refined Europeans'. He complained of how the Sabbath had been

> most impiously violated by the blows and cries of the Blacks, excited to uproar and outrage by the Whites, who take pleasure in the sufferings of their fellow men, and, who will propose and give a reward, that the unoffending may be slain, or injured, merely to gratify or indulge the diabolical passions of a base mind …[59]

Somewhere between the worlds of their tribal kinfolk and the destitute vagrants of Hobart Town was the 'tame mob', as contemporaries called the loose-knit band of detribalised Aborigines hailing mostly from Oyster Bay and Big River bands. According to 19th-century historian James Bonwick, 'Many of them had transgressed tribal laws in their own districts, and were obliged to live abroad for a season. The Superior attractions of town life may have seduced some from the forests'.[60] At Pitt Water in 1823, the Reverend William Horton encountered this group, which comprised

> 20 or 30 of both sexes and of different ages … who had
> absconded from their proper tribes in the interior …
> [they] have no settled place of abode, but wander about
> from one part to another, subsisting on what is given
> them by the benevolent, and on kangaroos, opossums,
> oysters, &c. which they procure for themselves, and
> lodging in all seasons around their fires in the open air.
> Though they have now been accustomed for several
> years to behold the superior comforts and pursuits of
> civilised man, they have not advanced one step from their
> original barbarism. All that they have imbibed from us
> is a smattering of our language and a fondness for our
> tobacco and spiritous liquors.[61]

We know that at least one and possibly several Poredareme spent time among the tame mob. Despite their uncompromising rejection of white society, the Poredareme's leadership did not necessarily banish those who flirted with the newcomers. It is not known whether Tongerlongeter was already heading the band when they killed John Kemp at Grindstone Bay in 1818, but as the survivors rowed away with the sealer's lifeless body, they observed among the jeering victors 'a native girl, who had been some time among those at present walking about the streets of Hobart Town …[who] in an apparent friendly, but artful manner entreated the party to return'.[62] Why had she gone to Hobart? Why had she returned? The circumstances of such comings and goings are frustratingly elusive, though certainly this woman and people like her communicated a trove of valuable information to their kinfolk. Tongerlongeter kept his distance from white society, but by maintaining relationships with those who didn't, he developed a detailed understanding of his enemy.

CHAPTER 6

A wayward brother

Nicholas Clements

The story of an Aboriginal warrior is never the story of just one man. Every aspect of Tongerlongeter's life was bound up with his kinfolk. Some of them played major roles in his story, and in the trajectory of the Black War. Most notable among these was Kickertopoller, or Black Tom as the whites called him. Tongerlongeter was maybe a decade older than the younger Poredareme man. Kickertopoller would have respected, even feared the chief.[1] Tongerlongeter and the other senior men taught him how to throw a spear with precision, and how to hold himself in combat. They would have guided him in ceremonies and revealed to him the many mysteries of the spirit world. Kickertopoller's upbringing would normally have been very similar to his mentor's, but these were not normal times. The difference between being born c. 1790 and c. 1800 was profound. Tongerlongeter came of age at a time when the white men were still a peripheral concern, a worrying novelty not an existential threat. Kickertopoller, by contrast, was shedding his adolescence just as the tide of white settlement started to lap ominously at his people's feet.

In only a few years, the Poredareme went from spying the odd colonist in the course of their migratory journeys to having to factor the sprawling invaders into their every move. There were reasons to avoid them and reasons to fraternise with them, but ignoring them had become untenable.

Kickertopoller was curious and brave and impulsive. Despite his fealty to the Poredareme, he was drawn to the whites, to their strangeness and power, but also to their exotic foods and heady stimulants. It's not clear how, but in February 1819, Kickertopoller found himself in Hobart. Although the sources are hazy, he seems to have spent time in the recently conceived 'Establishment for the Native People', recovering from what was probably dysentery.[2] While it masqueraded as evidence of the governor's 'humane intentions', the establishment was in reality just a single-room building rented for a pittance to shelter Aborigines in need of medical attention.[3] The short-lived clinic was overseen by the ailing drunkard Edward Luttrell, described by Governor Macquarie in New South Wales as 'criminally inattentive to his patients, extremely irritable, and violent in his temper'.[4] Still, despite the third-rate facilities and care, Kickertopoller recovered.

In running the establishment, Luttrell may have had some assistance, or at least discreet oversight, from a more reputable surgeon. Dr Thomas Birch was by then largely preoccupied with his business ventures, but the governor, long exasperated by Luttrell, may have asked his close friend to keep an eye on the makeshift clinic.[5] However it was that Birch came to meet Kickertopoller, he took a strong interest in the young convalescent. On 17 February 1819, Kickertopoller was christened with his patron's name.[6] Around the same time, 'Black Tom Birch' moved in with the doctor, his wife, Sarah, and their young family.[7]

The bond between Kickertopoller and his well-to-do foster family was evidently a warm one. Sarah Birch recalled their years together with fondness: 'He was so good and useful a lad, so obliging and gentle, so honest and careful, and so thoroughly devoted to his master … he gave promise of true civilization.'[8] Indeed, the Birches became so comfortable with Kickertopoller that they often left him in charge of their children.[9] For a time at least, he seems to have seriously entertained making a life among the whites.

The sudden death of Thomas Birch in December 1821 was a huge blow to Kickertopoller and to his will to persist with 'civilisation', though cracks were probably forming before this. Three months earlier, while guiding a survey party overland to Oyster Bay, he abandoned them and made his own way back to Hobart.[10] It's not clear why Kickertopoller agreed to lead the expedition, why he left it, or how returning to his country made him feel. It was around this time, though, that the spell of civilised life began to break. According to Sarah Birch:

He pictured the hopelessness and aimlessness of his future. What could he ever be but the slave of the Whites? Could he get a wife among them? Would they admit him on an equality with themselves? Did they not look upon him as a black dog? And would they not treat him very soon accordingly? Then temptations were placed before him. He was incited to drink. He was admitted into the licentious orgies of the roaming tribe. [We] saw the change coming over him, and strove to counteract the evil, but in vain.[11]

Despite Sarah's obvious affection for Kickertopoller, the death of her husband threw her life into disarray. A gulf developed between them. Now a wealthy widow, Sarah was soon engaged to her property manager, Edmund Hodgson. The quick-tempered Hodgson, who was at once unscrupulous and sanctimonious, did not share his predecessor's fondness for the young Aborigine.[12] He put him to work on their farm at Lovely Banks, where he treated him cruelly. Kickertopoller was also taunted by the convict servants he worked alongside, two of whom would come to feel his wrath.[13] Whether it was because of mistreatment or because, as George Augustus Robinson later claimed, 'a black girl had enticed him away',[14] Kickertopoller 'went bush' in 1822.

After Birch's death, Kickertopoller's disillusionment with white society deepened.[15] Casting off the white man's clothing, he returned to open-air living among the tame mob. Here he found solidarity with other disaffected or dislocated Aborigines.[16] But theirs was not a wholly traditional life. While they were sighted throughout Oyster Bay and Big River territories in the early 1820s, hunting and mixing with kin, they also visited farms and settlements.[17] Tongerlongeter had clearly not ostracised Kickertopoller, though the younger warrior's affinity for sugary tea and damper, as well as for tobacco and spirits, militated against his reintegration into the Poredareme. Even so, there is no evidence that Kickertopoller or his band of misfits felt ashamed of their decision to partly indulge in and partly eschew white society. Accounts of their interactions with white men show no obsequiousness. On the contrary, they typically intimidated the newcomers into giving them what they wanted and laughed in the faces of do-gooders who tut-tutted their lifestyle.[18] For the most part, though, they simply ignored the white men who attempted to engage them.[19]

There was, however, one among them who was fond of ingratiating himself with the white men. Musquito's stormy life had taken him from resistance fighter in Sydney to exile on Norfolk Island to labourer and tracker in Tasmania. He became a minor celebrity in 1818 when he helped track the notorious bushranger Michael Howe. As a reward, the governor promised to repatriate him to New South Wales and reunite him with his people, but this was never honoured. Bitter and dejected, Musquito joined the tame mob, in which he became an important figure alongside Kickertopoller. Contemporaries saw both as leaders of the mob,[20] but Kickertopoller had the real influence.[21] A host of factors undermined Musquito's sway with the locals. Before joining the tame mob, he had committed acts of violence against south-east bands.[22] Indeed, Bonwick wrote of a group of Oyster Bay warriors 'setting on him one day, and beating him nearly to death with their waddies'.[23] Even if this was not a barrier to his leadership, his inability to speak local dialects fluently or comprehend local beliefs and customs was.[24] Nevertheless, Kickertopoller had a genuine affinity for the exiled warrior.[25] This was probably due to their common experience of embracing and then being rejected by white society. They had learnt a lot from whites, but eventually they realised the whites would only ever see them as savages. They had a decision to make but it was scarcely a choice. They were warriors, and they would never be content with the scraps from the white man's table.

By late 1823, race relations in south-east Tasmania were combustible. The invasion of Aboriginal territory was proceeding so fast the survey department would be backdating land grants for years as settlers leapfrogged each other to claim the best acreage.[26] It was a frenzied advance that the Oyster Bay and Big River nations could not endure for long. The ignition point came in mid-November. Kickertopoller, Musquito and the tame mob had rendezvoused with 'the Oyster Bay tribe' at Grindstone Bay, in the heart of Tongerlongeter's country.[27] We know a number of Poredareme were present, and their chief, Tongerlongeter, was almost certainly among them.[28] The groups, which together numbered about seventy,[29] made camp near a hut occupied by three stockmen, John Radford, William Hollyoak, and a Tahitian named Mammoa. Grindstone Bay, which 'swarmed with large game, namely, emu and kangaroo', was a popular resort for Aborigines.[30] Its occupation by white intruders was undoubtedly a source of resentment, but it was the violation of an Aboriginal woman that triggered the attack widely considered to have initiated the Black War. Musquito was known to organise Aboriginal women to have sex with colonists in exchange for food, tobacco and other items.[31] This was likely the case at Grindstone Bay, though John Radford, the only white man who would come out alive, could obviously not admit this under oath.

On the second day, the Aborigines launched a vicious attack, which left Hollyoak and Mammoa dead and Radford seriously wounded. Radford claimed it was unprovoked,[32] but Kickertopoller and Musquito told a very different story. Musquito put it simply: 'some tak't away my "*gin*" [woman]: that make a fight'.[33] Kickertopoller was more specific. When he revisited the site with George Augustus Robinson in 1831, and 'saw the graves that contained the bodies of two white men', he recounted 'stopping at this hut with the mob and that as one of the women was walking away, they fired a quantity of small shot into her back which made a wound as broad as his hand. Tom said it was as cruel a thing as ever he saw done'.[34] Radford had every reason to lie; Kickertopoller had none.

One of the stockmen must have lost his temper and fired on the woman, because even armed with muskets, the stockmen were in a vulnerable position. The retaliation was a frenzy of violence. Warriors assailed Hollyoak and Mammoa with staggering ferocity. In the case of Mammoa, 'the head [was] beaten almost to pieces – the body pierced by spears in thirty-seven different places ... such was the force with which they cast their weapons at the body that many broken spears were afterwards found scattered about the ground where he died'.[35] Radford, despite being speared twice as he ran, made a miraculous escape. Neighbouring stockmen saved his life and got him to a hospital in Hobart, where he eventually recovered from his wounds. Even though Radford testified explicitly that Musquito did not participate in the violence, most contemporaries lazily blamed the killings on the devil they knew. This stemmed from the common assumption that the 'blacks of this Island are distinct from those of New South Wales, possessing more barbarous habits and more confirmed in their deplorable state of ignorance'.[36] As more insightful commentators appreciated, though, the Poredareme men had all the power at Grindstone Bay.[37]

Typically, the Poredareme would have cremated the fallen woman's body, but with Radford's escape, this may have been deemed too risky. The band moved quickly north to Oyster Bay. Local colonists rallied to send a clear message. Just four days after the killings, a revenge party discovered the band and opened fire. In the ensuing chaos, everyone 'scattered', leaving their dogs and weapons and fleeing across a lagoon.[38] Everyone, that is, except a woman who was captured and taken back to Grindstone Bay to point out the location of the now putrefying bodies. Then, on 14 December, the constable at Oyster Bay recorded in his diary:

> The natives who of late have been in the woods near
> my hut, have this day set the grass on fire near my
> farm … I sent my eldest son who was joined by two of
> Mr Meredith's men who fired at them and wounded one
> of the mobe [sic] who appeared numerous and fled over
> the hill. They pursued them for some time and returned
> after dark with a number of spears.[39]

Reprisal parties scoured the country for months afterwards.[40] Radford himself 'is said to have sworn not to rest two nights in his bed until he had taken a bloody revenge', and when he and 'a party of thirty constables, soldiers, and neighbours set off to execute his threat ... the number slain was considerable'.[41] But, while the Poredareme and the tame mob may have had their noses bloodied after Grindstone Bay, they were not cowed.

Kickertopoller experienced none of this retribution. Immediately following the killings at Grindstone Bay, he set out for Hobart, apparently on his own. Why is a mystery. Perhaps he was spooked by the sudden escalation. With his unique insight into the white man's power, he knew a dangerous line had been crossed. Maybe he had been close to the murdered woman, or maybe he was just pining for the security he had recently enjoyed with the Birches. Whatever his reasons, he soon ended up in custody.[42] The authorities decided to summarily exile Kickertopoller to the draconian penal settlement at Macquarie Harbour on Tasmania's west coast. Not for the last time, though, Sarah Birch interceded on his behalf, and around January 1824, the young warrior was quietly set free.[43]

That same month a warrant went out for Musquito's arrest.[44] By March, he had £100 on his head. It was a huge sum for the time — equivalent to a year's professional salary today — and it meant there were always several parties out in pursuit.[45] Meanwhile, a spate of Aboriginal violence was rippling through the south-east. In the twelve months following the Grindstone Bay incident, at least seven colonists were killed and four wounded in Oyster Bay country, and several more in Big River country. The pattern of the reported attacks was such that Musquito can be implicated in just one of them – the wounding of a man at Pitt Water in July 1824.[46] Kickertopoller, by contrast, was central to the rising violence.[47] On 10 June, for instance, Mr Osborne was killed and his wife severely wounded at Jericho. Mrs Osborne eventually recovered enough to make a statement, which is worth quoting at length as it speaks for the intensity of Kickertopoller's (Tom's) contempt of the invaders and the swagger with which he led. Mrs Osborne recalled she had been 'churning in the dairy' when

her husband rushed in and cried, 'O! Mary, Mary, the hill is covered with savages!' … In a few minutes the blacks had arrived within 50 yards [forty-five metres] of the door, Black Tom being their apparent leader; when Mr. Osborne addressed them by saying, 'What do you want? Are you hungry?' The answer was, 'Yes, white man, yes'. Then, said Mr. Osborne, 'Lay down your spears, and light a fire, and I'll give you some potatoes and butter'. At this time a large loaf was in the kitchen, which the deceased begged his wife to cut up, and distribute among them; but she was in such a nervous state as prevented her from doing more than breaking it in two pieces, and laying it before the sable tribe, with a request that they might fairly divide it. The deceased again said, 'Lay down your spears'. – 'We will,' answered Black Tom, 'If you, white man, put down your musket'. After a short discourse, the gun and spears were placed on the ground, the blacks (each of whom carried a fire-stick) came close to the house, were presented with some potatoes, which they began to roast, and seemed quite satisfied. Having eaten them, a party entered the house, and asked for more; the deceased went out to get some, and on his return, his musket was missing. Apprehensions of treachery were now awakened, and the deceased said, 'I'm a dead man!' A moment afterwards Black Tom entered, and after saying (as he pointed to many things in the house), I must have this, and I must have that, he took Mr. Osborne's hat off his head, and wore it himself. Two of the blacks then grasped, as if to shake in friendliness, the hands of the deceased, when a third, who stood at a little distance, forcibly drove a spear into his back, which convulsed him to such a degree, that with a scream he bounded several yards, and fell. Mrs. Osborne rushed wildly out, crying, 'murder! murder!' was pursued, and at length overtaken, after receiving three desperate wounds in the side and, neck.[48]

Mrs Osborne's account suggests Kickertopoller was animated by revenge. The couple was certainly known to him, having resided near the Birches during the time he had lived with them. He probably had payback in mind for his next target too. Edmund Hodgson had not only treated Kickertopoller poorly, he had also come between him and Sarah. But when his mob descended on the Lovely Banks property, he was surprised to find Hodgson absent. Instead, he was met by Sarah, who seems to have not only deterred him from attacking the property, but also convinced him to lay down his spears and rejoin her on the farm.[49] She even wrote to the local paper to provide her protégé with an alibi for the Osborne attacks. No one was about to question one of the colony's most influential settlers, so the matter was dropped.[50] How the rest of Kickertopoller's mob felt about his impromptu change of heart can only be guessed at, but they departed without violence. For the next five months, Kickertopoller worked for Sarah at Lovely Banks. When he was tasked in October with driving a bullock dray to Hobart, however, he discovered that his friends, Musquito and Jack, were in prison and awaiting trial. He returned the dray to Lovely Banks and walked off the property for the last time.[51] He had resolved, it seems, to make a stand, though for what is unclear. It may not even have been clear to him.

Whatever influence Musquito had on Tasmania's frontier violence, it was short-lived. In early August 1824, two constables and an 'Aboriginal youth' called Tegg surprised him at Oyster Bay. He had been absent when Kickertopoller and the others had attacked the Osbornes, and now it was just him and his two 'wives'. Unarmed, Musquito fled, but he didn't get far. Tegg, who had lived with a Hobart family for some years, unloaded his double-barrelled shotgun into the fugitive's groin and thigh. All three were apprehended.[52] Somehow, Musquito survived his wounds and the trip back to Hobart.[53] Together with another member of the tame mob known as 'Black Jack', about whom little is known, he was charged in connection with the Grindstone Bay killings. But just four weeks before their cases were heard, a remarkable event took place.

On 3 November 1824, sixty-four warriors appeared in Hobart.[54] Stunned officials scrambled to accommodate and reassure them. Observers noted that the delegation comprised members of the tame mob and two 'Oyster Bay' bands. They were headed by three 'leaders', one of whom 'could speak broken English'.[55] This was almost certainly Kickertopoller, and Tongerlongeter was probably one of the others. Why were they there? Liberating Musquito may have animated a few, but none of the first-hand accounts mentions this.[56] A close reading of the evidence suggests their primary motive was not to champion Musquito's release but to negotiate an accord that would pull the situation back from the precipice of war. These warriors would not have risked everything to come to the aid of a man most of them loathed. Moreover, Kickertopoller assured government officials that his delegation could 'come with many more' if things went well.[57] This suggests they were bargaining – and taking a great risk to do so. On the frontier, sixty-four warriors were an imposing force, but here they were dangerously exposed.[58] Only the desire to avert all-out war could have motivated such a bold attempt at peaceful communication. It seems they could already foresee the consequences of resisting the white juggernaut.

George Arthur, the colony's newly arrived governor, had 'frequent interviews' with the visiting warriors. Kickertopoller, who was likely pivotal in organising the delegations, undoubtedly acted as interpreter. Arthur was impressed by their intelligence and distributed army-issue caps and blankets as a gesture of good will, but it seems he was unmoved by their requests.[59] Once it became clear they would not be taken seriously, the group's mood shifted. According to one settler, 'upon the failure of their efforts, [they] returned to the bush with bitterer feelings'.[60] The governor's private secretary, however, had a more naïve interpretation of their departure: 'The third day they were rather sullen and refused to sing the Kangaroo song, and moved off the next morning', attempting to spear a man as they decamped.[61] The following month, sporting new caps, they resumed their premeditated attacks on colonists.[62]

On 1 December 1824, Musquito and Black Jack were tried in Hobart's Supreme Court by a jury comprised if not of their enemies then certainly not of their peers. Presumably neither man understood much of the proceedings. Neither was offered legal counsel or permitted to speak in his own defence. At the conclusion of this show trial, Musquito was sentenced to hang for 'aiding and abetting' the killers at Grindstone Bay. Although Radford testified that Black Jack was present, he was acquitted. His luck gave out, though, when he was found guilty the following month of murdering a hut-keeper at Sorell Plains. On the morning of 25 February 1825, Reverend William Bedford came to the prison and beseeched Black Jack to pray for forgiveness. He replied simply: 'You pray yourself. I'm too bloody frightened to pray.'[63] Later that day, to the great pleasure of the bustling crowd, Musquito, Black Jack and six white felons were executed in the name of justice.[64]

Had Musquito been 'the cruellest savage that ever tormented a colony,'[65] as some colonists believed, their problems would have been over. But he wasn't, and they weren't. The nascent resistance of Oyster Bay – Big River bands continued throughout 1825 and into 1826. Kickertopoller was in the thick of it. And while Tongerlongeter's name was not yet known to his victims, we can safely assume he too was involved. Moreover, circumstantial evidence points to some collaboration between Poredareme warriors and Kickertopoller's tame mob.[66] Their evolving resistance campaign will be the focus of the next chapter, but this one must close with the act that probably did more than anything to ignite Tongerlongeter's fury. If relations between whites and blacks in the south-east were strained by the hanging of Musquito and Black Jack, they were irreparably broken in September 1826 when the governor executed two Poredareme warriors. The whites called them Jack and Dick, and the latter was Tongerlongeter's brother.[67]

Jack and Dick were captured in April 1826 at Oyster Bay, where they had recently killed a stockman.[68] Escorted to Hobart in chains, they spent the frigid Tasmanian winter huddled in a dank cell. Remarkably, Jack, described as 'a youth, tall and erect', 'seemed quite unmoved at his awful situation'. It was even reported that 'he frequently imitates the marching of the sentry in the gaol-yard, with much accuracy'. Only in the forty-eight hours before his execution did the younger warrior's nerves begin to fray. In contrast, Dick was described as 'very old, has a long beard, long hair in ringlets, and is coloured with red ochre; he is ill and feeble, so much so, that he is only able to move about in the prison, by crawling on his hands and knees, with only a piece of loose blanket thrown over his body'. In addition to his decrepitude, Dick was 'suffering under a loathsome cutaneous [skin] disease, which almost covered his body'. He was, nevertheless, 'fully sensible of his impending fate'.[69]

Just after dawn on 13 September, the hangman began his work. One wonders what Jack and Dick made of this bizarre ritual murder. 'The old black died very hard', one observer wrote. Jack's end was even worse, 'the cord having slipped … up to his elbow, he reached up his hand to his neck, and bled profusely from the nose'.[70] The last thing they saw before the noose went tight was a sea of white faces, some pious and censorious, others giddy with schadenfreude.[71] Still, not everyone was comfortable with the idea of executing people according to laws they had never heard of – least of all for the 'crime' of defending their homeland. As the surveyor John Helder Wedge remarked:

> the executions were very questionable; for I am at a loss to imagine how he could be amenable to our Laws – no compact having been made with the natives nor did they directly, or indirectly ever acknowledge or submit to our jurisdiction – neither did they understand our language – The trial was therefore a mockery. The execution a bloody act of vengeance.[72]

News of the executions spread quickly among the bands.[73] They signalled a turning point in the war, and henceforth every encounter with the white man would be hostile.[74] To most Oyster Bay – Big River people, the hangings must have appeared like macabre human sacrifices, but Kickertopoller understood the full indignity of the noose, and he was livid.[75] He and Tongerlongeter surely felt vindicated in their decisions to take up arms against the invaders. But theirs was also a personal loss. Jack and Dick were friends and brothers. Their deaths surely had a searing effect on the close-knit Poredareme. It was one thing to lose a comrade in war, it was quite another to see their lives snuffed out by the cool hand of a government that preached one law for all but never held its own to account. Kickertopoller later told Gilbert Robertson that his people considered the hanged Aborigines 'as martyrs in the conquest of their country',[76] and together with Tongerlongeter, he put his bitterness into practice. He told Robertson that a number of killings were in direct response to the executions.[77] To surveyor James Calder's eye, the effect was beyond doubt: 'With the deaths of these four men, the estrangement of the two races, which before was never more than temporary and partial, became complete.'[78] According to a 'Gentleman in the interior' writing just two months after Jack and Dick's execution, 'Black Tom, and those with him, declare that they will murder every white man that they fall in with.'[79]

CHAPTER 7

Retribution: 1824–27

Nicholas Clements

Kickertopoller never rejoined the Poredareme. It's not clear why. Perhaps, after all that had happened, he simply felt he didn't belong anymore. He was still drawn to the white man's stimulants, even if he was no longer enchanted by his way of life. At a minimum, his faltering commitments must have disappointed Tongerlongeter, though the chief could ill afford to banish such a valuable informant. Kickertopoller was also a capable warrior and leader in his own right, and in the fight that was coming, Tongerlongeter needed every ally he had. While the sources are mute on the intricacies of their relationship, there is circumstantial evidence indicating that Tongerlongeter and Kickertopoller retained an enduring bond. Indeed, as we will see, it was this bond that allowed the war to be brought to a close eight years after Grindstone Bay. Yet before this could happen, both men had to survive the looming cataclysm. Ultimately, they would settle on very different strategies, but for the first half of the war, they fought together against the white intruders, not always side by side but as allies in an increasingly desperate struggle.

Why didn't Tongerlongeter and his allies just crush
the white men at the outset, when they had the upper
hand? If they were as 'tenacious of their hunting grounds' as
contemporaries claimed,[1] why did they allow even one settler
to establish himself? The Poredareme alone probably had
two or three dozen warriors. Had Tongerlongeter chosen to
unleash them on the first settlers, exposed and vulnerable as
they were, they wouldn't have survived their first week. Even
allowing for the fact that he didn't know how many settlers
would follow, Tongerlongeter's hesitation can be hard to make
sense of. One historian has even interpreted this delayed
resistance as evidence that Aborigines were neither attached
to their country nor resentful of its occupation; yet this view
is naïve.[2] While there may have been some complacency
early on, the reluctance of Tongerlongeter and others to
decisively repulse the first incursions makes perfect sense
given what they believed. The recent return of vast numbers
of grotesquely reincarnated ancestors was cause for grave
caution. Even with the insights provided by Kickertopoller,
their spiritual interpretation of the new arrivals prevented
Tongerlongeter and his ilk from appreciating their true nature
and purpose. Still, they fully understood that the white men
were dangerous. As much as they resented the strangers'
presence, they knew nothing good could come from further
escalating the violence.

Tongerlongeter's anxiety over the invaders' rapid advance
must have been intense, but in keeping with traditional
concepts of justice, he initially limited his warriors to avenging
specific grievances.[3] It's not that they were nonchalant about

the arrival of white men. They told numerous contemporaries that the invasion of their homelands animated them above all else.[4] But as long as there remained some hope of avoiding all-out war, Tongerlongeter and his allies appear to have grudgingly tolerated the strangers' presence provided they did them no violence. By the middle of the decade, though, enough colonists were actively seeking to harm them that bands like the Poredareme were regularly taking retributive action.[5]

In Oyster Bay – Big River territory between 1824 and 1827, sources describe eighteen assaults on Aborigines in which some thirty-one were killed, six wounded and twenty-one captured.[6] Of course, these were just the ones that made it into the historical record. There are several strong reasons to assume that Aboriginal casualties were chronically under-reported. For one, whenever Aborigines had the chance, they reported suffering incessant violence at the hands of white men. Another reason to doubt the completeness of the official record is that the government encouraged discretion by repeatedly, albeit emptily, threatening to hang anyone found guilty of killing an Aborigine. The high number of incidents recorded in private sources that never made it into official records is also telling. What's more, with no evidence of lethal disease among combatant bands, violence is the most obvious explanation for their decline.[7]

The Black War would obviously never have happened had Europeans not usurped Aboriginal lands. But while invasion was the war's ultimate cause, it was not its trigger. The Oyster Bay and Big River bands quickly notched up scores to settle, and once a conflict began there was little hope of it being resolved diplomatically. The result was mounting tit-for-tat violence that spanned the length and breadth of south-east Tasmania. Tongerlongeter, for instance, probably led the attacks in which two white men were killed and another wounded at Oyster Bay in March and April 1826.[8] Around the same time, more than a hundred kilometres to the south-west, Kickertopoller and his mob attacked a farm near Hamilton. They bashed one man to death with waddies, while another 'was so shockingly cut by them on the head, as to leave little hopes of his recovery'.[9] The attack had been provoked the same way most early violence was, the stockmen having 'pursued and carried off their women'.[10]

Dozens of contemporary sources assert that Aboriginal warriors were inspired to acts of violence by the abuse of their womenfolk.[11] By the mid-1820s, gangs of sealers and convicts were commonly abducting, raping and often killing Aboriginal women and girls. Occasionally, such men were able to surprise individual females or small groups during the day, though they generally acquired them by ambushing bands as they slept. The Oyster Bay – Big River nations could endure much in the name of preventing an unwinnable war, but this was too much to bear. Few men in any culture could stand by while their daughters, sisters and wives were violated and killed, and for patriarchal warriors like Tongerlongeter, it was impossible.

This practice was inexcusable, even by the standards of the day, but it is far from inexplicable. In 1822, there were six male colonists for every female. Among the convict population, the ratio was sixteen to one, and relatively few female convicts were assigned to frontier settlers.[12] Consequently, young male convicts predominated in settled districts. Often armed and rarely supervised, these men were in their sexual prime and with no legitimate sexual options. Not surprisingly, some were drawn to the naked black women who lived beyond the trees. Not only were they considered 'exotic', but their 'savagery' made them fair game in the eyes of many. In later life, one convict confessed: 'It was the custom of the sons and servants of the settlers to lie in ambush for "a mob" of native women and girls, and to seize and carry away the younger ones whenever an opportunity offered'. He went on to admit that when he and his mates got their hands on a female, 'we kept her for a few days before we shot her.'[13] Such shocking stories might be written off as hyperbole, were they not so widely attested to.

In December 1829, while preparing for his first conciliatory mission, George Augustus Robinson spoke with 'a settler from the neighbourhood of Oatlands', who 'observed that the natives had been shamefully treated; that the stockkeepers had chained the females to their huts with bullock chains for the purpose of fornication.'[14] And he soon learnt that these were not isolated incidents.[15] The women themselves left few accounts of their ordeals. All we have are a handful of testimonies given by women who were abducted by sealers.[16] Their accounts are harrowing, entailing unspeakable physical and sexual violence. There is every reason to believe women suffered similarly at the hands of convicts on mainland Tasmania, though the incentive to 'destroy the evidence' meant they rarely lived to tell the tale. In one case, Kickertopoller and the other envoys told Robinson about 'a female aborigine [who] was kept by a stockkeeper for about a month, after which she was taken out and shot'.[17] In another instance, Captain Donaldson was:

> told by a man at the westward at a remote stock hut that the natives had been shamefully treated: said ... he was witness of a barbarous transaction, that two stockkeepers kept a black woman and cohabited with her for some time, when they afterwards tied her up by the heels and left her to perish ...[18]

Warriors rescued their captive womenfolk when they could. In one case, Robinson's envoy Woorrady told him of a time when 'the white men took away the black women and that one night the natives came to the white men's hut when they was asleep, told the black women to run away, took away the musket, beat the white men on the head with a stone and run away'.[19] If the men responsible could be tracked and overpowered, they generally met a bloody end.[20] In 1823, for instance, a stockman on the southern escarpment of the Central Plateau kidnapped 'a black woman whom he had caught and chained to a log with a bullock chain'. But despite her captor's best efforts, the woman managed to slip her chains, even making off with his best linen shirt.[21] This was in the heart of Big River country, so not surprisingly, a local settler later reported that the woman's menfolk soon caught up with the stockman, 'who narrowly escaped with his life'.[22]

Naturally, these kinds of incidents produced intense emotions in warriors like Tongerlongeter, among them grief, anguish and emasculation. As we might expect, though, hatred and anger are those that emerge clearest from the records. When a stockkeeper in the Meander Valley asked an Aboriginal man 'the reason why they killed white men', his response was as profound as it was obvious: 'if black man came and took away his lubra [woman] and killed his piccaninnies [children], would he not kill black man for it?'[23] Incidentally, there is no record of Aborigines ever raping or molesting a white woman. It seems they had no interest in having sex with their ancestors.

The Black War's primary trigger was undoubtedly sexual violence. Tongerlongeter and his allies responded the only way they knew how. In the four years following the killings at Grindstone Bay in November 1823, Oyster Bay and Big River bands killed at least seventy white men in 157 attacks.[24] Compared to the second half of the war, this was a high mortality rate. What's more, with the exception of the tame mob, bands rarely engaged in plunder before 1826.[25] Retribution was clearly the dominant motive, but it seems they were also sending a message to the white men that they were trespassing on foreign country. This was made explicit on the Shannon River in November 1826, when the attacking band taunted its victims, calling them 'white buggers' and telling them to 'go away, go away'. They backed up their demand by killing one of the men, whom they 'speared, butchered and mangled, in a manner too horrible to relate'.[26]

Until almost the end of the war, Kickertopoller was the only Oyster Bay – Big River warrior known by name to the colonists.[27] Yet, based on volumes of circumstantial and retrospective evidence, we confidently assert that Tongerlongeter and the Poredareme were involved from the outset. Between 1824 and 1827, just in the settlements surrounding Oyster Bay, fourteen attacks were made in which seven whites were killed and four wounded, while only four instances of plunder were recorded.[28] This suggests revenge was the primary motive. So too does the savagery of the violence. In 1824, the wealthy Oyster Bay settler George Meredith wrote to the governor bemoaning 'the murder of one of my assigned servants':

> From the Confession of some of the native women, otherwise taken, it appears that the women and children were stationed on the adjoining Hill, whilst the men attacked the Hut. My poor man ran for his life, and as the women stated, might possibly have escaped, but for a Spear entering the Sole of his foot through a strong shoe while running, when he was instantly surrounded & put to Death. Sixteen spear wounds were counted in his body, his head was shockingly beat, and two fingers were carried off.[29]

Despite all the violence Tongerlongeter and his allies inflicted on the settlers of Oyster Bay during this period, the only known reprisal followed an attack on Thomas Buxton's property at Mayfield Bay, south of modern-day Swansea, in

March 1826. Once Buxton realised 'the natives' were attacking, he and three of his men raced to the house hoping to lay hold of the guns he kept inside. Buxton reached the house first, but by this time the attacking warriors had 'almost stripped it, taking also two guns'. As Buxton's daughter recalled:

The other men were speared [one fatally] before they could get to the hut. The Natives having taken the plunder to their camp, and knowing there were no more guns, came up boldly again, and one of them was about lighting a stick at a fire that was outside the hut for cooking. But it happened that a pistol was put away by one of the daughters, and this having been loaded T. B. fired at the Black who was going to the fire. Then the Natives took their wounded man away, and tried to throw firesticks at the thatch. But T. B., having cut port-holes in the hut, stationed the children and men at the holes to watch: and when any approached, the pistol was poked out of the hole. When night came the Blacks retired up the creek, and made a fire for the night. T. B. despatched a man to Waterloo Point for help, and George Meredith, jun. and some men came before morning. In the morning the Natives came again; and one with a firestick fixed to his spear came to the hut, and threw it on the stack of wheat. When those in the hut saw what the Blacks had done, they rushed out with their guns. The Natives, seeing the men with guns, immediately made off.

Having repelled the attack and saved his home, Buxton now prepared to go on the offensive. 'At night the fire of the Natives was seen up the creek, and the party going to it, killed several of the Blacks, and recovered some of the plunder.'[30]

Between 1821 and 1830, Buxton's property was attacked no less than nine times.[31] Adam Amos, Oyster Bay's beleaguered constable, expressed a curious mix of contempt and respect for those responsible:

> The natives are the very last in the human species in
> the arts or anything that is like comfort … the men
> however are mostly strong and agile and throw a wooden
> spear of a heavy kind of wood sharpened at one end
> to the distance of fifty yards [forty-five metres], with
> sufficient force to kill a man … They are very dangerous
> and troublesome if they fall in with a white man or two
> unarmed it is only a miracle if they escape.[32]

By this point, Amos was at his wits' end. After much pleading, a military outpost was established at Oyster Bay in September 1826. Initially, it was just four privates and a corporal, but when the violence worsened the following year, an additional twenty-two privates were sent.[33]

Kickertopoller may well have aided Tongerlongeter in some of the attacks at Oyster Bay. If the chief sought proof of where Kickertopoller's loyalties lay, the younger warrior gave him plenty. In 1826 alone, he was implicated in a dozen or more attacks. Six of these were in November, immediately following the execution of his friends Jack and Dick.[34] Based on when and where the violence took place, together with other circumstantial evidence, there is a strong chance the Poredareme were with him. For one thing, even the more conservative reports suggested a force of close to eighty warriors, far more than the tame mob's strength.[35] Some victims reported a much larger number, though terrified colonists often overestimated.[36] None of this is conclusive, but at least one band was bolstering the tame mob's number, and Tongerlongeter was the chief most likely to collaborate with Kickertopoller. We will assume as much here.

The attacks that month appear to have begun with a personal vendetta. The victim was John Guinea, one of the convicts with whom Kickertopoller had worked in 1822. The sole survivor testified that he and Guinea:

> observed at short distance an immense number of natives
> coming up armed with spears and waddies ... Guinea
> and myself went to the hut and locked up the house door
> ... Black Tom and two others appeared at the end of
> the hut and immediately threw their spears. Myself and
> Guinea was not more than 10 yards [9 metres]. Guinea
> received a spear wound from Black Tom in his left side;
> he was an extreme sufferer for about 30 hours until he
> expired in the greatest agonies. Guinea had a personal
> knowledge of Black Tom having lived twelve-months
> with him.[37]

Guinea had scarcely ceased breathing before Kickertopoller's war party attacked the neighbouring property, and killed the son of a prominent settler; his 'dead body was found at two miles [three kilometres] distance from the hut, transfixed with many spears and his head dreadfully shattered'.[38] After this, the mob moved south-east, avoiding several farms before they 'made a descent upon the shepherd's hut of L. Gilles, Esq. at the Elizabeth River which they robbed of every article, and beat the hut-keeper, who was an old man, to such a degree, that his life is despaired of'. Even though his assailants could have killed him quickly, this man, like so many of their victims, died in agony several days after receiving his injuries.[39] Indeed, many of those killed during these early campaigns suffered a lingering, torturous death. Either that, or they were beaten and stabbed in a frenzy that continued well after they had expired. Such impassioned violence, together with its highly selective nature, leaves no doubt that many of these victims were being singled out for revenge.

The mob then turned south-west towards Hamilton, where they killed three stockmen at a property Kickertopoller had hit just seven months earlier. Despite being speared in his neck, a fourth victim escaped and alerted his neighbours.[40] A pursuit party was quickly assembled. 'I instantly armed all my men some on horseback and some on foot', wrote one local settler. After a desperate search, he continued, 'we fell in with them on the top of a mountain [the following evening] and poured a strong fire into them'.[41] Another member of the party claimed 'two of them were shot dead on the spot. The rest ran away leaving 24 spears, some knives and tin pots'.[42] Following this reprisal, the mob appears to have split up. The

Hobart Town Gazette reported that 'the chief part of them has crossed the Derwent', and that a 'small party is however thought to have pursued their way towards the Coal River'.[43] Such a report is flimsy evidence, to be sure, but a split makes sense of the plotted movements of Kickertopoller's mob and of the band led, in all probability, by Tongerlongeter. It also explains the decreased size of each group.

According to the report by Chief District Constable Alexander Laing, Kickertopoller's mob set up camp on 8 December fewer than a hundred metres from his hut on the Orielton Rivulet. Kickertopoller accosted Laing's hut-keeper, Robert Grimes, demanding: 'You white bugger, give me some more bread, and fry some mutton for us'. Being 'afraid of them', Grimes,

> baked a peck [about 4 kilograms] or more of flour
> into bread, and cooked three-fourths of a sheep; they
> devoured the whole, and in the afternoon went out
> to catch opossums. On their return from the hunt,
> [Kickertopoller] came to the hut by himself, and ordered
> Grimes to get some more bread and mutton ready by the
> next morning.[44]

This was the kind of swagger that distinguished attacks led by Kickertopoller. He sought to dominate and humiliate his enemies, even if this meant taking extra risks, and on this occasion, he would pay for his carelessness. Grimes somehow got word to Laing, who immediately mustered an armed posse. The *Colonial Times* paraphrased the police report:

Laing left Sorell at 11 o'clock, p. m. with a party of four soldiers of His Majesty's 40th Regiment, and arrived at Grimes's hut, a little before day-break, on Saturday morning; and at daylight, they proceeded to the spot where Tom and his party lay, and got upon them unperceived. They secured Tom and his companions, consisting of four other black men, four women, and one male child.[45]

The captives were confined in the gaol at Sorell. In a most unusual act, Arthur made the day-long trip to see them. According to Laing, the governor 'held a long consultation' with Kickertopoller, after which he ordered the release of the infamous killer without charge.[46] It was an astonishing decision, especially in the face of considerable public pressure for Kickertopoller to 'be immediately gibbeted [hanged] on the very spot'.[47] Indeed, little more than a week before his capture, Arthur had issued a government notice stating that his capture was 'an object of the first importance'.[48] But the powerful Sarah Hodgson (née Birch) again interceded on her friend's behalf. She 'represented to the Governor the desirability of obtaining the help of so intelligent a native in his plan of Conciliation'.[49] It's also likely that Arthur didn't want this brash English-speaker taking the stand and revealing under oath what colonial forces had done to his people.[50] Whatever Arthur's reasoning, he would soon regret his decision.

A free man once more, Kickertopoller quickly rejoined the resistance and recommenced his attacks. On 12 April

1827, 'a tribe, with Black Tom at their head, visited Mr. Romney's Stock-hut at Jericho, in which were three of his servants – one, James Johnson, a free man, and two others'. Kickertopoller, the *Colonial Times* reported, 'beat Johnson most unmercifully, about the head and sides, with a waddy. His cries having reached the hut, the other two servants precipitately retreated … the cunning and wiles of the blacks are like those of Satan himself. The poor man, Johnson, lies in the Hospital, in a dangerous state'.[51]

Three months later, 'Black Tom's mob' attacked two men just east of Oatlands. One was Samuel May, another of the convicts Kickertopoller had worked alongside in 1822.[52] May 'received a spear-wound, two inches deep, in the breast; but … him and his companion escaped with difficulty'. The next morning, the mob attacked two more sawyers. According to the report,

> The natives came upon them by surprise as they were
> at work on the sawpit. One of them got away, but with
> seven or eight severe spear wounds. His companion
> was found on the following morning still alive, but so
> covered with bruises inflicted by waddies, that his life is
> despaired of.[53]

It was a bold series of attacks, especially because the invaders were becoming increasingly familiar with the country and the routes Aborigines took. What's more, attacking on consecutive days gave away the mob's speed and direction. Kickertopoller was more vulnerable than he realised. Two days later, a 'party, consisting of Mr. Bennett, [the] Chief District Constable ... with some soldiers, and Mr. Lackey and his men, fell in with them ... the natives fled precipitately, leaving behind upwards of 200 waddies, three spears and many dogs'.[54] But for Kickertopoller, this setback was just one more score to settle, and four months later his mob killed Bennett and severely wounded the man he was with.[55]

Kickertopoller led several more attacks in 1827, but in November his luck ran out. Following 'some skirmishing' at a farm near Russell Falls north-west of Hobart, in which a shepherd appears to have been killed, Kickertopoller was apprehended by a posse of constables acting on a tip-off.[56] He languished in gaol for eight months before he was again released by order of the governor,[57] an incredible act that further suggests humaneness was not Arthur's sole motive. By then, though, Kickertopoller had had enough. Rather than rejoin what was left of his people, he 'voluntarily returned to the gaol'. The perplexed sheriff was forced to send for 'His Excellency's instructions'.[58] Arthur's offer to resettle Kickertopoller in Sydney received a baffled reply from the sheriff: 'Black Tom ... refuses to go to New South Wales, but he will gladly go to England or live with a Master in Hobart Town'.[59] His demoralisation and abjection were understandable. By the time of his capture, he had lost nearly everyone. Dr Birch was dead, and Sarah had married a man he hated. Many of his friends and comrades had been killed, and in July 1827, he also lost 'Black Kit', the woman the *Colonial Times* called his 'queen'.[60] Nothing is known about their relationship, though at the very least Kit's death represented the passing of yet another person Kickertopoller had been close to. Perhaps as a result of all these factors, the man who had played such a pivotal role in the early resistance ran out of fight.

No doubt Tongerlongeter was also assailed by feelings of hopelessness, but his priority was defending his people and his country. Giving up was unthinkable. Kickertopoller did not lack talent; it was just that his history with the whites and his inability to wean himself off their allurements left him conflicted. Tongerlongeter's purpose was much clearer. Of the various attacks he may have led in 1827, one was likely the assault on George Meredith's house in late October. In the middle of Meredith's son's fifth birthday party, a breathless servant burst in to report that Aborigines had them surrounded. Meredith and his two eldest sons grabbed their guns and ran outside. They emerged to see their assailants hurling flaming spears at the roof of the homestead, which by then was already alight; 'the attackers were so jubilant that they showed fight, killing one convict and wounding another before they could be driven off'.[61] This attempt to burn out Oyster Bay's most prominent settler while everyone was at home sent a stark message to the white men – their intrusion would no longer be tolerated. Targeted retribution had proved futile, and despite Tongerlongeter's efforts to contain it, all-out war now seemed inevitable.

With this realisation sinking in, Oyster Bay and Big River bands ramped up their resistance. This dramatic shift happened quickly in late 1827, and settlers took notice. In a petition dated 30 November 1827, property owners along the Elizabeth and Macquarie rivers insisted that 'the murders they have committed are not so much the result of private revenge, as of a plan preconcerted by them as a nation, for the extirpation of the white inhabitants; with whom they doubtless consider themselves at war'.[62] In 1828, Oyster Bay and Big River war parties would make nearly three times as many attacks as they had the previous year. The character of their violence changed too. For reasons that will be explored in the coming chapters, the incidence of plunder soared. But it was their increasing use of arson that most terrified settlers, reliant as they were on dry harvests and timber housing.[63] Tongerlongeter and his allies were gaining an appreciation of the white man's vulnerabilities, and refining their tactics accordingly. The cost of this experience, though, had been shockingly high.

By the close of 1827, the white invaders had significantly reduced the Oyster Bay – Big River population and occupied most of their best hunting grounds. Because their hunting and foraging economy required a minimum group size and free movement to function, the surviving Tasmanians' traditional way of life was thrown into turmoil. Tongerlongeter's key ally, the Big River chief Montpelliatta, wryly observed after the war, that if his people 'left any place to go hunting elsewhere, when they returned in the course of eight days, they found a hut erected'.[64] Tongerlongeter undoubtedly felt the intense fear, sadness and hatred that anyone in his position would have. Robinson seemed to understand this: 'The children have witnessed the massacre of their parents and their relations carried away into captivity by these merciless invaders, their country has been taken from them and the kangaroo, their chief subsistence, have been slaughtered wholesale ... Can we wonder then at the hatred they bear to the white inhabitants?'[65]

The situation was becoming desperate, but it was precisely Tongerlongeter's capacity to lead under these conditions that would set him apart in the second half of the war.

1 *Tukalunginta (Tongerlongeter)*,
watercolour by Thomas Bock (1832).

British Museum, London,
Oc2006, Drg.72

2 *Tongerlongeter*, pencil sketch
by Thomas Bock (1832).

Queen Victoria Museum and Art Gallery,
Launceston, QVM:1968:FD:6G

3 *Muntipiliyata (Montpelliatta)*, watercolour
by Thomas Bock (1832). Montpelliatta, the
principal chief of the Big River people, was
Tongerlongeter's main ally in the Black War.

British Museum, London,
Oc2006, Drg.71

4 *Portrait of G. A. Robinson*, by Thomas Bock
(1832). George Augustus Robinson was a complex
man – intrepid, humane, pompous, self-righteous
and unwavering. While his character is disputed, his
role in ending the Black War, and in documenting the
cultures and experiences of the Tasmanians, is not.

State Library of New South Wales, Sydney,
PXE1004

Above **5** *The Conciliation,* by Benjamin Duterrau (1840). This iconic painting captures the scene, as imagined by the artist, in which Tongerlongeter and Montpelliatta agreed to the armistice with George Augustus Robinson.

Tasmanian Museum and Art Gallery, Hobart, AG79

Top right **6** *Residence of the Aborigines, Flinders Island,* watercolour by JS Prout (1840s). Wybalenna was the name given to the Flinders Island Aboriginal settlement. For all the investment in facilities and staff, disease took a dreadful toll on those who were exiled there. During its fifteen years of operation (1833–47), four-fifths of the Aborigines sent there died, mostly of influenza.

Allport Library and Museum of Fine Arts, Hobart, HA1105

Below right **7** *Aborigines attacking Milton Farm, Great Swanport, 14 December 1828,* unknown artist (1833). Occurring close to his homeland, this attack was probably led by Tongerlongeter.

Privately owned; held in Tasmanian Museum and Art Gallery, Hobart, AGloan29

8 *The Hazards, Freycinet Peninsula, 2015.* The Hazards, on the Freycinet Peninsula, are stunning monoliths that probably held special significance for Tongerlongeter and his people.

Jess Bond

9 *Lieutenant John Bowen and party arriving at Risdon* by Thomas Gregson (c. 1860).
Bowen's arrival heralded the start of a new and much darker period for
Tongerlongeter's people, though they could not have known that at the time.

WL Crowther Collection, Libraries Tasmania, Hobart

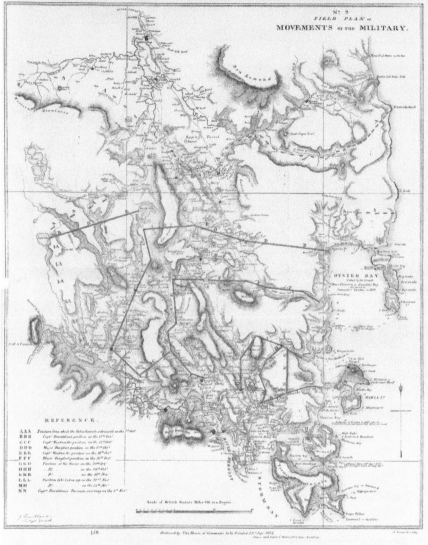

10 *Field plan of military operations against the Aboriginal inhabitants of Van Diemen's Land* by George Frankland (1830). This retrospective field plan illustrates the general pattern of divisional movements during the 'Black Line' campaign against the Aborigines in October and November 1830.

WL Crowther Collection, Libraries Tasmania, Hobart

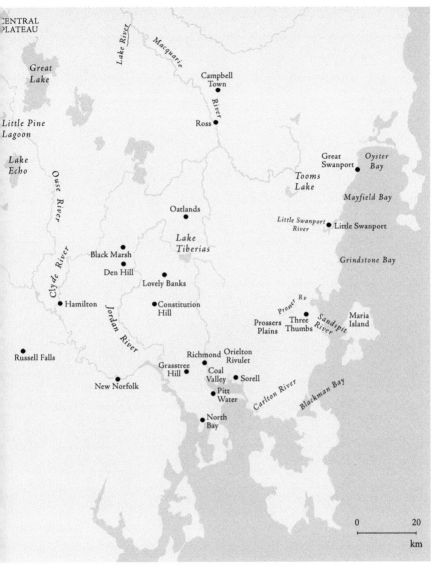

11 Map of south-east Tasmania with all relevant places mentioned in the text.

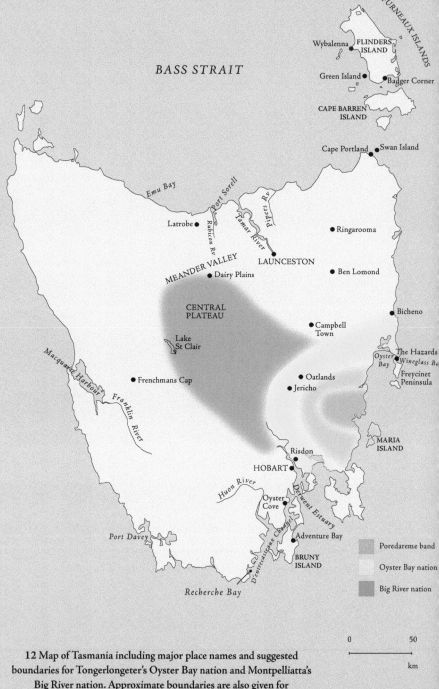

BASS STRAIT

FURNEAUX ISLANDS

Wybalenna ● FLINDERS ISLAND

Green Island ●
● Badger Corner

CAPE BARREN ISLAND

Cape Portland ● ● Swan Island

Emu Bay

Port Sorell

Pipers Rv

Tamar River

Rubicon Rv

Latrobe ●

● Ringarooma

MEANDER VALLEY

LAUNCESTON

● Dairy Plains

● Ben Lomond

CENTRAL PLATEAU

● Bicheno

Lake St Clair

Campbell ● Town

Oyster Bay

The Hazards
Wineglass B.

Freycinet Peninsula

● Frenchmans Cap

Macquarie Harbour

Franklin River

● Oatlands

● Jericho

MARIA ISLAND

Risdon ●

HOBART ●

Huon River

Oyster Cove

Derwent Estuary

Port Davey

D'entrecasteaux Channel

● Adventure Bay

BRUNY ISLAND

Recherche Bay

Poredareme band

Oyster Bay nation

Big River nation

0   50
km

12 Map of Tasmania including major place names and suggested
boundaries for Tongerlongeter's Oyster Bay nation and Montpelliatta's
Big River nation. Approximate boundaries are also given for
Tongerlongeter's band, the Poredareme, which probably ceased to exist as
an independent entity after about 1827.

CHAPTER 8

Resistance: 1828–30

Nicholas Clements

The Black War reached its zenith between 1828 and 1830. This time represents both the most violent period of frontier war in Australia's history, and the stiffest armed resistance ever mounted by Indigenous people on the continent. Post-war sources reveal that Tongerlongeter was at the forefront of this resistance, yet in the records for 1828–30, he is just one more 'savage chief'. Survivors of earlier attacks had often recognised Kickertopoller from his time in Hobart and his impressive grasp of English, but they generally had no way of identifying their assailants, whose features were difficult for European eyes to distinguish. For this reason, Tongerlongeter's actions can be difficult to disentangle from those of his allies. Because of the migratory nature of bands, even incidents occurring in Tongerlongeter's homeland cannot be attributed to him with certainty. It is fitting, to say nothing of ironic, that colonists came to liken Aborigines to ghosts who would materialise seemingly from nowhere and then 'vanish like spectres,'[1] because while we know Tongerlongeter was central to the resistance, he is like an apparition in this part of the story. And his ghostliness derived not just from his anonymity among his victims. In a very real sense, Tongerlongeter haunted his enemies. Charles Meredith, another of George Meredith's sons and one of Oyster Bay's first settlers, went so far as to liken the chief and his warriors to 'the shadows of a hideous dream'.[2]

Like most bands, the Poredareme had ceased to exist as a discrete entity by the late 1820s. Those who were left amalgamated with what remained of allied bands. Kickertopoller told Gilbert Robertson that by 1828, the various bands of the Oyster Bay nation had united, and that 'the murders on the coast were committed by all the tribes [bands] in a Body'.[3] Amid this regrouping, if not before, Tongerlongeter emerged as the nation's pre-eminent leader, transforming the war-hardened remnant into an even more effective guerrilla force.[4] The recorded attacks on colonists, just in Oyster Bay country, rose sharply from thirty-three in 1827 to 124 in 1830, and all this during a time when their numbers plummeted from several hundred to several dozen.[5] '[W]hile the natives diminished [in number]', the historian John West noted in 1852, 'they seemed to increase their activity, moving to various places with almost incredible swiftness'.[6] At first glance, it seems paradoxical that their resistance increased as their strength decreased. It certainly perplexed their enemy.[7] On closer inspection, though, the reasons become clear. As his knowledge and confidence grew, Tongerlongeter refined his tactics. Through trial and tragic error, he and his warriors became more effective resistance fighters. We will consider how they did this shortly, but first we must examine *why* they did it.

Before the Tasmanians could resist the invasion of their country and avenge the manifold wrongs perpetrated against them, they needed to eat. And eating had never been so difficult. There was a scarcity of game due to commercial hunting. West observed that, in 1831 and 'from Bothwell only, 100,000 [kangaroo] skins were sent to Hobart Town'.[8] It was no secret that convict stockkeepers, unsupervised for days or weeks at a stretch, enthusiastically hunted kangaroos and possums for their skins.[9] 'The extent to which it was carried on was enormous', West tells us. 'The skin of the kangaroo sold for a few pence, [and] was the perquisite of the stock-keepers, and long the chief object of their daily enterprise.'[10] Hunting dogs were ubiquitous on the frontier. A great number of them belonged to convicts, though many more roamed feral. They took a huge toll on game animal populations. By the late 1820s, emus had been all but wiped out and kangaroo numbers were waning.[11] Contemporaries well understood that this was inflaming frontier relations.[12] As 'the food, on which the [Aboriginal] people depended for subsistence, was diminished,' West recognised, 'the temptation to rob the settlers was regularly augmented'.[13] But it was an Aborigine who summed the situation up best: 'When I returned to my country, I went hunting but did not kill one head of game. The white men make their dogs wander, and kill all the game, and they only want the skins'.[14]

Even if game could be found, it was becoming increasingly dangerous to hunt it. The newcomers sought to establish their farms on flat or gently undulating country, lightly timbered, with plenty of grass and water – in other words, the best hunting grounds and migratory routes. By the late 1820s, almost all of this land had been alienated for settlement. Likewise, the increasing presence of settlers and sealers on the coast made beach visits perilous. And the precipitous loss of women, with their exceptional diving skills, made it difficult to procure shellfish, a staple for Tongerlongeter's people when on the coast. As opportunities to move and hunt unmolested shrank, plundering food could be safer than hunting it. As one observer wrote in the late 1820s:

> their latitude for procuring food by hunting and fishing, becomes more and more circumscribed every year, exactly in the same ratio as the farms are extended over the island; and in less than the period of one generation they will not have a single untenanted spot left. Starve they cannot, therefore it will always be a war of extermination.[15]

This is not to say that Tasmanians were never motivated by a fondness for the white man's foods and stimulants – they undoubtedly were – but as an Aborigine captured in 1830 revealed, the white man's food stores had, 'instead of being luxuries ... become necessities'.[16]

While hunger explains why Aborigines plundered food from the white man, only vengefulness explains why they so often killed him. From 1828, as grievances mounted, the hatred that had fuelled earlier, more selective reprisals intensified. By now, the remaining Oyster Bay and Big River bands were, according to one captive, determined 'to make repeated incursions, and to destroy all the whites [they] possibly can'.[17] No less rousing than the countless personal traumas they had experienced was the desire to defend their country – the home of their people, their culture and their spirits. Patriotic sentiments ran deep among the Tasmanians, and those with a smattering of English emphatically communicated their desire to expel the invaders. Following an attack on a Clyde River farm in February 1830, one victim testified:

> I was sitting in the front room when the servant called
> out 'Fire, fire, the natives', I immediately ran for water …
> I was then so determined to save the house, but, seeing
> this was impossible, so began to get what things we could
> from the house … Soon after this I saw a smoke arise
> about 6–700 yards [550 to 650 metres] from the house,
> then saw two natives walking alongside the fences setting
> fire to them at every twenty or thirty yards [eighteen or
> twenty-five metres] distance. Then two other natives
> appeared on the rock on the other side of the river,
> seeming to give direction whilst the other two continued
> to communicate fire to the cross fences & others bringing
> the fire closer to the river side. These two joined the
> others on the rock and began to leap and use much of
> their language – *'parrawar', 'parrawar', 'go away you white
> buggers, what business have you here'* – One of my men
> crossed the river with a musket [but when] I called to

him to come back the Natives immediately called out
'Ah – you coward'.[18]

But the demand to 'go away' was mere catharsis. While
they did force some settlers to abandon their land grants, and
occasionally several at once,[19] they knew by now that they
could never hope to eject them all. Tongerlongeter and his
allies 'do not suppose they can extirpate the white inhabitants. They entertain no such idea', Robinson learnt during
his quest to find the chief. 'No! They are actuated solely by
revenge'. For more than two decades they had suffered the
violation of their country and their people, and for these 'dire
enormities', Robinson was told, 'They bear a deadly animosity
to the white inhabitants'.[20]

The boldness of Tongerlongeter and his allies increased
with every year.[21] Officials and newspaper contributors all
noticed this, as did settlers testifying to the Aborigines Committee in March 1830. One observed that Oyster Bay – Big
River warriors

no longer confine their depredations to remote stock
huts and isolated dwellings, they now plunder houses
in populous places, where there are two or more
contiguous dwellings, in so insidious and crafty a
manner that they always escape with their booty, adding
murder to robbery whenever they meet a white man
unprepared to resist them; not sparing, except in rare
instances, even the women and children they find on the
habitations they attack. Lately they have commenced

a system of destruction, which if persevered in, will involve many families in utter ruin, by destroying houses and barns by fire.[22]

Likewise, Oatlands' police magistrate declared:

The Natives, during the last 12 months, have coined a spirit of enterprise and transition beyond that of any former year. The murders, in this District, have been less numerous, but the burnings of houses, corn stacks, fences have greatly increased. The Natives are becoming bolder and the Whites more timid.[23]

The *Colonial Times* put it more pithily: 'They have ceased to fear, and learned to abhor.'[24]

Emboldened though he was, Tongerlongeter knew carelessness would be paid for in the lives of his people. Through hard-won experience, he was becoming increasingly adept at exploiting the weaknesses of his enemy. He had grasped, for instance, that white men placed great value on their livestock, crops and buildings. Consequently, he and his warriors speared thousands of sheep and cattle (without ever eating them) and made dozens of arson attacks.[25] While they could arguably have brought the invaders to their knees by more systematically targeting such property,[26] their resistance nevertheless set the colony back years.[27] What's more, while guns remained fundamentally mysterious to them, they could now take advantage of their many shortcomings. The white men, despite their guns and their vastly superior numbers, lacked the martial training and local knowledge that Tongerlongeter and his people enjoyed. Robinson found that they 'entertain but a mean opinion of the white people's knowledge', and 'ridiculed the idea of white men following them in the woods'.[28]

Only one type of white man was spared this derision. The training and discipline of soldiers distinguished them from the other invaders, most of whom were farmers or petty criminals. Tongerlongeter and warriors like him were wary of these men in red. We know soldiers killed a significant number of Aborigines, but because so few military records have survived, we are left guessing as to the extent of their impact. Whatever it was, Robinson found that Aborigines had 'a rooted antipathy to the military', and 'an unconquerable aversion to soldiers'.[29]

However much fear and hatred Tongerlongeter may have felt, his enemies were no less afraid and no less bitter. There were many reasons he and his allies were able to evoke these emotions in colonists, but none more powerful than the sheer viciousness of their attacks. And nothing was more calculated to antagonise the invaders than attacks on women and children. Despite the fact that their own women and children had been systematically targeted by white men, Aborigines had, with the exception of Mrs Osborne in 1824, refrained from harming white women and children prior to 1828. That was about to change. On 9 October 1828, some twenty Oyster Bay warriors made a particularly harrowing attack on the Gough household near Oatlands. There is no way to know if Tongerlongeter led the attack in person, though there were only a few Oyster Bay bands left by this point.[30]

Two days later, a grief-stricken Patrick Gough made a statement to police. It is worth quoting at length as it sheds light on the kind of suffering Oyster Bay – Big River warriors could inflict on their usurpers.

At noon or a little after on Thursday last the 9th instant my wife said she heard the cries of a woman. I looked out at the door and saw the [now] deceased Anne Geary running towards my hut … When we got to her she appeared nearly exhausted and was in a great fright. She told me that she had seen the natives coming towards Mortimer's [her] hut [and wanted us] to prevent the natives from getting Mortimer's gun and ammunition. I and the two men went to Mortimer's hut with great speed. The hut is about a mile and a half from my hut. Bates carried a gun, and Jerry and myself carried each a black stick only. When we got to Mortimer's hut the door was open and many things were thrown around the floor and outside the door. I looked for the gun with the ammunition but could not find it. The blacks too were gone. We then returned towards my hut. On the way I thought I heard a shriek. I hastened towards home as fast as I could. About a mile from my hut I met my eldest girl Mary, covered with blood. She said to me 'Father, my mother and my sister are killed by the blacks – make haste'. I and the two men then ran as fast as we could. About half a mile from my hut I found my wife sitting on

the ground leaning with her back against a fence with my
child Esther in her lap. My wife said 'Gough, my Dear,
I am going, the Blacks have killed me'. She appeared to
me to be covered with wounds. I tore up my shirt to tie
round her head. My wife then fainted. I then ran to my
hut to look for my other child Alicia. I found her lying in
the ground in front of the door with her arms extended. I
thought she was dead. I carried her into the hut. I found
then she had a little life in her. On entering my hut I saw
the deceased Anne Geary lying on the floor of the hut,
with some gashes on her head. I lifted Anne Geary from
the ground and put her on a sofa, and then she vomited
much blood. About two hours afterwards Anne Geary
died. My daughter Alicia died about midnight of the
same day.[31]

Mrs Gough succumbed to her wounds three weeks after the
attack, by which time her assailants and their allies had killed
three more colonists and wounded another six.[32] Patrick
Gough tried to move on with his two surviving daughters,
but eleven months later, they were attacked again. All three
survived, but their house was burnt.[33]

In the three years that followed the Gough killings,
Oyster Bay – Big River warriors killed or wounded at least
twenty-five women and children, though even on a per capita
basis men were still more likely to be attacked.[34] Women and
children were therefore not being targeted in the latter half
of the war, they were just no longer being spared. The Oyster
Bay – Big River people had, after all, declared they would

kill or expel *all* whites. As Mrs Gough lay dying, she told her husband 'that she fell on her knees to the natives and said, "Spare the lives of my piccaninnies [children]", and that one of the assailants replied in good English: 'No you white bitch we'll kill you all'.[35] This new, indiscriminate attitude was every bit as understandable as it was harsh. Robinson noted:

> They have a tradition amongst them that white men have usurped their territory, have driven them into the forests, have killed their game and thus robbed them of their chief subsistence, have ravished their wives and daughters, have murdered and butchered their fellow countrymen; and ... whilst brooding over these complicated ills ... [they] goad each other on to acts of bloodshed and revenge.[36]

Tongerlongeter and his warriors often humiliated and tortured their victims. This may have been intended to terrorise the invaders into leaving, but it could just as easily have been the product of intense hatred. Either way, the records of coroners' reports read like the scripts of horror films. An Aboriginal woman from Bruny Island described to Robinson 'the manner of torture they adopted towards their fated victims, via breaking their arms or legs or cutting their heads, and when they did not kill they disabled or maimed'.[37] Attacks of this nature were commonplace. While there are far too many to enumerate here, it will suffice to illuminate two attacks that were most likely led by Tongerlongeter. The first occurred in September 1828. The *Tasmanian* reported:

On Saturday last, [James Stanton,] an assigned servant of Lieut. Hawkins at Little Swan Port, while out in quest of his Master's bullocks, was waylaid by a party of the Black Natives … and murdered in the most barbarous manner, his brains being literally dashed out … They then surrounded Lieut. Hawkins' house made fires around it, using threatening language, and counterfeiting the man's voice whom they had just killed, in hopes of enticing the Lieut. from his house.

This was, according to the *Tasmanian*, a crime of passion. 'These savages, in tolerable broken English used many opprobrious names towards the white men, and evinced a spirit of determined hostility.'[38] The coroner's report left no doubt:

the body of James Stanton was discovered with the head beaten in with waddies: the nails of the fingers were separated from the quicks apparently with a knife, the fleshy part of the outside of the hands was cut off, the eyebrows were cut off and the bones of the eyebrows beaten down to the eyes. The whole of the teeth were beaten out of the head and the body otherwise much mangled. During the time they beset Lieut. Hawkins' house they continued calling upon the dead man by name and laughing about it.[39]

A second case involved John Rayner, a freed convict in the service of George Meredith senior at Oyster Bay. Early in 1830, Rayner was out hunting when his dogs began to growl,

> as they always did whenever they saw or scented the blacks, and, on looking round, he perceived some of them near him. He jumped up and ran, but instantly received two spears, one in his breast, which he pulled out readily, and another in his back, which he wrenched at, and broke off short. He still ran as fast as he could, until, coming to a large log, he tripped, and fell over it in such a manner as to conceal him, for he knew nothing more, until, coming to himself at night, he by degrees recalled the circumstances, and with some difficulty made his way home. He remained ill for some time from the wounds.[40]

Rayner appears to have been sent to the hospital in Hobart to recuperate. Once sufficiently recovered, he began the long walk back to Oyster Bay. He would never make it. Near Grindstone Bay, on 28 March 1830, Rayner was assailed again, this time by 'about 30 black natives'. In his statement to police, he recounted how

> he had a fowling piece [i.e. shotgun] which he occasionally presented to intimidate [them] but did not wish to fire for fear of irritating them. They followed him about a mile and a half and occasionally discharged a spear at him. About dusk he received a spear between his shoulders and immediately after another on the back part of his right thigh. They then commenced to run

after him and throw vollies [sic] of stones and waddies by one of which he was knocked down senseless he came to himself about midnight when he found himself alone, he suffered much from thirst to alleviate which he pulled off his boot and voided his urine in it and when cold drank it. He also suffered much from cold they having stripped him of his jacket and waistcoat … About noon on Monday the 29th he crawled with the assistance of a stick in search of water and fell in with a hole in the middle of a marsh about 100 yards [90 metres] from the place where he was attacked of which he drank plentifully[;] he remained there until the 31st when at day break he heard the crowing of some cocks and with the assistance of a stick he proceeded in the direction from whence the sound proceeded … and shortly after he fell in with one of Mr Gatehouse's men.[41]

Horrified, Gatehouse's servants noted that Rayner was in 'unimaginable agony', having been 'cruelly maimed and wounded, with one eye knocked out, and the other quite blind, his frightful sores all festering, and alive with maggots!'[42] He was immediately shipped to the convict settlement on Maria Island to receive medical attention, but the surgeon there could do nothing, and he died soon after.[43]

Despite their insuperable hatred of the whites, Oyster Bay and Big River warriors did occasionally take pity on their victims.[44] During one attack in the Clyde River valley, they even had some fun with their quarry:

When they entered Mr. Young's hut there was only
one man in it, whom they desired to 'go, go!' motioning
him with their hands to go; upon the man's leaving the
hut, a native sprang suddenly before him from behind
a tree, brandishing a large waddy, and cried 'boo!'
grinned at him and laughed heartily at the fright he
had occasioned.[45]

Rare as their mercy was, they were more likely to show it
to women. In February 1830, for instance, 'a servant woman
with a child in her arms begged them to spare her life and
that of her child and [when] they promised to do so, she went
back into the house and brought them out cakes which they
accepted and offered her no violence.'[46]

Arguably the most remarkable instance of Aborigines
sparing a victim's life occurred on 1 November 1829, when
a Big River war party attacked a hut near Bothwell. Thomas
Clark and Ann Newport were inside. Newport was cleaning
when she was pierced in the breast by a spear. Shaken, though
not mortally wounded, she and Clark promptly barricaded
themselves inside the hut, but their assailants set fire to the
building. Just then, while 'looking out through a crack of the
shutter', Newport saw 'Mary Roberts coming towards the hut
with Henry Williams, she exclaimed "O Clark, I see a white
man and woman coming, we shall be saved", but directly
after, she heard the [now] deceased Mary Roberts screaming
"Murder" "Murder"!' Williams managed to escape. Newport

remained in the hut as long as she could, but her cap
and clothes being in a flame, and her arms dreadfully
scorched, she exclaimed, 'O Clark, I can remain no longer'
and went out. Directly after, she saw a 'Black' going to
spear her, but she went up to him imploring mercy, he
then lowered his spear, and lifting up his hand, spoke to
the others, who were also coming on to spear her, but
at his command the 'Black' (Apparently the chief) took
hold of her hand, and put the fire out, first on her head
and then down her back. He took her by the hand and
shaking it in a kind manner looked at her; he must have
perceived she was very large with child, and seemed
very sorry she had been hurt. She then motioned him to
go to the hut and get flour or something to eat, and as
she turned round, she saw the deceased Thomas Clark
coming out at the door. The Black immediately left her,
and lifting his spear ran at him, saying 'O you white
Bugger', the other Blacks following him in like manner.
She saw no more, but walked away …[47]

Mary Roberts had suffered 'a spear wound in the back of
the head, and two in the back'. Clark had been 'nearly burned
to ashes, only the trunk of the body remaining without the
head and limbs'. Two years after the incident, a Big River
woman told Robinson of how the 'tribe had attacked [the]
hut and set it on fire, and the woman run out from the flames
and begged of them not to kill her. MONTPELLIATTA the chief
took her in his arms and carried her away and would not let

Resistance: 1828–30

the rest hurt her. The man they killed, [they] chopped off his head and burnt him.'[48]

This is the first time the Big River chief appears in the historical record, but like Tongerlongeter, he had long been at the forefront of resistance in the south-east. Just as Tongerlongeter came to lead the remnant Oyster Bay warriors, Montpelliatta did the same for his Big River allies. While the majority of the violence occurred in Oyster Bay country and Tongerlongeter clearly became the dominant post-war figure, Montpelliatta appears to have been a wartime leader of comparable prowess. Moreover, it was the alliance between these two great men that made the resistance effort in southeast Tasmania more effective than any other in the history of colonial Australia.

145

Striking terror: 1828–30

Nicholas Clements

Tongerlongeter and Montpelliatta were well aware of the fear they inspired in their enemies. Under their leadership, Oyster Bay and Big River war parties relentlessly terrorised the intruders. Chiefs, who wore distinguishing war paint,[1] appeared doubly menacing. When Tongerlongeter and his warriors besieged their victims, they taunted them and shook their spears.[2] When they fell upon them, they hurt them in ways that sent a chill up the spines of every colonist. The fear they produced in the minds of exposed settlers and convicts was often paralysing. In a shaky hand, one servant wrote to his master:

> You have often been warning us against the natives. We always said they would never come here but alas they have made their appearance … poor Crowhurst and York [are] dreadfully speared. We don't expect Crowhurst to live but one of the men that came galloped off as fast as ever he could to Dr Paton. Now what is to be done? I am frightened out of my life.[3]

The archives brim with such accounts – hastily penned reports of 'prowling blacks', urgent appeals for military protection, petitions from community groups demanding the government 'do something', and of course the reams of testimony from traumatised victims. Fear was arguably the dominant sentiment expressed in war-related accounts by those living beyond the safety of the towns.[4] Being encircled by dozens of spear-wielding 'savages', their muscular bodies encrusted with ochre, their hate-filled eyes framed by heavy dreadlocks and clenched teeth, was a nightmare that came true for hundreds of colonists. Such imagery, together with the gruesome knowledge of what they did to their victims, dogged the minds of every man, woman and child.

Coordinated guerrilla warfare was what Tongerlongeter and his warriors did best. Their throwing skills had been honed over a lifetime, and courage was an unquestioned cultural obligation. But their greatest strength was teamwork. Years of hunting, fighting and living together gave warriors an uncanny ability to cooperate. In combat, they didn't just know where their comrades were, they knew what they were thinking. What's more, as the surveyor James Calder put it, 'they were a set of cunning fellows, and never attacked at a disadvantage'.[5] Why would they? They knew the country and could surprise their victims almost at will. Guerrilla bands like Tongerlongeter's would have been unstoppable, were it not for guns. When there was time for reconnaissance, they could often isolate unarmed targets, but wary frontiersmen rarely went far without a loaded gun. This meant there was no such thing as a safe or uncomplicated assault. In the heat of the action, plans often had to be changed or aborted. Mistakes meant losing friends and further weakening their fighting capacity. And the longer the conflict drew on, the harder everything became. Hunting, attacking, escaping, camping, simply moving – all was fraught with danger now. Yet this was when Tongerlongeter was at his most effective. Under his leadership, the harried remnants of the Oyster Bay people mounted an almost miraculous last stand.

'[I]t can no longer be doubted', declared the *Hobart Town Courier* in October 1828, 'that the natives have formed a systematic organised plan for carrying on a war of extermination against the white inhabitants of the colony'.[6] In 1830, the *Colonial Times* also referred to 'the increased system and organization which appear to mark their movements',[7] while Roderick O'Connor, one of the colony's widely travelled land commissioners, observed: 'The Natives have become so dexterous that it is now next to impossible to get a sight of them; they move with greater rapidity than formerly'.[8] It was apparent to everyone that something had changed. Tongerlongeter and his Big River allies were now executing a 'regular systematic plan of aggressions',[9] and using a tactical playbook that reliably frustrated their enemy, even though that enemy outnumbered them around 200 to one.

Oyster Bay and Big River bands sometimes attacked bullock drays or horse-drawn carts as they creaked along the island's potholed roads.[10] They even attacked mounted men when the opportunities arose,[11] but usually they targeted isolated huts. If those holed up inside were well armed, such attacks might become sieges, especially when the need for food or desire for revenge was strong. On one occasion, not far from Oyster Bay,

> two servants, each having a musket, defended
> themselves for five hours, in the best manner they
> could, from the spears and stones which were thrown
> at them, until at length the blacks pressed furiously on,
> and surrounded them with fires, through which, after
> much struggling, and with considerable hazard, the
> poor fellows (though followed for more than 5 miles
> [8 kilometres]) escaped ...[12]

Sieges of this kind were not uncommon,[13] but they were not as safe or efficient as hit-and-run ambushes.

Tongerlongeter clearly understood that speed and surprise were his best weapons. The quicker an attack and the more off guard the victims, the less room for error. At the height of the war, Oyster Bay – Big River warriors averaged one attack every three days, though they were careful to avoid obvious patterns, as predictability could be deadly.[14] A white man braced for an attack was far more dangerous than an unsuspecting one. Sometimes they would try to outpace the news of their last attack, hitting property after property in a series of rapid-fire assaults, usually over several days. Because settlement generally spread along river valleys, so too did these consecutive attacks. One settler observed: 'they invariably attack Mr Evan's hut first ... and proceed down the river plundering the different huts as they go'.[15] This was a convenient strategy used from early in the war.

They needed to get somewhere, but they also wanted to plunder and kill white men, so they did both at once. The only problem was that their adversaries sometimes figured this out and were able to head them off. The alternative was a more effective but far more complex offensive strategy.

Like the generals of the Great War of 1914–18, Tongerlongeter had to learn on the fly how to fight a new kind of war. While both sides evolved strategically over the course of the conflict, the Tasmanians' tactics were much more sophisticated than those of their adversaries. Nowhere was this more evident than when they executed coordinated, simultaneous attacks that both dumbfounded and devastated their enemies. '[C]onsiderable alarm prevails throughout the district,' wrote Bothwell's police magistrate in August 1830; 'the blacks instead of being awed … seem to be stimulated to greater acts of revenge, they divide themselves into small parties and attack different places at once widely apart, and then meet again, at some given place'.[16] Two weeks later, another blinding set of attacks was unleashed near Lake Tiberias south of Oatlands. An Aboriginal guide attached to a local roving party attributed them to 'the Big River mob', which he claimed was 'about 150 in number, and now divided into ten or a dozen small mobs, the better to effect their purposes'.[17]

Simultaneous attacks had, by the end of the 1820s, become the stock-in-trade of Oyster Bay – Big River warriors.[18] Such operations appear all the more impressive when one considers that leaders like Tongerlongeter were responsible for coordinating not only guerrilla fighters but also dozens of non-combatants. These people – women and children, the old and infirm – had to be factored into every move. Protecting them was at once a liability to the resistance movement and its underlying rationale. Tongerlongeter was not just a military leader – he was a chief, and his patriarchal obligations meant that fighting was never his only or even his main priority. To appreciate this, it helps to imagine what an average day looked like for Tongerlongeter – specifically, a day of offensive operations in the winter of 1829. In a meandering fashion, the remainder of this chapter will do just that.

Fatigued though they were, sleep no longer came easily to Tongerlongeter and his people. As we will later see, the night had become its own kind of hell. Mornings too were anything but restful. Lest they give away their position, the fire had to be doused before sunrise, leaving the chilled morning air to seep into their bones. Any meat left over from the previous night's meal would likely have been consumed by dogs or wildlife, and any damper would need to last them, so they probably began the day on an empty stomach. Thus, in addition to shouldering a constant and weighty burden of grief, hatred and anxiety, Tongerlongeter and his people were regularly cold, hungry and sleep-deprived. This was a recipe for bad moods and flared tempers. It didn't help that Tongerlongeter was no longer leading the Poredareme but rather a collection of survivors cobbled together from several allied bands. Despite their cultural and kin relations, most members of this group had not grown up together. Only with deft leadership could such a unit function at all, let alone effectively. Later accounts of Tongerlongeter paint a picture of a diplomatic and thoughtful leader who had no need to compel the loyalty of his people. This ability to inspire is surely what explains the otherwise inexplicable fact that 'the celebrated chief' was able so effectively to organise and rally this motley crew of traumatised yet decidedly unbroken people.[19]

The day would have begun as usual. Tongerlongeter would have surveyed the skyline and smelt the air. The Tasmanians' ability to forecast the weather was a source of astonishment to their usurpers. Robinson found 'they have numerous signs by which they judge [the weather] and I have seldom found them to err'.[20] Tongerlongeter's people may have been engaged in the fight of their lives, but the weather still dictated much of their day. A reliable source observed that they were 'not fond of travelling in the wet, nor will they do so, except in cases of necessity'.[21] Likewise, high winds made coordinating attacks perilously difficult, and if the day was intensely cold, they might hunker down with their dogs and blankets, waiting for the cloak of night so they could again warm themselves with fire. But they were vulnerable every minute they remained in camp. Thousands of white men were on the lookout for barking dogs or signs of fire. Many were now actively searching for them, some with Aboriginal trackers. The imperative to move was pressing, and so it fell to Tongerlongeter to review and initiate the day's plan.

After reapplying grease and ochre, they left camp cautiously. The men took the lead, dozens of skinny dogs pacing quietly beside them. These hounds, while indispensable at night, had to be controlled during the day lest they drew attention.[22] Because they had to camp as remotely as possible, it could be quite a journey to reach the settlements, which meant they generally attacked in the middle of the day.[23] The interior was by now crawling with white men, many of whom were familiar with the Aborigines' traditional migratory routes.[24] Farms had been established along every productive valley, and the white men who worked these properties were constantly vigilant. What's more, there were now probably two dozen military and civilian roving parties crisscrossing the interior in pursuit of the 'hostile blacks'.[25] While these marauding parties were generally ineffective, their sheer number made them a serious threat, and the beaten paths of old were no longer safe. Instead, as one Oyster Bay settler observed, 'the Blacks avoid, as much as they possibly can, taking the Hills, always keeping about the gullies, and rivers, where there is much scrub and stunted undergrowth'.[26] By this means, Tongerlongeter was usually able to evade roving parties and trigger-happy frontiersmen. But the going was tough. Thick scrub, scant access to food and water, and a lack of familiarity with the ground made his people's bleak situation all the more miserable.

Deciding where to attack involved a range of considerations. How long had it been since they were last in this area, and what surprises might they encounter? Whom did they owe a visit? Which huts were the most vulnerable? Which would likely be stocked with food? And, importantly, which offered the best approach and escape routes? A surveyor familiar with the interior told the Aborigines Committee: 'There is scarcely a distant stock hut in the colony that has not been visited, and the men attempted to be speared – especially if situated in a favourable place for an ambush, such as a scrub being near, or the country hilly and thickly wooded'.[27]

Once a plan was formulated, the women and children, elderly and incapacitated were sequestered at a safe rendezvous.[28] Kickertopoller revealed to the roving party leader Gilbert Robertson that 'they leave their women and children behind them, and send out parties to commit depredations'.[29] Likewise, an east coast settler who 'was frequently in the habit of heading parties in pursuit of the aboriginals', wrote: 'One thing seems to invariably be the practice of this tribe, which is, that the main body, women and children, are left some distance, from three to six miles [five to ten kilometres], in the Hills, while the detachments, as it were, go out in various directions hunting and doing mischief'.[30]

Tongerlongeter and his warriors were sometimes forced to go into an attack cold, unsure of what snags or defences awaited them. Wherever possible, though, they conducted reconnaissance, sending advance parties in the days or hours before an attack to reconnoitre potential targets.[31] Land commissioner Roderick O'Connor, insisted 'the Natives watch the stock-huts incessantly'.[32] The settler William Clark found they would 'for days and weeks, watch a house that they have marked out for plunder, till they find the whole of the males absent, they then pounce'.[33] In 1829, near Constitution Hill, Gilbert Robertson caught them in the act when his guides spied a war party 'sitting on a hill watching … Starkey's hut'.[34] Remarking on the deadly effectiveness of Aboriginal attacks, one settler insisted:

They accomplished this usually by watching the homestead on the farm, or the shepherd's huts, and taking advantage of a favourable opportunity to accomplish their purpose, when few or no men were about the place. They sneaked stealthily towards the house or hut, and murdered all the people, men, women or children, that were about the premises; and then made off with any provisions or clothing that they could carry.[35]

But just waiting for the right moment was not the only way Tongerlongeter improved his warriors' chances of success. There was a range of strategies he used to tip the scales against his gun-wielding adversaries. One was simply to seize the guns at the outset. It was difficult for colonists to carry these heavy weapons as they worked, so they often leant them against nearby trees, providing 'the cunning light-footed Aborigines' with the opportunity to sneak up and snatch them before their owners knew what had befallen them.[36]

Another way Tongerlongeter put his victims off balance was by decoying them. Based on a range of testimonies, the Aborigines Committee concluded: 'It has been clearly shown, by repeated instances, that the Natives have by artifice decoyed persons to quit their houses for the purposes of pursuit, who, on their return, have found their homes utterly destroyed by fire, and everything of value carried off'.[37] Tongerlongeter and his allies used several methods to lure their victims to where they wanted them.[38] Fire, which white men immediately associated with Aborigines, was frequently used. When Aborigines plundered George Meredith's hut in 1829, the *Colonial Times* noted that 'they set fire to the fence, to entice the men out of the hut!'[39] The following year, a clearly impressed Jordan River settler wrote:

> they are a most intricate [difficult] set of people to capture being a high witness to their exploits myself. No one can conjecture how crafty and subtle they act in the bush, they even made the fire and smoke in the bush to entice people from the buildings in order that they might plunder.[40]

Decoys were commonly used, sometimes to feign retreat, other times to approach their unwitting victims with a façade of friendliness.[41] Surveyor Thomas Scott recalled an instance in March 1830 in which 'they speared, or killed, with waddies, 60 sheep, within 2 miles [3 kilometres] of my tent, and threw a spear at the shepherd of Captain Smith. One woman who could talk English, came up to the door of the hut and asked for some bread, while the others were killing sheep'.[42] The colony's Executive Council referred to such ruses as 'the most consummate and deliberate treachery'. It decried

> those instances in which they have effected their purpose ... by sending some of their people, sometimes women, sometimes unarmed men, who have approached huts with apparently the most friendly disposition, and have succeeded in engaging the attention of the inmates, or in alluring some of them to a distance, and thus enabling

their armed confederates to fall suddenly upon their unsuspecting victims and destroy them.[43]

When the attack came, everyone knew their role. Tongerlongeter's warriors looked to him for more than just direction. Only a courageous and unerring chief could command the loyalty and sacrifice of his warriors. During his search for Tongerlongeter in 1831, Robinson learnt from shepherds at Bashan Plains near Lake Echo that Aborigines had, the previous year:

> burnt the soldiers' hut to the ground and piled up the
> stones for a battery [around the adjacent hut], from
> behind which they kept throwing fire at the hut and
> also stones, and calling in English, 'Fire at me, you white'
> ... the chief stood off in front and the chief kept giving
> directions how they ought to act. They were all round the
> hut behind stumps.[44]

A similar scene was reported two years earlier: 'A stock-keeper and a boy were near the[ir] hut, when all at once a sort of leader, with his hair thickly smeared with red ochre, was discovered crawling on his hands and knees, and directing about forty others to surround the hut'.[45] Similar examples of leadership in combat are well documented,[46] and as any field officer can attest, commanding operations of this kind requires considerable training, discipline and nerve. So critical was the role of the chief in such attacks that if anything happened to him, the operation was immediately aborted.[47]

Oyster Bay and Big River bands displayed remarkable strategy and discipline in their operations. In April 1828, the *Colonial Advocate* reported on an attack in Oyster Bay country in which the attacking warriors 'displayed a degree of discipline which was admirable, and according to Mr. Franks, "manoeuvred in the most beautiful style," in order to surround him'.[48] During another attack in the same region:

> The natives ran in two lines, one on either side of the men, with the view of surrounding them, and when parallel with them, began throwing their spears. The man who had the pistol then cocked it, and pulled the trigger, but it missed fire; on this the natives yelled, and ran with increased energy, calling to each other to close the lines, and surround their victims ...[49]

In an ambush, the most effective tactic was to simply kill everyone before they became a threat, such as when, 'at Mr Scott's, the attack was so sudden that the men were speared before they had any idea of natives even being near'.[50] After years of hard-won lessons, though, colonists had refined their defensive strategies. They now rarely went anywhere alone or without guns.[51] Most refused to work without such protections. Likewise, guard dogs were ubiquitous, making stealthy approaches difficult.[52] Yet, remarkably, few attacks were foiled by these obstacles. Guns posed the greatest threat, but even these could generally be negotiated by goading victims into prematurely pulling the trigger and then rushing them.[53] Indeed, Oyster Bay – Big River warriors had become so adroit in their resistance that even their victims developed a grudging respect for them. As the *Colonial Times* conceded in July 1830, 'the attacks and depredations of the Aborigines … assume a regular and alarming consistency, and evince on the part of the blacks a cunning and superiority of tactic which would not disgrace even some of the greatest military characters.'[54]

We can assume with some confidence that in the attacks on 6 June 1829, it was Tongerlongeter who divided his forces and descended upon the Carlton River settlements, some twenty-five kilometres east of Hobart. In short succession, his guerrilla bands killed four men at two properties and plundered huts at two others. Then, as suddenly as they came, they disappeared. Avoiding ridgelines and open tracts, they rendezvoused with their women and children and moved quickly from the scene. The next morning, they 'committed another murder near the lower settlement at Pitt Water. A servant of Mr. Downs was speared, and his brains beaten out with waddies within a few yards of his master's house.'[55] Again, they vanished. After days of searching the surrounding hills and valleys, a frustrated settler conceded: 'it was impossible to get sufficiently near ever to capture them', owing to 'their well known caution and cunning added to their extreme quickness of sight.'[56] The local magistrate added:

> Every soldier and constable that can be spared has been
> out in pursuit but the peculiar nature and habits of these
> savages gave them a decided superiority over Europeans
> … they instantly vanished like spectres and baffled all

pursuit. The Systematic Stratagems by which their
operations are conducted render them every day more
and more dangerous …[57]

The previous year, Kickertopoller had told Gilbert
Robertson 'that after having committed a murder or other
outrage they invariably retreat to some remote situation in
the interior'.[58] And this is exactly what his old comrade did.
Tongerlongeter quickly gathered up his people and turned
north-east, putting distance between them and the wasps'
nest of angry white men they had just kicked. It had been
an intense twenty-four hours, but rest was not an option.
They hadn't time to hunt kangaroo as they moved; instead
they would have snacked on plundered food. They had just
killed five men and harassed several others, so they probably
needed to rearm with fresh spears and waddies. It was a
familiar problem, and one they had solved in recent years by
littering the landscape with caches of weapons.[59] They did
the same with the dozens of firearms they seized, ensuring
they would never again be used against them.[60] It seems a fair
assumption, then, that Tongerlongeter's retreating band had
enough food and weapons. All that remained was to make
certain they weren't followed or spotted.

The ability of Oyster Bay and Big River bands to simply
'vanish' was a source of great astonishment among colonists.[61]
Even with Tongerlongeter's encyclopaedic knowledge of
the country, leading his people through difficult terrain,
harried as they were by armed parties, must have been
extremely challenging. 'The rapid movements of the blacks

was remarkable,' recalled one party leader, 'forty or fifty miles [sixty to eighty kilometres] a day must have been travelled by them at the height of the war'.[62] But such feats were not always possible when a band was encumbered by wounded kin or heavy plunder. They later explained their strategy to Robinson:

> The hostile natives have the greatest confidence in
> themselves and when pursued will, contrary to the
> general notion of the whites, secrete themselves and
> allow their pursuers to pass them, and then go in a
> contrary direction; and as a proof of their confidence
> they Walk deliberately away with heavy loads of flour in
> the face of their crime.[63]

Grappling to explain their uncanny evasiveness, another party leader pointed to 'their extreme cunning and vivid senses – their adroitness in concealment,' to which he added their 'quickness of sight, hearing, and smell, the agility, and their knowledge of the rough and thickly wooded country'.[64] They also had tricks to confuse the Aboriginal trackers many parties were now using. Jorgenson, a roving party leader whose guides were regularly hoodwinked, concluded that the bands they were pursuing 'point their sticks [used to direct slower members of the band] towards a wrong direction for the purpose of deception'.[65]

Before darkness fell, a safe campsite had to be located. 'The hostile natives', Robinson's guides explained, make their camps 'in the obscure recess of the forest or fastness of the hills between the rugged tiers.'[66] The same was obvious to those who discovered their used campsites: 'Their rendezvous are always very difficult to access, and they generally choose a spot for their nocturnal resting place, which will command a view of the approaches.'[67] Once he arrived at a campsite, Tongerlongeter first had to check for any signs that white men had discovered it since they were last there. He then directed sentries to keep watch while the rest got to work preparing food, shelter and weapons. Rollicking evenings of dance and song were a thing of the past now. Staying alive meant staying quiet. Hungrily, they waited for dusk to fade so the small fires they had set could be lit. Huddled around the life-giving warmth, women held tightly to their few surviving children as damper and possums roasted over the coals. Dogs panted in the shadows waiting for scraps. Men discussed the day's operation. This particular night, having now put five days and forty kilometres between themselves and their Carlton and Pitt Water attacks, Tongerlongeter had good reason to assume they were safe – but he was wrong.

Maybe they were glimpsed snaking their way along a hillside, or maybe the cold June air tempted them to light their fires too early, but somehow they were spotted. What happened next was reported in the *Hobart Town Courier*:

> After the late outrages at the Carlton ... a man named Douglas Evans [Hibbens], succeeded in observing them encamp for the night on Friday last, under a hill called 'the Three Thumbs,' on very rocky ground, with thick brush. A party of ten set out about 11 o'clock in hopes

of surrounding them, and taking them alive. On arriving within 300 yards [270 metres] of the spot, about one o'clock they advanced very cautiously in order to avoid giving alarm, but when within 20 yards [18 metres], one of the dogs which was with the blacks began barking, and they all instantly rose up, and the attacking party rushed on them, threatening to shoot them if they did not surrender. But they fled precipitately in all directions. Six of the party immediately fired at them (the guns carried by the other 4 missed fire). Douglas Evans pursued them alone into the bush for a few minutes, and fired a second shot, having been surrounded by them on separating from his companions.[68]

According to the official report, 'eight or ten of the natives were severely wounded, blood in considerable quantities having been traced in the direction they took. 49 spears, more then one hundred waddies, and forty blankets fell into possession of the party'.[69] Many colonists participated in this kind of campsite ambush; some made quite the sport of it. Hibbens was one such man. In 1830, it was suggested to the Aborigines Committee that he 'would soon put an end to the eastern mob if he were employed; he has killed half that tribe by creeping upon them and firing amongst them with his double-barrelled gun'.[70] The endless influx of white invaders meant Tongerlongeter and his allies would never win the Black War, but men like Hibbens made sure they lost it.

CHAPTER 10

White devils

Nicholas Clements

Tongerlongeter and his allies always attacked during daylight hours, but as soon as the sun went down, the tables of vulnerability turned; the hunters became the hunted.[1] So strong was the Tasmanians' fear of nocturnal spirits that only necessity could tempt them from their fires. The problem wasn't the night per se but the darkness, which gave cover to the evil spirit Wrageowrapper and other malevolent spectres. The white men were also believed to be evil spirits, and they too came at night. Both tormented the Tasmanians' minds; the latter assaulted their bodies. After the war, Robinson took stock of the mangled survivors: 'there is not an aborigine on the settlement nor an aborigine that has been at the settlement but what bears marks of violence perpetrated upon them by the depraved whites … Some of the natives have slugs in their bodies and others contusions, all inflicted by the whites.'[2]

Some of these battle scars were received in offensive operations or during chance encounters,[3] and some were inflicted by enemy spears.[4] Most, however, were incurred at night or at dawn, when white men ambushed their campsites.

It was usually fire that gave them away. Frontiersmen eager for black women or black blood developed a keen eye for scanning the horizon. 'It was', wrote Jorgen Jorgenson, 'always an easy matter at a very long distance to distinguish the fires of the Blacks from those of a white party – smoke from the former would ascend in many separate small and faint columns'.[5] But spotting a campsite was just the beginning. Executing a successful ambush was tricky, and most attempts seem to have failed.[6] Could the site be found once darkness descended? Could they get close enough without disturbing the Aborigines or their dogs? And, if they made it that far, would their guns work?

The Brown Bess musket – the most affordable and common firearm on the frontier – was a relic of the previous century.[7] Long and heavy, the gun was described by one party leader as 'very inconvenient in the bush'.[8] Beyond fifty metres, it was difficult to hit anything smaller than a stout tree, and that was *if* it fired; misfires were common.[9] One frustrated settler, describing a failed ambush, wrote: 'The 5 men all levelled at these 20 Blacks, but lamentable to tell, only one gun went off, the percussions all missed, and the whole of the Blacks made off'.[10] Even when the guns did go off, reloading was so complicated that assailants rarely got a second shot. Instead, they lunged forward using their musket as a club or, if they had a bayonet, a pike. But for all their faults, muskets that hit their mark could do truly horrific damage. They fired a nineteen millimetre lead ball at low velocity, shattering bones and tearing scrappily through soft tissue. Even if victims survived the initial trauma, they frequently succumbed to some combination of shock, blood loss and infection. Anything but a glancing wound would usually be fatal without rest and good medical care, neither of which was available at the height of the war.

By 1828, there were still some Oyster Bay and Big River Aborigines who hadn't themselves been shot, but none had been spared the carnage of campsite ambushes. As the only effective tactic in the white man's arsenal, these clandestine attacks were common. Undoubtedly, they account for the majority of violent Aboriginal deaths during the war. The early historian John West described the practice with disturbing clarity:

> no one will question the atrocities committed by commandoes, first formed by stock-keepers, and some settlers, under the influence of anger, and then continued from habit. The smoke of a fire was the signal for a black hunt. The sportsmen having taken up their positions, perhaps, on a precipitous hill, would first discharge their guns, then rush towards the fires and sweep away the whole party. The wounded were brained; the infant cast into the flames; the musket was driven into the quivering flesh; and the social fire, around which the natives gathered to slumber, became, before morning, their funeral pile [sic].[11]

Evidence for the ubiquity of camp-fire ambushes is overwhelming. Dozens were documented and many more undoubtedly weren't.[12] On 6 December 1828, for instance, a party of the 40th Regiment ambushed a band near Tooms Lake, east of Oatlands. One of the men described how 'we got near as possible to them that night', and the next day:

> at daybreak we formed ourselves to surround them, one of them getting up from a smaller fire to a larger one discovered us and gave the alarm to the rest, and the whole of them jumped up immediately and attempted to take up their spears in defence and seeing that, we immediately fired and repeated it, because we saw that they were on the defensive part, they were about twenty in number, and several of whom were killed, only two, unfortunately, were taken alive.[13]

When officials pressed for clarification, 'several' turned out to be 'ten',[14] but even this might have been an understatement. Witnessing the soldiers' jubilant return to Oatlands, Corporal Robert Ayton 'heard many of them boast that they had killed sixteen of the natives, one man in particular boasted that he had run his bayonet through two of them, and that they had gathered them into a heap and burned their bodies'.[15]

This ambush was executed by an official party, but most were unofficial. Some years after the war, an east coast settler who prided himself on killing Aborigines recounted his most successful 'hunt'. Other than the higher than usual and probably inflated death toll, his detailed account, transcribed by a fellow settler, reads like a blueprint for the typical ambush:

As soon as evening approached, I mustered our men to watch for the resting-place of the natives on the tiers. We had six muskets in good working order, and a good supply of ammunition, with ball and heavy slugs. The men posted themselves in good positions for making observations; and at last, in the grey twilight, one of them detected a light smoke rising from a gully two miles [three kilometres] distant. We carefully noted the spot and waited until near midnight, when we all sallied out together in search of our game. We took no dogs with us, lest they might be heard by the watchful dogs of the natives. Keeping the open country we soon reached the tier, and proceeded stealthily along until we stood over the little gully, from whence we then distinctly saw the smoke arising. It was now necessary to move along as quietly as possible; and, by observing every precaution, we succeeded in getting a pretty near view of the lighted fire, with a mob of natives and their dogs fast asleep around it. Having arranged our muskets and pistols for the fray, the former being loaded with heavy charges of slug and grape shot, we all six noiselessly approached to within a few yards of the wretches, when all of a sudden the dogs gave the alarm by raising a great commotion and furious barking. The natives were on their feet like electricity, but they looked stupefied, and never attempted to run. It would have been all the same if they had, for we had them nearly all under cover of our guns, which we discharged at once, and dropped some eight or ten like crows. Then there was a jolly scramble to make off, but we dropped a few more as they bolted away into the scrub. Our night's sport made a dozen less natives, whom we left there to rot, and we sent away several wounded.[16]

Aborigines told Robinson about a number of these attacks. During the search for Tongerlongeter, for instance, a Big River woman from among Robinson's envoys recounted an incident in which

> a party of white people followed them and came upon them at night and fired in among them and killed one woman and one man. The woman was shot dead, but the man walked a short distance to a thicket and dropped down dead. This the woman informed me who belonged to them and was with them at the fire when they were attacked. Said the white people had watched and waited till they made their fire and then came and fired in among them.[17]

Tongerlongeter's people believed that certain spirits would warn them when white men were approaching, and their success in evading pursuers must have confirmed this belief.[18] But their vastly more numerous enemies only had to get lucky occasionally to present a serious threat.

The defensive strategies of Oyster Bay and Big River bands were as sophisticated as their offensive strategies. They had to be. The risk of ambush was ever-present, especially when moving through the settled districts. They began by carefully selecting a secluded campsite with good defensive features.[19] The priority was to protect the most vulnerable.

'After a long chase of two days and a night of very wet weather', one settler described how his party 'found their fires at night but in such a scrubby place that they could not approach them undiscovered; in fact one of the men says they could not find the way to their fires through it'. He noted how, when his party came upon them, they were 'seated at no less than 7 fires, at the nearest of which there were 20 able men; no woman, nor any children were with them. They all crept up until they got very close to this group of 20, which they could not get by to the others, without being discovered'.[20]

Because plumes of camp-fire smoke gave away their location, Robinson found the tribes had learnt to 'do with small fires, the smoke of which is scarcely perceptible. They will collect the small dry sticks for this purpose'.[21] Although clean-burning fires helped, the safest option was to wait until dark to light them. Yet, even if they could tolerate the spookiness of twilight, they could not always withstand its icy temperatures. Anyone familiar with Tasmania's fickle climate can scarcely believe Aborigines went about naked. A lathering of animal fat and ochre gave their bodies some insulation, but during the war both ingredients could be hard to come by. Even when they weren't, the crusty paste alone was unequal to the bone-chilling night air, which can dip below freezing most months of the year. The white man's blankets offered some protection, though they were useless when damp. Marsupial skins were better but difficult to prepare and transport in wartime conditions.[22] Sometimes their only option was to light their fires before dark and keep them burning past dawn.[23]

Traditionally, Aboriginal fires were dotted around a sprawling campsite, giving each family its space. But when the white men learnt to look out for smoke that 'descends in so many distinct columns',[24] bands were forced to camp in closer proximity. To protect these sites, chiefs posted lookouts to cover the most likely approaches.[25] Kickertopoller and another Poredareme guide told Gilbert Robertson that Tongerlongeter's bands 'always keep regular sentries'.[26] One roving party 'came within 200 yards [180 metres] of a tribe, then in the act of cooking kangaroo. The party proceeded along a gulley through a scrub, but when approaching the tribe, two blacks watching on the hills on both sides of the gulley, gave the alarm, and the tribe fled'.[27]

Sentry duty wasn't only performed by warriors. One of the key reasons bands kept dogs was to act as an early warning system for ambushes.[28] These 'dogs are always on the alert,' wrote one colonist, 'and alarm the tribe instantly on the approach of a party'.[29] What's more, these large and ferocious animals often turned on assailants, undoubtedly saving many Aboriginal lives.[30] After one ambush, a member of the attacking party wrote: 'it would have astonished you to have witnessed the dogs when the attack was first made, how they bravely defended their masters'.[31]

While such measures made it difficult for colonists to ambush Tongerlongeter and his allies, the burden of being constantly pursued was a heavy one. Before the war, they had selected comfortable campsites with abundant water, game and shelter.[32] By 1828, though, hunting and gathering had become so difficult that they often went to sleep hungry, while the need to move and camp inconspicuously meant thirst too could be a problem. In some cases, they solved this by utilising 'glass bottles full of water with strings tied round their necks.'[33] But the greatest challenge was staying warm. This was especially true when, in the latter years of the war, they were forced to seek refuge in the high country.[34] Surviving here in the colder months was extremely difficult, but a brief reprieve from the bullets and bayonets was worth the hardship. Sheltering from the cold was also difficult in the settled low country. Where traditionally they had slept in enclosed shelters during the winter, these 'huts' now made them vulnerable to the stealthy approach of white men. Any Aborigine still alive in 1828 had, while fleeing an ambush, heard the muffled screams of their kin being butchered inside a hut. It was a prospect of which they were rightly terrified. In the end, Bonwick observed, they were 'so harassed by Europeans, they left off building huts and were satisfied with break-winds.'[35]

Sleeping alongside dogs was often the only thing between Tongerlongeter's people and hypothermia.[36] They also grew fond of these hounds, who in turn were loyal to them. But whether they realised it or not, these warm, furry companions were also the source of great suffering. By the late 1820s, there was scarcely an Aborigine on the island who was not tormented by canine scabies, a ghastly skin disease acquired from dogs.[37] Colonists often remarked on the 'scabby appearance of the natives.'[38] Robinson noted that every time his party stopped, his guides 'employ themselves in puncturing with a small sharp pointed stick the small pustules with which their skin is covered, the patient under those operations groaning as though he was suffering considerable pain.'[39] 'I have', he wrote, 'seen these poor creatures in the greatest torment and scratching themselves as if they would tear the flesh, the blood trickling down their naked bodies.'[40] When Robinson himself caught it, he declared he would 'sooner face a thousand hostile natives than have this horrid infection'. The demands of the war served as a distraction during the day, but at night the misery of this affliction was inescapable. Even on Flinders Island in 1832, James Backhouse observed that the exiles regularly awoke to stand by the fire and scratch themselves.[41]

With all this – the cold, the hunger, the maddening itch, and the groans of the wounded – nights could be a hellish experience. And if this weren't enough, there were the spectres lurking beyond the glow of the fire. To the minds of Tongerlongeter and his people, the darkness had always harboured evil spirits, but what kept them awake were the white ghouls who might, on any night, be stalking them. No campsite was entirely safe, and the constant fear of an ambush gnawed at their weary minds.[42] It didn't help that the Tasmanian bush comes alive at night with the sounds of rustling marsupials – sounds scarcely distinguishable from the creeping advance of an enemy. The fear could be suffocating, especially for children. Little was recorded of their experience, though much can be inferred. The few children who were still alive in 1828 had experienced unimaginable trauma.[43] They had seen most of their siblings and playmates killed or abducted. Their parents too were likely dead. In the north-west, Robinson noted the 'terror' experienced by children: 'I observed that the natives, when they wanted to quiet their children, told them that the NUM LAGGER, i.e. the white man come, which always was sufficient to quiet the children'.[44]

Aborigines of all ages had reason to be afraid. By the height of the war, bands like Tongerlongeter's could probably expect to be ambushed several times a year. Generally they escaped with minimal casualties, but occasionally their losses were crushing.[45] In 1830, the *Colonial Times* described 'the custom that has been almost universal amongst certain Settlers and their servants, whenever the Natives have visited their neighbourhood, to consider the men as wild beasts whom it is praiseworthy to hunt down and destroy, and the women as only fit to be used for the worst purposes'.[46] This was certainly not true of all or even most colonists but, as John West noted, 'Among the whites, there were men distinguished for the malicious vigour with which they tracked and murdered the native people'.[47] One settler admitted 'that it was a favourite amusement to hunt the aborigines'.[48] When another later bragged about participating in massacres, his interlocuter rebuked him: 'I call that murder'! Surprised and indignant, he retorted:

Nothing of the sort, you don't know anything about it. It was doing a noble service to shoot them down. Of course, we used to spare a young female occasionally when we got a chance, and kept her for a few days before we shot her.[49]

Once the first shots were fired, panic ensued. How many were out there? Where were they? Was there any hope of rescuing the wounded? These were not questions that could be deliberated on – they had to be decided in seconds by minds foggy from sleep and fear. Escape meant running a gauntlet of guns and bayonets. Women and children sometimes froze with terror.[50] There was scarcely time to account for one's closest kin let alone to gather supplies or weapons. So chaotic was the scene that warriors were rarely able to counterattack.[51] For those who escaped, the ordeal was just beginning. Rendezvous were probably prearranged, but disorientated by grief and fear and darkness, regrouping would have been difficult. And without the warmth of fires, dogs or coverings, hypothermia was a real danger. The situation for the wounded was critical, and oftentimes hopeless. For a leader like Tongerlongeter, finding and reassuring his people became an urgent imperative. By the time everyone was together, there would have been a pressing need to get warm, find food, make new spears, and put distance between themselves and their assailants.

Leadership under these conditions took serious mettle, especially when the victims of the ambush were loved ones. Talking to Robinson on Flinders Island after the War, Tongerlongeter recounted the night his wife was abducted. He told him of how the white men 'came near to them [as they slept] at night; then stopped [hiding in the darkness] till morning and that when it was little day light [the waiting assailants] came and fired at them. Took away his wife, also DROMETEHENNER. This was near the Lakes. On this occasion

they shot DROMETEHENNER's husband through the head;
his name was MAR.TRO.LIB.BEN.NER'.[52] The whole thing
would have happened in seconds. And at some point during
the blurry struggle, Tongerlongeter must have seen that
attempting to rescue his wife was suicidal. Still, abandoning
her to the white predators must have been a heart-rending
decision. Nothing is recorded about how the abduction of his
wife affected the chief. It is almost impossible to imagine his
pain. Had she been killed it might have been easier to process
her loss. The band would have been in disarray, lacking food
and weapons. The white men knew this too. However much
Tongerlongeter wanted to liberate his wife, his people were
in no shape to go on the offensive. It is unknown whether
Tongerlongeter saw his wife again, but his silence on the point
is suggestive, and a broader view of the sources indicates that
few men in his situation ever did.[53]

There would be no funeral for Martrolibbenner. As
important as funerals were for Tasmanians, retrieving bodies
in the wake of ambushes was rarely possible. This displeased
the spirits of the dead and compounded the grief of the living.
In a note titled 'Grief or lamentation of the aborigines',
Robinson observed that 'they give themselves up to grief.
They break their spears and necklace, throw away kangaroo
skins, cut their baskets, don't red ochre themselves, are quite
neglectful and mourn'.[54] In the immediate wake of Martrolibbenner's death, there would have been an outpouring of
grief and anger. And while necessity always propelled them
back into action, the sadness never went away – it sat in the
pit of their stomachs growing heavier and heavier with every

death. This way of life was gruelling in the extreme. There was little to take pleasure in besides slaking their thirst for revenge against those who had robbed them of every reason to smile.

Tongerlongeter's wife was one of hundreds of women who became victims in campsite ambushes. Aside from the emotional trauma this inflicted on everyone involved, the continuing loss of women had devastating economic and political ramifications for Oyster Bay– Big River society. So that men could hunt, fight and make spears, women performed nearly every other role. Now that there were so few of them, men were forced to do much more at a time when they were least able to.[55] 'An aborigine of this Colony without a female partner is a poor dejected being,'[56] Robinson observed. As their numbers declined, competition over women created tensions within and among the remnant bands. Every band Robinson encountered during his friendly mission 'complained in the strongest terms … of the hardships incumbent upon the deprivation of their women.'[57]

Tongerlongeter went to ever greater lengths to protect his people. This was on display the night of 25 October 1830, when his people suffered one of the most notable ambushes of the war. By now, Tongerlongeter and Montpelliatta had fused what remained of their bands and were primarily operating as one unit.[58] Just a week earlier, they had been in the Sorell district, where they made ten attacks over two days, plundering eight homes, wounding three colonists and killing one. Saddled with plunder, they had made their way to the rugged and sparsely populated Sandspit River valley, five kilometres from the east coast. On the afternoon before the attack, they hunted, their dogs barking as they flushed out game. They must have thought themselves safe, but they were not. A heavily armed party led by the settler Edward Walpole was watching. The men were still watching as the light faded and the band established its camp. During the night, as rain set in, Walpole brought up reinforcements. The stage was set for a slaughter, but that wasn't what happened.

Tongerlongeter and Montpelliatta had been caught unawares before, but this night they had the time to prepare a strong defensive position and guard the only access point with a detachment of five warriors. When dawn came, Walpole realised: 'There were five other huts across the creek in the centre of a very thick scrub – I had fully intended to attack the main body but I found it impossible to get near enough with[out] being heard. The hut with the 5 men appeared to have been a look out … The natives in the other huts fled on hearing the shots.'[59] The only losses were the sentries who, after a long night of keeping watch in the rain and cold, had fallen asleep under their blankets. Seeing his opportunity, Walpole gave the signal to his party and the men rushed forward. As they seized hold of the sleeping warriors, a desperate fight broke out:

> they endeavoured to make their escape. The man whose foot he [Walpole] had hold of made a violent effort to escape, and darted through the back of the hut, carrying Mr. Walpole with him into the gully or creek behind – here he again tried to make his escape by twisting his legs and biting, and would have succeeded had Mr. Walpole

not drawn a small dagger from his belt and inflicted
a slight wound, which so frightened him that he was
secured. The other taken, was a boy of about 15 years of
age ... Two others were shot by the party in making their
escape into the scrub.[60]

Tongerlongeter and Montpelliatta probably saved many
lives by arranging the camp the way they had, which allowed
the main body time to escape. They couldn't have known it
as they scrambled up the escarpment to the sound of gunfire,
but the men who had just attacked them were an advance
party of the so-called Black Line, the largest military offensive
ever mounted on Australian soil. Two thousand two hundred
soldiers, settlers and convicts under the direct command of
Governor Arthur now blocked their escape, with military
posts spaced 180 metres apart and armed men patrolling
between them. Three weeks earlier, the line had stretched
several hundred kilometres, lassoing the greater part of
south-east and central Tasmania. Beginning on 7 October,
the parties had advanced southward and eastward, the cordon
contracting each day until it extended in a thirty kilometre arc
from Sorell to the Sandspit. The foremost goal of this 'Grand
Army' was to capture or otherwise suppress the Oyster
Bay – Big River people, whose strategic and highly effective
resistance had left the colony in a state of desperation. For
their part, Tongerlongeter and Montpelliatta probably never
realised the full scope of the Black Line, but as they hastened
to the top of the tiers that morning and saw twin rows of fires
burning on the horizon, they knew something big was afoot.

They were encircled, and they were going to have to break out.

As they got closer, Tongerlongeter and Montpelliatta realised this escape would not be as easy as most. Crude fortifications made from the surrounding foliage obstructed the obvious routes between the military posts.[61] Speed was paramount. They resolved to split up and penetrate the line at different points. Bringing their dogs was too risky, so they made the painful decision to tie up their canine friends and abandon them.[62] It was another 'tempestuous night', wrote the *Hobart Town Courier*'s correspondent. At 2 am:

> the natives attempted to force their way through the
> line where Lieut. Oven's division was posted, upon a
> rocky hill on the south bank of Prosser's river, about five
> miles [eight kilometres] from the sea. The men on guard
> observed a black man in a stooping attitude, and with
> a fire stick in his hand running past … Several other
> lights were observed at a short distance on the hill, so
> that it is probable a considerable body of the natives was
> endeavouring to force their way [through].[63]

Tongerlongeter appears to have made it through that night, telling Robinson 'he went through the Line when they had fires.'[64] But the next morning, at least six warriors were still inside the line. It could be they failed in their initial attempt, though there is some evidence that they acted as decoys while the others slipped through.[65] Either way, at 11 am, they took their opportunity. That afternoon, Major

Douglas scribbled a note to the governor: 'the natives have attacked a sentry at Mr Weiss's hut no.5 Richmond party and severely wounded him in two places'.[66] According to one correspondent, 'so daring were the natives that, after throwing their spears, they came and drew them out themselves, and then made off, dangling their blankets in the air as a kind of bravado'.[67] Such bravado suggests they were contemptuous of the line. Certainly, when Robinson's envoys passed the site three months later, they 'laughed heartily at this scheme', and when he later asked a woman who 'was there at the time', she 'said they had no trouble in getting away'.[68]

This confidence was expressed in hindsight, however. The fact that they abandoned their dogs and broke through at night is telling. As mentioned earlier, the darkness gave cover to frightful spirits and only in extremis would they have ventured into it. It really had been a close call – too close for four of their number. Once out, they made a beeline for the Central Plateau.[69] To get there, they took a traditional Aboriginal route through Black Marsh, just east of Bothwell. While this was the quickest way, it was also one of the most densely settled districts. It had seen a great deal of violence over the preceding half-decade, but with most of the guns behind them, Tongerlongeter probably felt confident they could slip through in relative safety.

CHAPTER 11

Things fall apart

Nicholas Clements

Tongerlongeter would have felt his arm explode before he heard the crack of the musket. The pain had to have been excruciating.[1] His once powerful limb now dangled from his elbow, a hideous spectacle of splintered bone and gouged flesh. As he would later tell it, he

> was with his tribe in the neighbourhood of the Den Hill and that there was men cutting wood. The men were frightened and run away. At night they came back with plenty of white men (it was moonlight), and they looked and saw our fires. Then they shot at us, shot my arm, killed two men and three women. The women they beat on the head and killed them; they then burnt them in the fire …[2]

Considerable evidence indicates that this ambush took place almost a week after Tongerlongeter and his people had escaped the Black Line.[3] For example, Tongerlongeter said 'it was moonlight', and their route would have taken them past Den Hill on or about the full moon of 31 October. What's more, a local settler reported that Miles Opening, on the northern edge of Den Hill, 'was where the natives got through at the time of the Line'.[4] This means they were spotted, which also means an armed party would have been mustered. Certainly, this mountain pass offered the quickest route to the Central Plateau, which is where we know they were heading,[5] but it was also full of white men. It was a gamble that almost proved fatal for Tongerlongeter.

Shards of moonlight pierced the canopy as the chief and the other survivors fled the campsite where they had moments earlier been sleeping. Tongerlongeter wouldn't have got far before collapsing from loss of blood. His arm was irreparably smashed, though the wound must not have ruptured both of the arteries in his forearm, or else he would have bled to death within minutes. Even so, he was bleeding profusely and his comrades had to have used a tourniquet – it's the only way they could have saved his life.[6] They then carried him to a safe distance and lay the delirious chief down. Those who gathered around him knew the score: no one survived such wounds. But Tongerlongeter was an extraordinary case; he was their leader. Tactically and symbolically, he was essential to their continued resistance, and to their sense of hope. He knew it too. They must have been shaking with fear and grief, having just seen five of their friends shot and bludgeoned to death, but they had to at least try to save the chief's life.

One or more warriors had to have gone back to the campsite. The white men having gone, they were confronted with the smouldering bodies of their dead friends. Retrieving a firestick and a cutting tool, they quickly fled the gruesome scene and returned to the chief.[7] His shattered arm had to come off, and it would have to be done quietly. Whoever performed the operation knew what they were doing. Years later, the surgeon who undertook Tongerlongeter's post-mortem remarked that the radius bone had been 'violently torn away – not a vestige of it remaining – the shattered end of the other bone [the ulna] having been scraped down into its present form, which is conical, with a blunt apex, and certainly a very excellent cushion was made of the soft parts.'[8] That his comrades saved his life is remarkable; how they were able to perform such a neat and professional amputation under those conditions is nothing short of miraculous.

As his friends held him down and sliced off what remained of his arm, Tongerlongeter's pain would have been stupefying.[9] But the worst was yet to come. Someone had to then take the splintered remnant of his ulna forearm bone and grind it down to a smooth, rounded end. All they had available to them was abrasive rock, which they must have scoured repeatedly over the stump. The difficulty of this part of the operation, conducted by the light of a small flame, is scarcely imaginable. The shortened bone, now just a few centimetres long, would have been almost impossible to grip, not least of all because it was recessed into the surrounding flesh. By the time it was over, the wound would have been a bloody pulp of flesh, bone and grit. Then, in an attempt to stem the bleeding, a final torture was inflicted. When discussing it with Robinson on Flinders Island, Tongerlongeter simply said they 'burnt the end.'[10] But this matter-of-fact description belies the true horror of cauterisation without anaesthetic. He may already have lost consciousness, but if not, he would have been subjected to an unimaginable test of fortitude.

Having survived the operation, Tongerlongeter needed to rest. But he couldn't stay where he was. He and his people likely had no food or spears, and their enemy knew their general whereabouts. In his weakened state, Tongerlongeter would have struggled to walk unaided. Slowed by its ailing chief, the band probably took a week or more to get free of the settlements. Resting where he could, Tongerlongeter somehow kept death at bay. The cauterisation of the wound helped stem the blood loss, but it also raised the risk of infection.[11] There is no record of his arm becoming infected, though under the circumstances it was very likely, and this probably posed an even greater risk to his life than the original trauma. Still, against incredible odds, he recovered. Gunshot wounds were commonplace during the Black War, so we can assume many amputations were attempted, but Tongerlongeter is the only Aborigine known to have survived such an operation. While this probably owes as much to luck and the devotion of his carers as it does to his resolve; he certainly needed all three.

As 1831 began, Tongerlongeter's arm would have been mostly healed, his pain manageable.[12] He could have returned to Oyster Bay country and resumed the offensive, but he didn't. For so long, despite unbearable loss and hardship, Tongerlongeter's spirit of resistance had been irrepressible, but something had changed. In the first eight months of 1830, eighty-eight attacks were recorded in Oyster Bay territory; in the first eight months of 1831, there was one.[13] The two remnant nations restricted themselves to raiding within Big River country and in the neighbouring country north of the Central Plateau. In January, Montpelliatta led a war party north to Dairy Plains near Deloraine, where he and his son 'most barbarously murdered' Mrs McCasker.[14] Two months later, they went north again, attacking six properties in five hours along the Lake River.[15] In May they launched two attacks in the frigid high country, where they speared and bludgeoned two men to death,[16] and in June, they made five attacks in one day along the Ouse River, killing one woman and wounding another. For the most part, though, they lay low in the first half of 1831, making only a quarter of the attacks they had made during the same period the previous year.[17]

If this signalled that they were in trouble, their decision to spend winter in the high country confirmed it. Because relatively few white men lived there, the Central Plateau was the safest region in Oyster Bay – Big River country, yet it is almost impossible to comprehend how Aborigines could survive in such a forbidding alpine region during winter, a time when they would normally be in the relatively hospitable lowland valleys and coastlines. The plateau is a labyrinth of lakes and scrub where the average daily minimum temperature from May to October is minus one degree Celsius, but it often gets much colder.[18] Rain and snow compete almost daily for the right to oppress the landscape. A few stoic trees, their backs arched, brace themselves against the unremitting winds. Only the ubiquitous dolerite boulders seem at peace in the landscape. Tongerlongeter probably knew some of his people wouldn't survive this ordeal, but he also knew that many more would die if they returned to the settled districts.

Forty or fifty people – predominantly men – were now all that remained of the Oyster Bay and Big River nations, whose combined pre-invasion population was surely well in excess of 1000 and maybe as high as 2000.[19] This exhausted remnant was composed of individuals from numerous bands. Some were literally the last of their bands,[20] and several were hangers-on from decimated foreign nations. While traversing Oyster Bay country in 1829, Gilbert Robertson noted the signs of this decline in his journal:

> the country between the Windfalls and Maloney's Sugar
> Loaf has undoubtedly been the chief haunt of another
> Tribe, for in this latter District, there were ranges of
> old Huts within almost every mile for thirty miles [fifty
> kilometres]. The huts at the oldest encampments that
> we saw appeared sufficient to contain Two Hundred
> natives, but their encampments appeared to decrease in
> size every year, and those of last winter could not contain
> Thirty people. We remarked the same decrease in the
> extent of encampments on the Forest which we this day
> explored.[21]

For every survivor, the day eventually came when he lost one too many of his kinfolk, and the band he had grown up in could no longer sustain itself as an economic unit. This set in motion a search reminiscent of a post-apocalyptic novel.

Wanderers returned to familiar rendezvous and scanned the horizon for smoke in the hope of locating fellow survivors – friends, allies, or even traditional enemies who might now take them in.[22] John West put it poignantly:

> Some, who gave themselves up, stated that they had been very unhappy; they had gone over the country, searching for their lost friends, of whom they could gain no tidings. We realise a softening scene, in contemplating these fragmentary tribes, traversing their ancient haunts, and uttering the unanswered, and then melancholy call which distinguishes their race.[23]

It was a scene echoed by a Big River exile, who told confidants on Flinders Island how:

> by innumerable affrays with the white man, they were at last reduced to three men, exclusive of women and piccaninies, and a few months since, they were suddenly surprised, and two of the men were killed; and they wandered all over the island for the purpose of joining some other tribe, feeling themselves too weak to exist, and under constant dread that the remaining man would be killed, and the rest, who, it appears, could not get food for themselves, starved. They wandered over the island in every direction, but found no traces of black men; they began to despond, and led a miserable existence, feeling themselves to be the last natives in the whole island, and that the white man had rooted them out.

Scared and tired, 'they were very glad when they were taken'.[24] Most would have had no idea that men like Robinson and Robertson were out there proffering a peaceful end to the war. Tongerlongeter, Montpelliatta and the others holding out on the Central Plateau that winter must have struggled to see how they would escape their predicament alive. By now they surely saw the conflict as a war of extermination, one in which they were squarely on the losing side.[25]

Even as the end neared, though, the white ghosts were not Tongerlongeter's only foe. Intertribal relations weighed heavily on his mind. Despite moments of tension over how best to combat the interlopers,[26] the alliance between Oyster Bay and Big River nations held firm.[27] But relations with north-eastern bands were reliably hostile.[28] Longstanding animosities between the different language groups had clearly been exacerbated by the white invaders, who had driven bands onto the country of their enemies, and kidnapped or killed most of their women.[29] In 1828, Gilbert Robertson learnt from his Aboriginal guides and captives that an alliance had been made between Tongerlongeter's Oyster Bay nation and the Stoney Creek nation to the north (key observers used 'tribe' and 'nation' interchangeably). They had agreed 'to make war on the Port Dalrymple tribe. Their war originated in two causes – first – to capture wives for the Oyster Bay and Stoney Creek tribes who had lost nearly all their women and – secondly – to repel an invasion which the Port Dalrymple [tribe had made into an Oyster Bay hunting ground]'.[30]

As would become obvious after the war, diplomacy was one of Tongerlongeter's greatest strengths as a leader. The

Stoney Creek nation was a traditional enemy and yet he was able to make common cause with them. It also seems that, even though the Port Dalrymple people had killed 'many of the Oyster Bay mob',[31] Tongerlongeter's true purpose at the meeting was not violence. Rather, as Gilbert Robertson's informants revealed,

> they met without committing any act of Hostility and
> … have made some sort of treaty by which the [Oyster
> Bay] tribe have given all the others to hunt on their
> grounds – From whence each tribe sends small parties to
> rob and hinder the inhabitants of the remote huts – I am
> informed that they are now on their way to Fight the Big
> River tribe for the purpose of compelling them to give
> up their hunting ground for the common good and make
> common cause in carrying on their warfare against the
> white inhabitants.[32]

From at least 1827, resisting the white invaders had become Tongerlongeter's overriding objective. His 'was a savage people', warned the Bruny Island envoy Woorrady, adding that they 'no like white man; that they hate him'.[33] If he were ever going to rid his country of the white scourge, Tongerlongeter knew it would require a pan-Aboriginal alliance. Still, the task of uniting the nations was immense. They had grudges going back generations, and they distrusted each other intensely. They had no common language. The territory of one was a foreign country to another. And before any of these obstacles could be negotiated, the nations –

or what was left of them – had to coordinate meetings. All this had to be accomplished at the height of a war of unprecedented scale and intensity. Somehow, though, they seem to have managed it.

The alliance-building project lasted from mid-1828 to mid-1830. In addition to the diplomatic efforts made in 1828, Aborigines taken captive at Oyster Bay in November 1829 revealed 'that a general meeting of the tribes was to be held near the Big Lake about this time'.[34] The Big Lake was Great Lake, on the Central Plateau. If Tongerlongeter had attended, we would expect to see a cessation of attacks on the east coast and a surge of attacks on the plateau and its approaches during this period, which is exactly what the record shows.[35] The summit appears to have been successful. In February 1830, an Aboriginal guide in Jorgen Jorgenson's roving party revealed that the different nations had 'suspended their own internal broils, and formed a regular systematic plan of offensive aggressions against the white colonists'.[36] The same year, a settler close to Launceston noted: 'one fellow taken a short time ago who could speak a little English said that the different tribes had leagued together sinking their own disputes and determined to exterminate the whites if possible'.[37]

These efforts to unite the nations, in which Tongerlongeter must have played a central role, were unprecedented. That they occurred at all speaks of the imagination and courage of the leaders involved. Ultimately, though, their efforts had little effect. The various nations probably never intended to coordinate their offensive actions. There is almost no evidence of this,[38] and it would be difficult to make sense of it if there were. Country was central to how and why Tasmanians fought. No nation wanted to abandon its own country to fight for someone else's. Tongerlongeter sometimes fought in Big River territory because his people had a long, reciprocal connection with that country and its people. But he had little incentive to defend the country of northern tribes who, until recently, had been his avowed enemies. Even if reciprocal assistance could be counted upon, a warrior's effectiveness depended heavily on his knowledge of the land. Rather, the purpose of the alliances forged in 1828 and 1829 must have been to relax intertribal tensions so that each of the various nations could focus solely on resisting their mutual enemy.

These compacts were sound in theory, but they were too little too late. The white invasion had already broken the economic and cultural spine of the eastern nations. This was most apparent in the north-east, which had been almost completely stripped of women and girls by the rapacious sealers. In November 1830, Robinson interviewed the survivors from that region and took a census that included 'all the aborigines in a line from the Tamar [River] to the Derwent [River]… parts of different nations, some of Prossers Plains, Ben Lomond, Oyster Bay, Piper[s] River, Cape Portland &c'. The list he recorded, while omitting a number of the women with Tongerlongeter, provides a chilling snapshot of the devastation wrought by the invasion: 'out of 74 persons there are only 3 females'.[39]

Without women and the crucial economic roles they

played, the remnant north-eastern bands could not function. More poignantly, they could not see a future. Some of their wives and daughters were still alive, enslaved on the islands of Bass Strait, but they were powerless to liberate them. In one of the more wrenching scenes recorded from this period, Robinson describes a group of north-eastern men sending smoke signals to their enslaved womenfolk from atop a coastal rise. 'The females of the island make smoke in answer to the men', who in turn 'dance on these hills and sing an aboriginal song which is a relation to love complaints. What a wretched existence, all their females gone, torn from them'.[40]

It was a grim situation for the north-east remnant, as unsustainable as it was unbearable. Without women, their fate was sealed. They had to abduct some, even if it meant breaking the pact they had made with their southern rivals. In 1830, the Oyster Bay – Big River nations had probably only two dozen women between them, yet at that point these constituted almost the entire female population of eastern Tasmania. That year, the northerners went on the offensive, scaling the Central Plateau to attack the Big River people at 'the Lakes'. On their return, ten warriors took refuge at John Batman's farm at the foot of Ben Lomond before heading to the coast, where they gave themselves up to Robinson's envoys. They told both Robinson and those at Batman's that they had recently been embroiled in strife with their enemies on the plateau,[41] where they claimed to have 'killed 3 of their opponents and put the rest to flight'.[42] If so, their victory was an expensive one with little pay-off. Not only did they return without any captives, but one of their own women was killed on the expedition.[43]

It's not clear whether Tongerlongeter was involved in this particular battle, though there are reasons to think his Oyster Bay warriors did clash with north-eastern bands in 1830. One of the warriors captured by Walpole in October told an interpreter that his people had recently 'fought the Stony [sic] Creek tribe and killed a great number'.[44] That same month, the refugees at Batman's railed against the Oyster Bay people, who they claimed had 'killed off' most of their band.[45] They were certainly in bad shape, with 'spear wounds all over them … and two of them have lost an eye each'.[46] The various accounts of intertribal conflict in 1830 don't jibe perfectly, no doubt owing to conflicted perspectives and the difficulty of cross-cultural communication. It's not even clear whether they refer to separate conflicts.[47] What is clear, though, is that the fragile accords negotiated in 1828 and 1829 had unravelled.

By 1831, Aboriginal society in eastern Tasmania was in ruins. Further resistance may have been cathartic, but it was futile. Tongerlongeter and his allies had put up a valiant fight, but what hope was there now? They had been deprived of nearly everything that had made life worth living. They could no longer hunt and roam freely on the country of their birth. They could no longer build their huts in the lush river valleys. They could no longer observe the rituals that ensured balance in this world and the next. What's more, they could no longer hold ceremonies with friends, both because such gatherings were too dangerous, and because their friends were almost all

dead.[48] The absence of these ceremonies and the closing in of
the white demons undoubtedly precipitated a spiritual crisis.
What had they done to deserve this? What would become
of them when they too joined the dead? While the record is
silent on these questions, they had to have been asked.

Tongerlongeter's people had been made to live like
fugitives in their own country, moving rapidly through thick
scrub and over rugged tiers to elude the invaders. Possibly the
cruellest aspect of this predicament was the heartbreaking
decisions they were forced to make. Staying still wasn't an
option, but not everyone could keep up. The elderly and
severely wounded faced a sombre choice. This was made
starkly apparent to Robinson in 1829 when he arrived on
Bruny Island to begin his work with the Aborigines. In one
of his earliest journal entries he noted that when a person
was mortally afflicted, their kin 'put water into a piece of kelp
and a few shellfish alongside the afflicted persons and leave
them to their fate'.[49] He observed this practice several times
in southern and western Tasmania,[50] and Tongerlongeter's
people almost certainly employed similar expedients.

In nomadic societies, mobility is a matter of life and
death, which is why abandoning invalid or dying kin was
sometimes resorted to, especially in times of hardship.[51]
As the missionary James Backhouse pointed out, following
conversations with Aborigines exiled on Flinders Island,
they appear to have observed this practice only 'as a matter
of necessity'.[52] The war increased the speed and difficulty of
movement at the same time as it produced large numbers of
wounded. Leaving such people behind may or may not have

been a traditional practice,[53] but it was now an unavoidable one. If there is one image that captures the tragedy of this war, it is surely one of tearful men and women reluctantly forsaking their dying loved ones.

Perhaps, though, there is an even more tragic image. In Robinson's November 1830 census of Aborigines 'at large' in eastern Tasmania, not a single child appears,[54] and when his mission encountered these peoples, they were almost invariably childless. It was an absence that hadn't gone unnoticed by the newcomers. 'The disappearance of all the young children among the natives', ventured one Oyster Bay settler, 'compels us to the inference that they were destroyed, doubtless on account of the difficulty of conveying them about in their rapid flights from place to place'.[55] But this is neither the only nor even the most obvious explanation. Girls of all ages were quickly picked off by sealers and other sexual predators. Boys in their teens had a better chance, but inexperience made them more vulnerable than their adult counterparts. Younger children, just like their elderly kin, would have struggled to escape the incessant ambushes.[56] Still, the vulnerability of and danger posed by very small children does raise the spectre of infanticide.

When on campaign in the low country, Tongerlongeter was sometimes able to leave Oyster Bay children with his allies in the high country,[57] but this was not always an option, and it was never a sustainable one. While Robinson only recorded the practice of infanticide among women abducted by the sealers,[58] a number of other sources suggest that it was sometimes resorted to as a wartime expedient.[59] When attempting to move stealthily through the settled districts, a crying child could jeopardise the entire band. One settler claimed that 'the marked decrease of children arose from the policy of the tribes, who finding themselves hard pressed, and who feared the betrayal of their haunts from the cry of their little ones, resolved upon themselves the destruction of their children'.[60] Whether or not such claims were well founded, we know that protecting young children from the ravages of the Black War was next to impossible. We can be just as certain that the parents of these forlorn children suffered indescribable agony.

Tongerlongeter would come to know this heartache all too well. Following the abduction of his wife described in the previous chapter, he, as chief, had the pick of available women.[61] He chose Droomteemetyer. A diminutive woman in her early twenties, Droomteemetyer had presumably been Tongerlongeter's primary carer following the amputation of his arm. As the chief recuperated in the summer of 1830–31, the couple conceived a child. By the time Droomteemetyer had begun to show, the plateau's brief window of hospitable weather, if it can be said to have one, was closing fast. As the remnant nations braced for the bone-chilling highland winter, Droomteemetyer and Tongerlongeter must have felt mixed emotions. On the one hand, their people had no future without children; on the other, how could they ever hope to preserve the life of such a vulnerable being under these conditions? They resolved to try.

Somehow, Droomteemetyer and her unborn child survived the indifferent savagery of that long winter. It had been gruelling for everyone, but as the warmer weather beckoned, it seemed only logical that they would remain in their highland sanctuary. Safety was not their only concern, though. Whether by fiat or frustration, the group split. In late August, the Big River remnant, together with a few Port Sorell people and at least one Oyster Bay man, pushed northward again, plundering farms and exacting revenge at several properties. Continuing north along the Rubicon River, the band advanced on Port Sorell, where they made the most high-profile attack of the war, killing Captain Bartholomew Thomas, brother of the colonial treasurer, and his overseer James Parker.[62] The panicked colonial press saw this as evidence that the hostile tribes had returned stronger than ever, but nothing could have been further from the truth. As the bodies of the two men lay at their feet, a fierce argument broke out. Three of the women stormed off. Three warriors followed and were attempting to entice them back when all six were apprehended by Thomas's men.

Robinson and his guides, who arrived in the area soon after, were summoned to interrogate the captives and locate the bodies. The ensuing conversations revealed that the Oyster Bay and Big River nations – or at least, what was left of them – were in a desperate state. One of the women claimed 'that MONT.PE.LI.ATTER, chief of the Big River tribe, had gone to the Big River back of Hobart Town out of the way and a long way back in the bush, and that he intended remaining there'.[63] Kickertopoller was told that he was not with them at Port Sorell, that he was stopping in his own place taking care of a man that had been speared by another native and that when the man was dead MONTPELIERATTER proposed going away by himself with his wife and stopping in the bush, that jealousy was the cause of this measure.[64]

But these claims were false. Made at a time when it looked like the men responsible for killing Thomas and Parker would hang, they were probably an attempt to provide Montpelliatta with an alibi. The chief had not remained at the Big River. Rather, he and his band had turned south-west from Port Sorell and, as Robinson's one-time assistant, Alexander McKay soon discovered, 'Monte Pelati' and his people spent September and October hiding out in the Surrey Hills north-west of the Central Plateau. Robinson heard they were there for ochre.[65] McKay, however, who had his own Aboriginal guides, discovered they had been 'driven there by the activity of the parties in the settled districts but detained there latterly against their will by the [swollen] state of the Rivers and only waiting an opportunity to return'.[66] McKay came by this intelligence in late October, when he and his party ambushed the band, killing four and capturing two men, a woman and a child.[67]

Tongerlongeter was not with Montpelliatta during this period.[68] Around the time Thomas and Parker were killed, he and about two dozen of his people had set out for Oyster Bay. On the face of it, it was an unnecessary and risky journey. With warm weather on the way and a pregnant wife, why not remain in relative safety on the plateau? The sources cannot answer this question definitively, but one explanation stands out. Tongerlongeter had seen enough to know that his days were numbered, and he would have wanted to see his country one last time. He probably also had strong feelings about where his child should be born. His people's rites and beliefs associated with childbirth were never recorded, but a culture so steeped in ritual and creed undoubtedly had them. It seems almost certain that the Freycinet Peninsula, with its spectacular granite monoliths, was a special place for the Oyster Bay people. Why else would Tongerlongeter have led them into the most densely populated settlement on the east coast and, once there, onto a narrow isthmus past the whaling station of his old nemesis, George Meredith? Whatever the cultural significance of the peninsula, going there in October 1831 was taking an audacious risk.

Droomteemetyer was heavily pregnant when she crossed onto the peninsula. There were no settlers past the neck, so if the band could be careful with its fires, Droomteemetyer might hide for a time and give birth in that majestic place. But they had made several attacks en route, putting the settlement on high alert. As the band approached the isthmus, it was spotted. Vague reports of an Aboriginal group numbering between twelve and thirty roused the authorities to action. Despite the failure of the Black Line twelve months earlier, they moved fast to establish a cordon over the steep, narrow pass through the Hazards, roughly following the line of today's popular walking track into Wineglass Bay.[69] The operation, which became known as the Freycinet Line, began on 21 October. An estimated 100 soldiers and civilians took up positions across the neck, patrolling between their posts and sending in parties to flush out the enemy. Makeshift fortifications reinforced the cordon, while a chain of blazing fires illuminated it at night. The men guarding the line felt confident that escape was impossible.[70]

Finding they were hemmed in, Tongerlongeter seems to have abandoned his plans on the peninsula and turned his mind to escaping before even more white men arrived. Just as with the Black Line, he and his band had no trouble outfoxing their adversaries. Luckily, for a people wary of the dark, the moon was almost full on the night they attempted their escape.[71] The local settler John Lyne provides the best account of that evening:

> at the end of the fourth night the moon didn't rise until 10 pm and the fires were becoming low. It was my turn to patrol, I was at the time [urging] the men to keep good watch as the native dogs were seen amongst the fires in front, and after passing one of the soldiers on duty about 50 yards [forty-five metres] I heard him call 'Halt'. He comes there firing off his gun to give the alarm and on my running quick I heard a rustle as though a mob of wild cattle were passing but could see nothing … [the] next morning we tracked their foot marks very plain, the ground being soft from previous rain.[72]

No doubt shaken by yet another impressive show of force, Tongerlongeter wasted no time clearing out. The thought that he might never see his homeland again surely occurred to him, but right now he had to get Droomteemetyer away from the guns. Using attacks as a proxy for movement, he appears to have headed straight for the Ouse River on the western fringe of the settled districts, and we know it was here that Droomteemetyer gave birth to their son, Parperermanener.[73]

Three attacks were made along the Ouse in mid-November. Three more were made a few weeks later and about forty kilometres to the east; then the violence ceased. Robinson later discovered that around this time the remaining Big River people journeyed to the Ouse 'to see the old chief TONGELONGTER'.[74] From there, the remnant Oyster Bay and Big River people, now numbering fewer than thirty, made their way together to the high plateau. Clearly, they wanted to spend the summer as far away from the white men as possible; but what then? Was this not just a temporary solution to a problem that was ultimately unsolvable? They must have realised they were on the losing side of an apocalyptic struggle, that the white devils who had killed most of their friends and family were coming for them too. Tongerlongeter surely appreciated what this meant. It wasn't just him and his family who were about to die. He could foresee his whole world – his religion, his culture, his history – being snuffed out forever. It was a grave but unavoidable conclusion, for he had no idea that his old comrade and wayward kinsman Kickertopoller was about to reappear in his life, this time offering a reprieve – one literally too good to be true.

CHAPTER 12

Armistice

Nicholas Clements

With the birth of Parperermanener, a small and delicate flame had been kindled from the dying embers of Tongerlongeter's people. But he and his newborn son were not the last of the Poredareme. There was Kallerromter, who was captured after the Port Sorell killings, and several women who had been liberated from the sealers.[1] Most importantly, though, Kickertopoller was still alive. And now we must rewind four years and briefly return to the story of this conflicted warrior, as he leads us back to Tongerlongeter and the dramatic closing scene of the war.

After being captured for a second time in November 1827, Kickertopoller had languished in the dank, vermin-infested Hobart Gaol. A notorious killer, he was expected to hang for multiple counts of murder. Yet, when his case went before the Supreme Court on 17 July 1828, an extraordinary thing happened. The prosecution presented no evidence and no witnesses, and so to the vexation of colonists everywhere, the 'treacherous and infamous leader, Black Tom – that despicable creature' was released.[2] In all likelihood, the hand of Sarah Hodgson (née Birch) was again involved, though this has not been proven.

Then something even more remarkable happened. The very next day, the sheriff of Van Diemen's Land wrote to the governor with an unusual problem: 'I have the honour of informing you that the 4th Session of the Criminal Court finished yesterday, when Black Tom (a native Black) was discharged by proclamation, but voluntarily returned to the Gaol … I have therefore to request His Excellency's instructions as to his disposal'.[3] In response, Arthur asked 'whether Black Tom would voluntarily go to N.S. Wales – if so, the Governor [of that colony] I have no doubt will place him in a situation to obtain his livelihood – I will order him to be forwarded by the *Mermaid*',[4] which was then about to sail. But Kickertopoller was having none of it. 'In reply to your Letter of yesterday', Fereday wrote, 'I beg to state for the information of His Excellency that this individual refuses to go to New South Wales, but he will go to England or live with a Master in Hobart Town'.[5]

So why did Kickertopoller not return to the bush as he had before? What had changed? His rationale, while not explicitly recorded, can be guessed at with some confidence. By now, the 'tame mob' had, like most of the other 'hostile' bands, been effectively destroyed. If Kickertopoller were to rejoin the resistance it would be under Tongerlongeter, not as a leader in his own right. And the relationship between these two men was at best complicated. Tongerlongeter seemed to take a forgiving stance towards the younger warrior in the mid-1820s. The valuable information Kickertopoller trafficked in surely helped, though the chief's magnanimity probably had more to do with the strength of the bond between hunters and warriors from the same band. Even if their relationships were robust enough to cope with Kickertopoller vacillating commitments, the young warrior had lost his appetite for war. He knew he would be lucky to survive another year if he rejoined the fight. And while he seems to have admired Tongerlongeter's resolve, he understood something the chief probably didn't – the white invaders were not returned ancestors; they were real men from a real place, and they would never stop coming.

Removal to New South Wales was never a viable option either. Kickertopoller knew all too well from Musquito that the white men there were just as menacing. At least in Van Diemen's Land he knew his way. What's more, he had skills the white men needed – the ability to speak English and to track and parley with the hostile bands. He wagered that if he stayed he could leverage these skills to ensure his safety, as well as a ready supply of sugar, tobacco and other allurements. So that's what he did, and sure enough, he was immediately earmarked to guide a roving party. His commander would be Gilbert Robertson, the Coal Valley settler who had been friendly to him and the tame mob in the early 1820s. Robertson took several months to organise and outfit his men, but by late October 1828, it was time for Kickertopoller to head to Richmond, where the party was preparing to move out.

Robertson's roving party consisted of himself and six soldiers together with Kickertopoller and his cellmate,

Thomas Arthur, who joined the outfit at Kickertopoller's request. They set out on 5 November, just four days after the government had declared martial law, officially allowing what had always been tacitly accepted – Aborigines could be shot on sight.[7] As it happened, they met the governor just a few days into the expedition. He and his entourage were on their way to Oyster Bay and, that night, as the two parties camped together, Arthur asked to speak with the resistance-fighter-turned-tracker.[8] Kickertopoller agreed to meet the white chief, though the transcript of their conversation shows he was anything but deferential.[9] He opened with a rhetorical question: 'Ant your stock-keeper been a kill plenty black fellow?' When Arthur responded with, 'I want to be friendly and kind to them [your kinfolk], yet they would spear me if they met me', Kickertopoller laughed in his face. He laughed again when Arthur read his proclamation giving Aborigines the right to enter the settled areas if they had a government-authorised pass.[10] He derided the scheme as 'foolish', not least because an Aborigine had no way of learning about it. Sensitive to that problem, Arthur asked: 'Can't you tell him, Tom?' Kickertopoller explained that if he did the white man's bidding, his kinfolk would 'very soon *spear me*'. He continued in an insolent and sarcastic tone until an exasperated Arthur declared, 'Well, Tom, I will put them in prison, and keep them there'. Now angry, Kickertopoller retorted: 'Put him in a gaol, Mata Guberna! You take his country, take his black woman, kill her right out, all his little child – then you put him in your gaol ... You better [to] kill him right out'. But for all his bitter rejoinders, Arthur held the cards, and Kickertopoller knew it.

Over the next twelve months, Kickertopoller accompanied Gilbert Robertson on several expeditions. Robertson was a unique figure in Tasmania in that he was both 'respectable' and black. The son of a West Indian slave and her white master, Gilbert Robertson senior, who belonged to one of the most powerful Scottish clans, not only took the controversial step of acknowledging his son as his own, but also sent him to be educated in Scotland. Yet despite his auspicious beginnings, Robertson went broke in 1822. Seeking a fresh start, he emigrated with his wife and child to Van Diemen's Land.[11] His improbable story helps explain his outspoken sympathies for the island's Aborigines. He took an immediate liking to Kickertopoller when they met in 1823, and asked for him by name five years later when proposing the idea of a roving party to Arthur. The affection seems to have been mutual. Now, Robertson and Kickertopoller took the lead in the government's newest attempt to suppress the intensifying resistance of Tongerlongeter and his allies. They were two black men elevated in a white man's world because of their promise to pacify other black men.

Regardless of how much he liked Robertson, Kickertopoller was not about to betray Tongerlongeter. As the party's guide, he sometimes pretended to get lost in country with which he was familiar, while at other times he actively led Robertson astray.[12] Jorgen Jorgenson attributed the general ineffectiveness of the roving parties to

Black Tom and the other blacks accompanying the expedition not being willing to bring the parties to where the natives would be very likely to be – I have this from general opinion chiefly, and also that the moment I entered Swanport [Oyster Bay] I found that the natives had been in that district for a length of time and yet none of the parties had ever thought of entering that district.[13]

Kickertopoller only seemed to find his bearings when tracking enemy peoples. His one success as Robertson's guide came just a week into their first expedition, when he led the party to the camp of his old foe, Umarrah, a northern midlands chief, who was captured along with four others.[14] Robertson attributed his success to Kickertopoller, 'of whom I cannot speak with enough praise',[15] but when it came to tracking the two main players in the black resistance – the Oyster Bay and Big River nations – his distinguished guide was far less helpful.

Kickertopoller's attempts to assist his people during this period were not just passive. He had influence now, and he did what he could to use it for his people's benefit. After seeing the appalling diet and cramped conditions of a group of Oyster Bay captives being held in the Richmond Gaol, he demanded that Robertson intervene. 'Last week an Aboriginal Native called Black Tom joined me', Robertson began his letter to the Richmond magistrate:

> he complained that the Aborigines at present confined in
> the Richmond Gaol were not supplied with fresh meat
> and their allowance of food was not Sufficient ... Tom
> also complained that the gaoler had confined the Native

called the Lawyer, handcuffed in a Cell, and requested
me to lay the matter before the Governor, which I did
through Mr Anstey, the Police Magistrate at Oatlands.[16]

Keen to keep Kickertopoller on side, Arthur ordered the
gaoler to meet his requests.[17]

Thanks in large part to Kickertopoller's shrewd tactics,
Robertson's initial success in capturing Umarrah was not
followed up. His roving party and others like it produced
roundly disappointing results. Despite the vast and coordinated
efforts of these paramilitary parties, Tongerlongeter and his
allies were launching more attacks than ever. Frustrated, the
governor recalled Kickertopoller to Hobart in December
1829. He was to be reassigned to guide another expedition,
only this one had a different philosophy, dreamed up by an
altogether different kind of man.

George Augustus Robinson's 'friendly mission' differed
from the roving parties in important ways. Robinson had no
intention of capturing or killing Aborigines.[18] Rather, the purpose of his twenty-nine-person expedition was simply 'to point
out to the tribes the benevolent intentions of the government
towards them and to open a channel of communication with
them'.[19] The primary instruments of Robinson's conciliatory
endeavours were thirteen Aboriginal envoys recruited from
several different nations.[20] Over more than six years, the
mission would undertake almost a dozen expeditions, and
contemporaries would come to see it as a spectacular success,
but in the beginning, they scorned it as a laughable waste of
time and money.[21]

Kickertopoller may have had doubts too. After all, the first expedition was to proceed south of Hobart and then west – that is, in the opposite direction from the conflict it was supposed to suppress. Robinson had convinced Arthur, if not himself, that the war was being waged primarily by western tribes penetrating into the settled districts. It was a bizarre theory, but Kickertopoller seems to have done nothing to disabuse him of it. Maybe he just wanted a break from the conflict and uncertainty that had plagued his young life thus far, though he could also have been motivated by the governor's promise of a boat and – as perverse as it was ironic – a grant of land if he accompanied Robinson.[22] Whatever his reasoning, Kickertopoller willingly set out with Robinson from Recherche Bay on 3 February 1830.

Robinson's self-righteous pomposity repelled nearly everyone he met. Still, he was unquestionably an intrepid and humane man who had genuine sympathy for the Aborigines. Although his attitudes are recognised as paternalistic if not racist today, he was a bleeding heart by the standards of his time. Kickertopoller's initial impression of him is unknown, but Robinson had confidence in their relationship. In January 1830, he wrote: 'I entertain great hopes of the assistance of the aboriginal Tom who ... is a famous interpreter and this is the stronghold on which I build my chief hopes'.[23] While he certainly proved valuable, Kickertopoller soon got under Robinson's skin. Recalcitrant by nature, he often deceived his boss, whether to protect the people they were pursuing or simply to have casual sex with a female envoy away from Robinson's puritanical eye. In his journal, Robinson regularly vented his frustrations.[24] In Kickertopoller's presence, however, he usually held his tongue. By his own admission, he was wholly dependent on him and the other envoys, not just to locate and negotiate with the 'wild natives', but also to find food.[25]

Over the course of eight months, Robinson's party walked around fully half of Tasmania, searching the coastlines and hinterlands of the island's south, west and north-west. It achieved several nervous audiences with local bands, but this of course did nothing to suppress the violence that was raging out of control in the east. When he reached Launceston in September 1830, Robinson found the town abuzz with preparations for the Black Line. Horrified by the operation and the murderous sentiments being thrown about, he again took his mission in the opposite direction, this time deep into the unsettled north-east. With redoubled urgency, Robinson adopted a new strategy. Frontier relations were, he now told himself, beyond repair. For everyone's safety, the remaining bands would need to be removed from the island. But Robinson understood their attachment to country better than anyone; he knew they might well fight to the death before assenting to permanent banishment. He would need to reassure them that removal would only be temporary, just until peace could be restored. And as a deeply pious man, he would also need to convince himself that he could deliver on this promise.

As the Black Line pressed southward, Robinson's refitted expedition moved north. He soon established a base on Swan Island, four kilometres off the north-east tip of Tasmania, and from here his party scoured the hinterland for remnant bands. Results didn't take long. By 15 November, Robinson's envoys had negotiated the removal of thirteen Aborigines. The contrast between the friendly mission's success and the Black Line's failure was stark. The colony had thrown everything it had at the Oyster Bay – Big River people and failed. Dejected and grasping for solutions, Arthur looked to Robinson's friendly mission to deliver the results that 2200 armed men had not. After considerable stalling and several small expeditions, one of which led to the surrender of Umarrah and six others,[26] the mission set out from Campbell Town on 15 October 1831 in quest of the main prize: the Oyster Bay – Big River people.

Tongerlongeter and Montpelliatta had always been the colonists' deadliest adversaries – now they were the last of them. If Robinson could convince these chiefs to lay down their arms, he could put an end to the Black War. His envoys lent legitimacy to the mission, but he would need more than their endorsement to placate this, 'the most savage of all the aboriginal tribes'.[27] The sweetener would be Robinson's assurance that he

> was commissioned by the Governor to inform them that,
> if the natives would desist from their wanton outrages
> upon the whites, they would be allowed to remain in
> their respective districts and would have flour, tea and
> sugar, clothes &c given them; that a good white man
> would dwell with them who would take care of them and
> would not allow any bad white man to shoot them, and

he would go with them about the bush like myself and
they then could hunt.[28]

He had made this promise to his envoys and to 'wild
Aborigines' on several occasions. 'I omit no opportunity of
impressing upon the mind of the ... natives that they are to
remain in their own country'.[29]

Arthur explicitly endorsed every aspect of Robinson's
offer, except perhaps for the critical part about staying on
their country accompanied by a government envoy.[30] The
closest Robinson came to receiving such instructions in
writing was in April 1831, when the colonial secretary wrote:
'whether the natives will or will not go to the establishment
[in Bass Strait] they should be conciliated by every possible
means and promised food, clothing and protection if they will
only be pacific and desist from the outrages which they have
been in the habit of committing'.[31] Desperate for the biggest
bargaining chip he could get, Robinson took what he wanted
from these vague instructions. Still, when he explicitly told
Arthur in August that he was promising the Aborigines they
could, once tensions had subsided, return to their country,
the governor did not correct him.[32]

But for Robinson to promise Tongerlongeter anything,
he first had to find him. For this, he was entirely dependent
on his envoys – two in particular. Of the fourteen who
accompanied him on this, his most famous expedition,
Kickertopoller and a Big River woman named Polare were
the most important. Other than Tanlebonyer, the Oyster
Bay woman rescued with her sister Tekartee (see chapter 5)

from sealers, these were the only Oyster Bay or Big River people in the mission. Perhaps because of her many years in captivity, Tanlebonyer seems not to have been useful to Robinson, who rarely ever mentioned her. He did, however, rely heavily on Kickertopoller and Polare.[33] Polare's understanding of Tongerlongeter and Montpelliatta's strategy was critical. She had been with them when they escaped the Black Line but had been captured at Port Sorell following the killing of Thomas and Parker back in August. Polare and Kickertopoller would eventually lead Robinson to Tongerlongeter and Montpelliatta, though they would do it in their own time and on their own terms.

From October to December 1831, Robinson's guides led him on a zigzagging tour of south-east and central Tasmania. The aspiring conciliator grew increasingly frustrated. While the envoys made the most of the ruse, hunting daily and enjoying a steady stream of flour, tea and sugar, it would be wrong to portray them as gleefully sharing an in-joke. They had much in common, yet they also harboured very real animosities towards each other.[34] Kickertopoller was in the thick of these tensions, as were his traditional rivals, Umarrah and the famed north-east chief Mannalargenna. The latter had given himself up the previous year. Hailing from an unsettled region, he probably played only a minor role in the Black War, though few had suffered more from the ravages of the sealers. His initial attempts to establish cordial relations with these men had blown up in his face. At various times, they had shot him, taken his sister and three of his daughters, and abducted almost all the females from his and other north-east bands.[35]

But these predatory men had taken much more than that – they had robbed Mannalargenna of all hope for his people's future. Now, all this old man had left was his reputation as a wily shaman and a once great warrior. He and Kickertopoller had a turbulent history, and they occasionally clashed, but they were united in their efforts to bamboozle Robinson.

Working himself into a convulsive state, Mannalargenna regularly summoned his 'devil'. This spirit guide, Kickertopoller solemnly assured Robinson, would show them the way.[36] And while Robinson turned his nose up at what he considered to be a 'satanic delusion', he was initially awed by the chief's theatrics.[37] The envoys too seemed to respect his shamanic credentials. But was Mannalargenna, who was now in cahoots with Kickertopoller, sincere in his quest to find the Oyster Bay – Big River people? It is impossible to be sure, but as weeks turned into months, Robinson noticed that the chief's spirit guide seemed more interested in finding good hunting spots than in locating Tongerlongeter and Montpelliatta. 'The chief said his devil told him the natives was at this hill', Robinson wrote on 23 November, but 'now we had arrived here he said they were gone to Swanport [90 kilometres away]. I was not to be deceived by this nonsense, but at the same time I knew they would not be controlled'.[38]

Mannalargenna wasn't the only one who seemed to be playing Robinson, who constantly suspected his envoys of 'lead[ing] me considerably astray'.[39] On 7 December, after nearly two months of fruitless searching, he lost his temper:

After the natives had taken their refreshment I requested
them to proceed, when they appeared perfectly
indifferent and I could no longer suppress my feelings
at the careless and utter indifference manifested by
these people, and rather too freely gave vent to that just
indignation which such ungrateful conduct is sure to call
forth and which it so justly deserved, and reprehended
them in severe terms for their shameful proceedings, to
all of which reproof they appeared utterly indifferent, and
what still added to my mortification was that savage grin
of satisfaction which sat on their countenances [faces].[40]

Infuriated as he was, Robinson recognised that most of
his envoys 'were afraid of leading me to the tribes I was seeking
from an apprehension of their own destruction'.[41] Although
this was true, the one who did the most to undermine his
mission had the least to fear. Kickertopoller, who could expect
to be welcomed by his old comrades,[42] became a source of
intense frustration for Robinson. This 'bad man', he railed,
continued to 'sacrifice my interest to his'.[43] As they approached
Lake Echo on 7 November, for instance, 'Tom behaved in a
very disgraceful manner by setting fire to the grass in two or
three places'. Almost certainly he was signalling a warning
to Tongerlongeter, because two days later the mission came
across a recently vacated Aboriginal campsite.[44]

The envoys held most of the cards, though not all of
them. To overpower his guides' fear of Tongerlongeter and
Montpelliatta, Robinson used a range of threats. He regularly
reminded them of the Black Line and the force of arms the

government was capable of arraying against them. He insisted he was the only thing between them and the soldiers,[45] and they may well have believed him. As it was, though, the white men were not their most immediate threat. Robinson's party consisted of several unarmed white men and eight Aboriginal men. Not only were they outnumbered, these eight warriors were anything but united. Their loyalties were as varied as their languages. If Tongerlongeter and Montpelliatta had a mind to kill this motley crew, they could easily have done so. Not surprisingly, the envoys' enthusiasm for finding them was lukewarm.

Kickertopoller and Polare posed a different challenge. Robinson had to convince them that the government was sincere in its promises, or at least that their kinfolk would be no worse off for accepting its terms. Kickertopoller surely found it hard to believe the government would deliver on its promises. He had seen too much to be sanguine about the white man's sincerity. He also understood that Hobart had little control over what happened on the frontier. But, like Robinson, he may have seen exile as preferable to annihilation.[46] Polare too was evidently conflicted,[47] not least because of a strong attachment to her brother who was still fighting with Montpelliatta. When, in mid-November, she 'saw the tracks of her brother she wept much'. Her tears, Robinson was told, were because she 'loved him'.[48] So much so, it seems, that on 14 December she asked three other female envoys 'to run away [with her] into the bush and go to her brother'.[49] Her plot was foiled, but she obviously knew how to find him.

About this time, a change came over the envoys. At least some of them started acting like they actually wanted to find the Oyster Bay – Big River people. The mood picked up as well. On 21 December, Robinson remarked: 'Tonight some of the natives indulged in a little hilarity in dancing and singing … This was the first time that they had so amused themselves since leaving Campbell Town [ten weeks earlier]'.[50] Any number of things could explain this change, none of which stands out in the evidence. It could have been as simple as the recognition that Robinson was not going to give up and that they couldn't mislead him forever. Whatever it was, things started to happen quickly in late December. While not everyone was on board, the cooperation of Kickertopoller, Polare and several others allowed Robinson to close in on his quarry.

On 30 December, near Little Pine Lagoon on the Central Plateau, the party observed 'native smoke in a westerly direction. It did not appear far off'.[51] Robinson sent six envoys to reconnoitre. Kickertopoller and Polare were to initiate the parley. Two months earlier, Kickertopoller had told Robinson that the pair 'would go first to them, lest they might suppose it was a strange tribe, the Port Dalrymple tribe, come to fight with them'.[52] Later that day, the envoys returned with the news that it was indeed the Oyster Bay – Big River people. They had seen their 'tracks and tracks of their dogs which were numerous. The woman [Polare] saw her brother's tracks and MONTPELIERATTA's'.[53] Excitement and dread filled the air in equal measure. At first light the following morning, the parley group went forward again. The rest of the mission waited and listened, their nerves fraying with each passing minute. Everyone knew that if they had miscalculated, they could be massacred.

Sure enough, with his young wife and infant child in camp, Tongerlongeter was quick to go for his spear. In an instant, he and his comrades were poised for combat. It was an instinctive response, conditioned by years of warfare, but even in that moment he would have sensed something was different. Familiar voices could be made out. His old comrade Kickertopoller came into view. A surprise no doubt, but not completely unexpected. Accompanying Tongerlongeter was the northern midlands warrior Parwarehetar, who had deserted the friendly mission nineteen months earlier. He would surely have informed Tongerlongeter and Montpelliatta that the mission existed, and that Kickertopoller was one of its principal guides. When they were eventually introduced, it was clear to Robinson 'that they had heard of him'.[54] Still, since first learning about Robinson, Tongerlongeter had experienced the Black Line, the Freycinet Line, and the ambush in which he lost his arm. While he may have hoped to encounter this 'good white man',[55] experience had taught him to be wary. Tongerlongeter and Monpelliatta listened as Kickertopoller and Polare explained the situation, but they weren't taking any chances.

Back at Robinson's camp, Mannalargenna was growing increasingly agitated. Ominously, they had camped on the site of a bloody battle that had taken place between his band and Montpelliatta's.[56] Mannalargenna had 'killed many black people and … among the rest he had killed a female belonging to the Big River tribe'.[57] Further inflaming matters, Montpelliatta had speared Mannalargenna's son.[58] This gave the old shaman every reason to believe he was about to be killed. As Robinson told it:

> I heard their war whoop by which I knew they were
> advancing towards me. I also heard them rattle
> their spears as they drew nearer. At this moment
> MANNALARGENNA the principal chief leaped on
> his feet in great alarm saying that the natives were
> coming to spear us. He urged me to run away.
> Finding I would not do so he immediately took up
> his spears and kangaroo rug and went away. Some of
> the other natives were about to follow his example
> but I prevailed upon them to stop … The chief
> MANNALARGENNA would not return until some time
> after all this had taken place.[59]

What happened at this meeting is not entirely clear. In his account, Robinson was at pains to inflate his own bravery and importance, but neither he nor the author of the other surviving account, his assistant Alexander McGeary, were present at the initial meeting. The purpose of McGeary's account was primarily to smear Robinson, whom he loathed, and to seek a reward for his own efforts.[60] Still, when all this is taken into consideration, a picture presents itself. Robinson claimed that:

on observing my people the whole of them jumped up
and seized hold of their spears of which they had a vast
number and then boldly advanced upon my people in
a menacing attitude poising their spears in the air and
quivering them and advancing to the attack. My people
then called to them not to spear them and took hold of
their arms.[61]

A less dramatic account is given by McGeary, who insisted
'there was little or no danger, for they found that we had
with us their own sons and brothers and sisters [Polare,
Kickertopoller and Tanlebonyer] travelling comfortably with
us, and they talked to them and were glad to join us, and
kissed and hugged one another'.[62]

Tongerlongeter would have been flooded with conflicting
emotions. Old friends, enemy chiefs, west coast people, white
men, and all of them together so far from the settlements must
have seemed strange in the extreme. In the air was something
he had scarcely considered possible – the prospect of peace.
However unappealing it may have been to strike an accord
with the beings who had so callously wrecked his world, the
weary chief understood the futility of continued resistance.
Like any defeated commander, he knew that to keep fighting
was to needlessly sacrifice the lives of those he commanded.
The only difference was that, if he and Montpelliatta chose
to fight on, they were risking the wholesale erasure of their
people, culture and history. The precariousness of their situation could not have escaped them. This was an existential

crisis in the truest sense. But while Tongerlongeter's heart must have been leaden, he presented a stoic front. He would listen to what this white man had to say.

Kickertopoller almost certainly made the introductions and translated Robinson's offer. Years later, when writing to Arthur's successor about 'the compact made to the aborigines', Robinson claimed they had been

> guaranteed by me on behalf of the government that they
> should be protected and cared for generally, and that
> as far as practicable they were in the summer months
> under proper protection to occasionally visit their native
> districts and further that myself and family should reside
> with them until those stipulations were completed.[63]

This is a far cry from the promise he had repeated so often in 1831, namely that they could stay on their land if they lived in peace and travelled with a government envoy. The latter was almost certainly the deal Kickertopoller translated to Tongerlongeter and Montpelliatta on New Year's Eve 1831. Removal to Bass Strait probably wasn't mentioned until the party arrived in Hobart a week later. Either way, it had to have been pitched as a temporary 'cooling off' period, as no one so attached to their country would have accepted terms of permanent exile. The roving party leader Jorgen Jorgenson was undoubtedly right when he asserted that Robinson 'invariably' told [the Aborigines] they would be placed on some spacious hunting ground, and that they would remain within their own boundaries unmolested. Had he even hinted at any intention of sending them to some other island his mission would have totally failed'.[64]

The plan to remove remnant Tasmanians to Bass Strait was hatched six months after Parwarehetar had absconded from Robinson, so however it was pitched, Tongerlongeter couldn't have known he would be faced with such a choice. Still, there probably wasn't much to deliberate on. 'They were', as 19th-century historian John West put it, 'the worn out relics of their nation'.[65] Simply feeding themselves without getting shot had become an ordeal.[66] Their bodies bore the scars from years of fighting, there being 'scarcely one among them – man, woman, or child, but had been wounded by the whites'.[67] The deepest scars, though, were psychological. Almost everything that had once brought meaning and joy to their lives had vanished – the blue-water diving and bountiful hunts, the raucous corroborees and solemn rites, the laughter of children and the old people's stories. Such memories brought the emptiness and hopelessness of their situation into sharp relief. How would this bleak story end? Tongerlongeter must have grappled fiercely with that question. Maybe there was no hope, but if there was, Robinson appeared to be it.

Could he be trusted though? There were certainly reasons for Tongerlongeter and Montpelliatta to be incredulous. They had little to no experience of good white men. It was hard to believe Robinson was an exception, and even harder to believe that he spoke for the governor. If the white chief wanted peace, then the recent military campaigns were an odd way to communicate that. And yet, here was Robinson, putting his life in their hands and offering them a way to end the nightmare. What's more, he had with him shrewd men and women, who would surely not have aided someone they distrusted. Perhaps sensing his wariness, Robinson gifted Tongerlongeter his boat cloak as 'a pledge of inviolable friendship'.[68] A boat cloak was the hardiest of outdoor clothing at the time. A full-length hooded poncho, it was made from wool and lined with either linen or a finer-weave wool.[69] Its value was such that, when it was stolen from Robinson at Campbell Town in October, an investigation was undertaken and a 'warrant was issued against a man suspected'.[70] Twelve days later, he received word that his cloak and its thief had been apprehended.[71] Robinson's decision to give Tongerlongeter this valuable garment suggests that it was the Oyster Bay chief who led the negotiations.[72] It was a significant gesture on Robinson's part, and one by which Tongerlongeter was clearly moved.[73] An agreement was reached.

As soon as he could, Robinson scribbled a message to Arthur informing him that he had negotiated an armistice to end the war, and that he was en route to Hobart with an additional '16 men, 9 women and one child including the celebrated chief MONTPEILLIATTER of the Big River tribe and TONGER.LONGTER of the Oyster Bay tribe'. He added that 'No restraint in any way has been placed upon them'.[74] 'The chiefs', he reported:

> assigned as a reason for their outrages upon the white
> inhabitants that they and their forefathers had been
> cruelly abused, that their country had been taken from

them, their wives and daughters had been violated and taken away, and that they had experienced a multitude of wrongs from a variety of sources. They were willing however to accept the offers of the government.[75]

He forewarned Arthur that he had

promised them a conference with the Lieut Govr and that the Governor will be sure to redress all their grievances. I earnestly hope that every possible kindness and attention may be shewn to these people for they cannot and ought not to be looked upon as captives. They have placed themselves under my protection and are desirous for peace.[76]

CHAPTER 13

Exile

Nicholas Clements

After eight gruelling years, the fighting was over.[1] The armistice Robinson forged with Tongerlongeter and Montpelliatta was, 19th-century historian James Bonwick declared, 'by far the grandest feature of the war'.[2] The chiefs had, in Arthur's words, led 'the two worst Tribes which had infected the Settled Districts', having 'always shown themselves to be the most blood-thirsty'.[3] Still, the governor had developed a grudging respect for this 'crafty foe', conceding that 'their cunning and intelligence are remarkable'.[4] And now, on this the first Saturday of the new year, he would finally get to meet them face to face. As his staff busied themselves with preparations, Arthur heard the sound of the cheering crowd grow louder and louder as the procession made its way down Elizabeth Street towards Government House. When they came into view, Tongerlongeter, with his imposing stature and his missing arm, was unmistakable. He wore his new cloak – a symbol of the pact he had made with Robinson. Behind him was the unbeaten remnant of one of history's most enduring peoples. Their maimed bodies and lined faces told a fearful story, and yet they stood tall, spears in hand. Arthur lavished them with hospitality, even wheeling out the military band, but it was all too much. They were there to be heard, not serenaded. The band was silenced, and the delegations moved inside.[5]

We will never know what was said in that meeting. Would the chiefs have agreed to simply abandon their beloved country for permanent exile on an alien and inhospitable island? Such a concession, especially after Robinson's lofty promises, seems inconceivable. All we know is that ten days later the whole party set sail for Flinders Island. Onlookers surely recognised the significance of the moment. Here were the island's vanquished original owners, exiled from the country of their birth. The feelings of the townspeople were conflicted.[6] On the one hand, many were inspired by the 'lost cause' narrative of determined warriors defending their country against impossible odds, and very nearly to the last man; on the other hand, the removal of this stubborn enemy relieved them of an enormous burden. The fear that had filled the air for so long was finally gone, and the colony's stultified economy was now free to grow.[7] In the interior, shaken colonists tried to put 'those days of terror' behind them.[8] The firing holes that had been hacked into the walls of every exposed hut could now be boarded up, and the guns issued to convicts repossessed. 'A complete change took place in the island', one settler recalled; 'the remote stock stations were again resorted to, and guns were no longer carried between the handles of the plough'.[9]

The land itself bore the marks of war. The Black Line had

cut a swathe through more than a million hectares of bush-
land, the evidence of which remained for years after.[10] Dozens
of newly and half-constructed 'trap huts' – Arthur's latest
plan for surprising Aboriginal war parties by hiding armed
men in secluded huts – were abandoned to the wildlife.[11]
And some 259 graves, all that remained of the men, women
and children killed by Aborigines, littered the landscape as a
memorial to the cost of free land.[12] But the greatest change to
the Tasmanian landscape wasn't the presence of any of these
things; it was the absence of the people who had created that
landscape. Tasmania's mosaics of distinctive vegetation were
in no way 'natural'. They were the sophisticated handiwork of
Aborigines, who used fire to sculpt a land rich in resources.
Now that they were gone, their usurpers soon noticed the
proliferation of forest undergrowth, and consequently of
uncontrollable bushfires – a scourge that haunts the island
to this day.[13]

The question of who would care for the land was one of
many that must have plagued Tongerlongeter's mind as the
strange floating islands began to drift out into the channel.
It being so far from their country, most Oyster Bay – Big
River people had probably never sighted Flinders Island.
Was it the isle of the dead from whence the white devils
came? It was obvious to Tongerlongeter and his people that
the forces of evil were at play. As the sails were unfurled,
'they were much terrified at the ship's movement, and rattled
their sacred bones to prevent the devil from running away
with it'.[14] According to Jorgenson: 'They thought they were
proceeding to England, where, they said, they would be

starved to death, for if white people had anything to eat at home they would never come so far as Van Diemen's Land'.[15] If Tongerlongeter held out any hope for the journey, it surely came from Tanlebonyer, whom he had not seen since she was abducted years earlier. By now she had surely told the chief of the cruel system of slavery carried on in Bass Strait by the sealers, and how Robinson had liberated her. If all those enslaved women were about to be freed, then maybe there was hope for his people after all.

James Bonwick discovered that 'On their way to the Straits they suffered much from seasickness. The captain of the vessel assured me that it was pitiable to witness their distress. Their moaning was sad indeed. They appeared to feel themselves forsaken and helpless, and abandoned themselves to despair'.[16] The most heart-rending stretch of the voyage was sailing past their homeland. The captain of Tongerlongeter's vessel remarked that, 'during the whole passage they sat on the vessel's bulwark, shaking little bags of human bones, apparently as a charm against the danger to which they felt exposed'.[17] And their sense of foreboding was well founded. They were headed for a desolate land that had been uninhabited for millennia. Despite its rugged beauty, Flinders Island was prone to tempestuous weather and lacked reliable fresh water. It may not have been the isle of the dead, as many of the new arrivals imagined, but death would soon be its defining feature.

Severe seasickness had dehydrated Droomteemetyer, which made breastfeeding difficult. Her infant son grew weaker as the voyage progressed. Parperermanener's condition worsened as his homeland receded into the distance, a fact that must have appeared ominous to his parents. Soon after the nauseous travellers disembarked at Flinders Island, a great wailing went up. Parperermanener's tiny body had gone limp. Droomteemetyer and Tongerlongeter mourned as only parents do, with pain deep and suffocating. No community takes the death of a child lightly, but for the Oyster Bay – Big River people, this was no ordinary tragedy. It wasn't just that a child had died, or even that it was the child of a chief – it was that there were no more children.[18] Whether it was said or not, they all knew what Parperermanener's death meant for their future.

In keeping with traditional mourning practices, Droom-teemetyer 'took some of the child's bones and burnt them, after which she pounded them and rubbed the powder over her face and body'.[19] But there was more to this ritual. Robinson learnt that she 'cut off [Parperermanener's] head and the skull she had then suspended to her neck'. In Tasmanian cultures, the bones of the deceased were thought to harbour powerful spirits with the capacity for communing and healing.[20] Skulls were considered especially potent.[21] Repelled by the whole spectacle, the officers administering the settlement insisted the child be buried whole. They ordered a grave to be dug, but Droomteemetyer was having none of it. The officers, Robinson later discovered, were 'consulting where the head should be laid, when the mother advanced with the body wrapped in a blanket and deposited the remains in the grave. The whites did not know at this time that it was a headless trunk'.[22] In time, Parperermanener's skull would become a notable feature of the settlement, 'frequently to be seen suspended upon the breast of its father or mother'.[23]

As the fog of grief lifted, Tongerlongeter was able to take stock of his new surroundings. There was little to buoy his spirits. The settlement was on the south-west coast of Flinders Island, at an uninspiring location known as 'the Lagoons'. An inexplicable choice, the site was buffeted by Bass Strait's notorious westerlies, and the flat heathland offered little shelter. When the wind relented, mosquitoes breeding in the adjacent lagoon arose in force to torment the inhabitants. The water, bucketed from holes dug above the high-tide line, was sickly brackish. Provisions, if they arrived at all, were often rotten or infested with vermin, and crops refused to grow in the thin soil. To make matters worse, the settlement was overseen by Sergeant Alexander Wight, a cruel and inept man who focused solely on minimising his own discomforts.[24]

Robinson briefly visited the Lagoons in February 1832 to investigate reports of Wight's abuses, but he could not stay. Arthur had ordered him and his envoys to immediately turn their 'attention and talents' to the western tribes. Spurred on by the promise of handsome rewards, Robinson now impatiently set about removing every last Aborigine from mainland Tasmania. Over the next three years, he and his notably less friendly mission sent a steady stream of western survivors to the settlement. In total, 244 Aborigines were exiled to Flinders Island between 1830 and 1842, 114 from the west and 130 from the east.[25] Many of the easterners were slave women liberated from the sealers or remnant peoples from the north and north-east. Scarcely more than forty were Oyster Bay – Big River people.

Mercifully, Wight was replaced as commandant by Second Lieutenant William Darling about a month after Tongerlongeter's arrival.[26] From the outset, Darling proved to be proactive and relatively humane. Many of the exiles seemed to appreciate the young officer's sincere efforts, which included continuing to emancipate women from the sealers.[27] Darling's attempts to improve conditions at the settlement were, however, hindered by innumerable natural and bureaucratic obstacles. In October 1832, the visiting missionaries Backhouse and Walker noted that for shelter, the Aborigines had just three dirt-floored, A-frame huts made from boughs and thatched with grass. Since there were then eighty-two of them at the Lagoons and the floorspace of these huts was just three by six metres, twenty-seven people were forced to share a space no bigger than a modest master bedroom.[28] Despite Darling's best efforts, the exiles were miserable. For the men, hunting was the only reprieve, and to his credit, Darling respected their autonomy, ordering that 'no restraint of any type to be put upon them; [so that] they [might] go hunting when ever they like and for as long as they like.'[29]

Soon after his arrival, Darling began scouting for a better site for the settlement. In November 1832, he decided to relocate the exiles to Pea Jacket Point, twenty kilometres to the north.[30] The new site, which Darling named Wybalenna (an Aboriginal word for 'black man's huts'), was far from ideal. There were no safe anchorages nearby, and the sparse foliage did little to temper the ferocious westerlies. Still, the water and soil quality were better, and with a sizeable contingent of soldiers and convicts at his disposal, Darling quickly set about installing basic amenities. The first order of business was accommodating the Aborigines, and within a year, nine 8.5 by 4.5 metre huts had been erected.[31] When they felt like it, the Aborigines occasionally helped with such work, but only if they received extra rations and the doctor or commandant worked alongside them. The eastern tribes in particular repeatedly stressed their status as 'free men'.[32] Work was for the convicts at the settlement. This was the agreement they believed they had with the colonial government, that 'white men work and not they'.[33]

What became of Montpelliatta in exile is not known. Until at least the final year of the war, he seems to have been regarded as Tongerlongeter's equal. But their significance diverged sharply after this. Tongerlongeter quickly became the most prominent Aborigine on Flinders Island, and is regularly referred to in the records, whereas Montpelliatta seems to have faded into obscurity. He appears occasionally in lists, but this is the only evidence he was even at the settlement; neither Robinson nor any visitors or staff commented on him. Not even his death, which occurred sometime in 1836, was recorded. What explains this? While he had fought hard for his people throughout the war, it would be perfectly understandable if the devastation of that conflict and the desolation of exile had caused him to lose heart. Like many of the exiled men, Montpelliatta probably felt emasculated and depressed by a loss of purpose. As a provider, warrior and military leader he had distinguished himself, but he needed different skills and a different mentality to make the most of his new circumstances. Maybe he didn't have these, or maybe he just couldn't stomach learning the white man's language or sharing pleasantries with him. Either way, the leadership of his people now fell exclusively to Tongerlongeter.

Just two months into his tenure as commandant, Darling revealed that Tongerlongeter had walk-in access to his quarters. While writing to Arthur, he broke off mid-report to note that the chief had arrived and 'desired me to tell you to send down plenty of tobacco and clay pipes for the weiba's and lubra's (men and women)'.[34] While in charge of the settlement from 1832 to 1834, Darling 'seldom sat down to breakfast or tea … without having some aborigines as guests'.[35] Tongerlongeter developed a particularly good rapport with the lieutenant, who referred to him as 'the Governor' and considered him 'a very intelligent and good tempered man'.[36] The chief's attitude towards Darling and those who came after him was probably genuine, but it was also strategic. A man of impressive presence and charisma, he garnered influence with anyone who could help his people. While there were relatively few Oyster Bay – Big River exiles at the settlement, Tongerlongeter was quickly able to establish their dominance.[37] By securing the support of settlement officials, he cemented his people's position and deterred challengers. There were perks as well. For example, the Oyster Bay and Big River exiles received the first and best accommodations at Wybalenna, which were also those closest to the commandant's office.[38] From the outset,

Tongerlongeter himself was accorded special privileges,[39] and by February 1834, James Backhouse could state that he was 'now the principal chief at Flinders'.[40]

While Tongerlongeter's ascendancy and the favouritism extended to his people cannot have been popular with everyone, most came to accept the new order. Incredibly, given the generational hatreds that existed between them, the various nations never resorted to violence in exile. In time, the remnants coalesced into two main factions. The larger of these rallied around Tongerlongeter, the other around Rolepa, the 'Ben Lomond Chief', whose 'tribe' consisted mostly of north-east peoples. 'The Western natives', it was noted, 'attached themselves to either one … as their inclination led them'.[41] While the men respected each other as warriors, and their shared adversity often led to collaboration, old grudges were not easily effaced.[42] Wary of a confrontation when armed, the two factions wisely refused to hunt together 'unless the Commandant or doctor be with them'.[43] Darling's arbitration was clearly part of the reason hostilities were kept in check, because they soon resurfaced when he was recalled in July 1834.

Henry Nicholls replaced Darling in September of that year. Although his intentions were admirable, they came to little. As a civilian, he lacked control over the soldiers posted at the settlement. What's more, Arthur distrusted the new commandant and obstructed his efforts at every turn. But most insidious of all was the appointment of catechist Robert Clark in August 1834. Clark, who was charged with instructing the Aborigines in religion, was a conniving man who seeded discontent on all sides.[44] And Nicholls didn't just fail to improve things. In his year as commandant, he came close to losing control of the situation entirely. In July 1835, he reported that 'It requires very great vigilance to prevent their breaking into open hostilities. A very little would set them aflame they are so very jealous of each other'.[45]

These tensions may have erupted were it not for the timely return of George Augustus Robinson, the man in whom they had all placed their trust. Robinson's arrival in October 1835, after he had removed most of the remaining western and north-western bands from their country, was cause for celebration. The exiles held a 'grand dance' to mark the occasion, and intertribal relations soon began to improve.[46] It's not always easy to see through the self-aggrandisement in Robinson's reports, but we have no reason to doubt his claim that, by July 1836, 'there is now no bad feeling, no spear and waddy making for hostile purposes, no slandering'.[47] Two months later he proclaimed that relations were 'very considerably improved – There is the greatest cordiality and harmony existing among them'.[48] And while this latter claim was overstated, the improvement was real.[49]

There are a few key reasons why Robinson was able to restore a measure of harmony to the settlement. For all his flaws, and there were many, he genuinely cared about the Aborigines.[50] By the time he arrived to take up his post at Wybalenna, Robinson had lived alongside Aborigines for more than six years. He knew them better than any other white man. There were surely things about him they despised, but they also understood that he was their only hope of getting back to their country – or at least of getting off the cursed island to which they had been condemned. His arrival had an immediate calming effect on the settlement. He was also a relatively competent administrator, who was brimming with ideas for improving the settlement and the Aborigines' wellbeing. As paternalistic and eccentric as most of these ideas were, they at least injected some energy into the settlement.

Governor Arthur did not want the extinction of the Tasmanians on his conscience or his record. He insisted they be well taken care of. They received a generous food ration in comparison to the convicts. Adults were allowed 450 grams salted beef, 450 grams flour, 230 grams biscuit, 7 grams tea, 45 grams sugar, and 14 grams soap per day, but due to the incompetence of low-rung officials, shipments of food were irregular and often spoiled during the settlement's early years. Even when they weren't, for people accustomed to a healthy diet of red meat, seafood and plants, much of the food was hard to stomach. They found salted meat especially inedible, preferring to feed it to their dogs.[51] In quest of a more palatable diet, the women dived for shellfish and the men embarked on 'frequent hunting excursions'.[52] On occasion, though, the imperative to find food went beyond mere preference. When Arthur commissioned Major Thomas Ryan to review Wybalenna in April 1836, he 'drew attention to the neglect in keeping the settlement supplied with provisions, which in the past had led on three occasions to "semi-starvation", the natives being obliged to take to the bush to forage for themselves'.[53] This took a severe toll on game numbers, and before long hunting parties were regularly returning empty-handed.[54]

The scarcity of game didn't faze Robinson. To him, traditional practices like hunting only hindered his plan to turn the Aborigines into Christian ladies and gentlemen. One of his first orders of business was to rename them after renowned mythical or historical figures, such as Cleopatra, Napoleon and Achilles. The sealers and convicts, finding the tribal names difficult to pronounce or remember, had given some exiles crude nicknames, such as Peacock, Jumbo, Boatswain, Poll and Goose. Robinson detested these and hoped the lofty new names would renew their pride in themselves. Tongerlongeter, receiving a name more befitting his status at the settlement, was to be called King William, after Britain's reigning monarch. Accordingly, Droomteemetyer became Queen Adelaide. While modern observers naturally recoil at the cultural insensitivity of such renaming, the exiles appear to have embraced it.[55] Their traditional naming conventions are poorly understood, but we know that most already had two or more names.[56] Robinson's were just one more.

Other changes were more consequential. Robinson put great emphasis on education. His primary focus was on the children, none of whom belonged to Tongerlongeter's people. They attended school during the day and at night they slept under Robert Clark's roof. The rationale for housing children with the physically and verbally abusive catechist was to segregate them from their 'uncivilised' parents. Remarkably, there is no record of parents protesting against this practice.

Perhaps it was because segregation was preferable to the policy of Robinson's predecessors, who had sent at least fourteen children to the King's Orphan School near Hobart. Six died before Robinson returned the survivors to Flinders Island when he arrived in October 1835.[57] Parents were assured it was in their children's best interests to board with their white tutors, whether in Hobart or on the island, and at least in the beginning they seem to have reluctantly accepted this. Whatever their rationalisation, we know that these separations were the source of immense sadness.[58]

The purpose of educating the Aborigines was to Christianise and civilise them. School was compulsory for children, while adults were pressured to attend in the evenings and on Sundays. Most were unenthusiastic. On the eve of Robinson's arrival, Nicholls reported that the Aborigines had 'a perfect horror of everything connected with religious instruction.'[59] Some, like Tongerlongeter, simply opted out.[60] When probed about whether he had accepted Christianity, the chief was shrewdly non-committal.[61] Once, he supposedly told Robinson that 'God made everything'. But this may have been wishful thinking, because on this occasion 'King William spoke in his own language', which Robinson understood very little of.[62] What's more, Tongerlongeter had by now learnt passable English,[63] so his choice to respond in his native tongue may even have been subversive. While he and the other exiles learnt to humour the evangelising white men, few, if any, relinquished their traditional beliefs.[64]

Over time, though, the exiles did make 'advances in civilisation.'[65] Most learnt to speak and write some English.

A majority wore clothes and lived in permanent huts. On Sundays they typically put in an appearance at 'divine service', and when dining at the commandant's table they observed a measure of 'polite etiquette', but it was in promoting commerce that Robinson saw the greatest success. The Aborigines earned money in several ways. In an effort to induce greater 'industriousness', he paid them for doing everything from carrying wood and building roads to cooking and singing.[66] At a weekly market started in 1836, they sold manufactured goods such as clothes and necklaces. Tongerlongeter readily involved himself. When Robinson brought visitors to one of these early markets, 'Mr Wright bought two fowls from the King of Oyster Bay for 4/4 and Mr Davis bought necklaces to the amount of 2/6'.[67] The exiles found customers beyond Flinders Island too. Robinson established an 'Aboriginal Fund' for the proceeds of goods sold by agents in Launceston. These goods included mutton birds, shell necklaces, woven baskets, kangaroo and wallaby skins, and a range of manufactured items.[68] While the fund was 'appropriated for general purposes',[69] profits made locally were theirs to spend, very often on ochre or tobacco.[70]

Commerce may have been embraced by the exiles, but other impositions were less popular. For instance, in an effort to promote a more sedentary lifestyle, Robinson prohibited unauthorised excursions beyond the settlement.[71] This injunction seems to have been roundly ignored. If anything, it encouraged even more lengthy pilgrimages to distant parts of the island. The same was true of their practice of shedding their clothes, painting themselves with ochre, and engaging in 'wild corrobborees'. Richard Davies, who captained the settlement's supply vessel from 1832 to 1837, observed: 'Their principal amusement consists in their corrobories or dances … I have seen as many as ninety joined in one corroborie'.[72] Davies admired these events, but Robinson saw them as an obstacle to his civilising poject, and strongly discouraged them. Undeterred, the Aborigines simply conducted them at a remove.[73] To his constant frustration, the exiles refused to abandon their culture.[74] Open defiance was rare though. Aware of their relative powerlessness, and of the advantages of staying in the commandant's good graces, they went along with many of his civilising schemes, sometimes in earnest, oftentimes not.

To fill their days, the men played marbles and went hunting, even when there was little game to be found. The women swam, made clothing and crafts, and went on long walks, often for days at a time.[75] 'In the evening,' Walker revealed, 'they sit round the fire and talk, or one sings, while the rest listen with deep interest and attention, frequently applauding by a general shout'.[76] We have no idea what they discussed in these intense fireside meetings. The stories and legends that had entertained them in better times were surely retold. So too, presumably, were humorous anecdotes from the day. But undoubtedly they also discussed the calamity that had befallen them. Suggestions would have been raised and explanations offered. Elders deliberated and clever men prophesied. Despair and disorder were never far below the surface, which is why steady leadership was so important.

The role of elders has always been central to the maintenance of culture and law in Aboriginal societies. Nowhere were these stabilising figures more necessary than on Flinders Island, where the temptation to lose hope was powerful. Walker observed that: 'The chiefs are called fathers. The rest of the tribe term themselves brothers and sisters.'[77] Tongerlongeter unquestionably played the role of father to the Oyster Bay – Big River survivors. But his influence went beyond his own people. Whether everyone was happy about it or not, the Aborigines at the settlement appear to have accepted his status as the overall leader. There is certainly no evidence of his authority being questioned during Robinson's well-documented tenure. One reason for this was surely that, even though he led the largest and most influential faction, he did not press this advantage against his rivals. Once Robinson became commandant, Tongerlongeter's position was secure, and he no longer needed to jostle for control. Instead, a period of order and relative self-determination ensued.[78]

Without question, Robinson and his predecessors con-tributed to Tongerlongeter's power, but this was no accident. The patronage he received was the result of deft diplomacy. Tongerlongeter was proactive, making the effort to under-stand the white man. He was also held in high regard by the other exiles. Everyone, including his enemies, seemed to respect him as a warrior and leader. Tongerlongeter manoeuvred himself to the top and then managed to stay there, not because he was sly, but because he was a skilled communicator and ambassador. What's more, his friendships with the successive commandants appear to have been genuine.[79] While these men were unable to shake off their sense of cultural superiority, Tongerlongeter could see they respected him. He is discussed dozens of times in the settlement records but never once in a negative tone. This is all the more remarkable given Robinson's pathological habit of complaining about everyone. Moreover, Tongerlongeter could see that exile would be more bearable and repatriation more likely if they worked *with* the white men rather than against them.

In Robinson's effort to get the most powerful of the exiled men on side, he bestowed upon them titles and authority. He named six 'kings'. King Alfred (Purngerpar), King Alexander, King Alphonso and King Tippoo were minor chiefs. The most senior positions went to the leaders of the two main factions, King William (Tongerlongeter) and King George (Rolepa).[80] This hierarchy was on display at a grand dinner hosted by Robinson in August 1836. Everyone sat at one long table with Tongerlongeter and his wife 'at the head and foot'.[81] From the outset, Robinson recognised that Tongerlongeter was the most powerful Aborigine on the island. As soon as he disembarked, he sought the chief out and in him alone confided his intentions.[82] Robinson knew Tongerlongeter's support would be essential in the battle of hearts and minds he hoped to win. He immediately ordered a new house to be built for the chief and his wife.[83]

This wasn't the only way Robinson attempted to ingratiate himself. In July 1836, 'The King of Oyster Bay was presented with his new garment neatly embroidered, made into a frock coat with Prussian collar, the colour grey. The king was highly pleased'.[84] The following week, Robinson also 'Gave the king of Oyster Bay a fine turban made under directions of Mrs Clark', and 'a gilt chain and cross'.[85] In fawning over Tongerlongeter, Robinson was in lock step with colonial administrators the world over. Still, a healthy relationship between the commandant and the chief was in everyone's interest. Robinson 'frequently conferred with the king', who in turn supported him in maintaining order at the settlement.[86] The arrangement generally worked well for the exiles too, who used Tongerlongeter's influence to further their own agendas.[87]

The establishment of the 'Aboriginal police' in August 1836 was one of Robinson's more important and successful initiatives.[88] He was adamant that the Aborigines should 'preserve order amongst them-selves, and decide all disagreements which might arise amongst them'.[89] Looked at more cynically, it appeared to be a textbook case of divide and conquer. An uprising would be far less likely if he had eyes among the exiles. Be that as it may, Robinson was sincere in his desire 'to give them a voice in the management of their own concerns', and establishing the police did just that.[90] The other key benefit was that it distributed power among the tribes. Robinson tells us that the force initially comprised 'three of the most active and intelligent [men] ... chosen viva voce by their own people assembled for the occasion'.[91] These were Tongerlongeter, Rolepa and, so that all three major language groups were represented, a west coast man named Noemy. The arrangement worked so well that six months later, Robinson asked Tongerlongeter and Rolepa to select two more constables from among the exiles, each choosing one of their own warriors. The new recruits gladly accepted their appointments, and when the assembled men were asked if they approved, 'they all with one voice said they did'.[92]

The constables were charged with two main tasks. The first was to preserve order and harmony, not just among the 113 Aborigines then at the settlement, but also among the convict labourers and trespassing sealers. In February 1837, for instance, Robinson ordered the constables to arrest Samuel Jones, a convict servant who had gone to Badger Corner to engage in illicit dealings with sealers. They assured the commandant that:

> they would soon find him and would bring him to the settlement. King William said they must frighten him, for which purpose they took their spears. King W said they must walk like soldiers and keep the PERINTYER i.e. convict in the midst of them whilst the other party hunted kangaroo, that is, they would walk on each side of him.[93]

The other primary function of the police was to adjudicate disputes and pass judgment on cases of misconduct. Minor cases were decided by the chiefs, but Robinson states that 'in all matters of an urgent and important character ... I judged it prudent to recommend that the two principal chiefs [Tongerlongeter and Rolepa] should sit with me on those occasions and by whose fiat the cases should be determined – This met with universal concurrence'.[94] In one such instance, the court

tried Peter for stealing before King William and the four
constables. Peter's guilt was proven and he was sentenced
to one night in the cell. Two other boys was also tried
but on account of their youth they were ordered to wear
fool's caps and to be marched round the settlement. Their
offences was for stealing from the carpenter's box … The
chief King William evinced great tact and judgement and
carried it off with a majestic air.[95]

There is a sense, however, in which all of this – the police,
the markets, the schooling – was mere distraction. To the
extent that it was, it was surely a necessary one. The reality
of what was happening to these survivors was almost too
painful to face. But face it they had to, for this was the devil's
island and he seemed to be coming for every last one of them.

CHAPTER 14

'Till all the black men are dead'

Nicholas Clements

On 21 March 1837, Tongerlongeter and his main rival on the island, Rolepa, put aside their differences and approached the commandant together. They demanded 'to leave this place of sickness'. They then posed a question that Robinson found deeply unsettling: 'do you mean to stay till all the black men are dead?'[1] Deaths, by this stage, were terrifyingly common. During the five and a half years Tongerlongeter was at the settlement, there were four births but well over a hundred deaths.[2] Most were from 'lung complaints' – almost certainly influenza resulting in fatal pneumonia. The virus was clearly novel to the Tasmanians. Lacking immunity, they were all but helpless to resist the onslaught of disease or, as they saw it, possession by the evil spirit that haunted the island.[3]

The story of how disease affected the Tasmanians following the arrival of Europeans is a murky one. Around the time of first settlement, there was a deadly epidemic in the Huon Valley south of Hobart,[4] but after this, there is no evidence of introduced diseases until 1827, when a detribalised Aboriginal woman died at the Coal River, allegedly of a sinus infection.[5] The next mention of Aborigines getting sick is on Bruny Island in 1829, and not again until 1831, when Robinson's exiles began to die at an alarming rate. striking. Remarkably, in over a thousand documented encounters, no one ever reported coming across a sick Aborigine.[6] While this does not mean disease had no impact on the Tasmanians before or during the Black War, the absence of evidence is striking. What's more, if the Aborigines on Flinders had suffered significant outbreaks before their exile, it is reasonable to assume it would have come up in one of the hundreds of conversations Robinson and others recorded with them, many on the topic of disease. Whatever the case, few of the war's survivors appeared to have much resistance to the strains that wreaked havoc on Flinders Island.

Kickertopoller was, as far as we know, the first of Tongerlongeter's people to get sick. He briefly visited the Lagoons with Robinson soon after the Oyster Bay – Big River remnant had disembarked in January 1832. Little was recorded of his six weeks on the island, so we are left to wonder what transpired between him and Tongerlongeter. The chief had just lost his country and his son, and was now struggling to come to terms with the bleak situation into which he had been lured. He could easily have blamed Kickertopoller, who had presumably vouched for Robinson's promises, but no disagreements were recorded. Perhaps both men appreciated the dearth of options that led them to make their respective choices. Whatever Tongerlongeter thought of the younger Poredareme man, he was soon gone from his life. Just two months after leaving the island on 9 March, and only five weeks into the friendly mission's latest expedition, Kickertopoller and Polare both fell ill. Robinson was in too much of a hurry to wait. He left them both at Emu Bay (today's Burnie), which he admitted was 'a miserable place for invalids'. Within a few days, the two envoys who had been most instrumental in bringing him fame and wealth, were dead.[7]

It was some time before word of Kickertopoller's death reached Tongerlongeter. By then, disease was already making inroads among the exiles. There had been only a handful of deaths at the Lagoons, but in the first year at Wybalenna, thirty-two Aborigines died. It was the first of several major epidemics that battered the settlement between 1833 and 1839.[8] The mortality was not a matter of neglect by the colonial authorities. While the accommodations and resources provided to the exiles were poor compared to the comforts of a modern home, they were quite good by the standards of the day. The settlement had been provided with a full-time surgeon, something to which few settlers had ready access.[9] Nevertheless, the medical wisdom of the time was so backward that being treated by a doctor often increased one's chance of dying. Regular enemas, designed to purge the body of 'contaminants', were as dehydrating as they were degrading, while the practice of bleeding the 'bad blood' from dangerously ill patients often hastened death.[10]

In January 1836, there were 116 Aborigines at the settlement. By that point, around seventy had already perished, and worse was yet to come.[11] Europeans by now understood that such afflictions were physical maladies, though they had almost no grasp of epidemiology. The Tasmanians, who perceived the workings of the spirits in everything, made sense of the tragedy in the only way they could. Each language group had its own name for the evil spirit who was responsible, but Robinson used the Bruny Islander term, Wrageowrapper.[12] While the exiles definitely associated Wrageowrapper with the white man, the evidence provides no clear picture of how they understood the connection. Robinson notes: 'It is universally believed amongst the aborigines that their afflictions are caused by RAEGEOWRAPPER (devil or evil spirit)'.[13] Darling too noted their attachment to 'the idea that when sickness comes upon them, an evil spirit has got possession of them'. Perhaps for this reason, he found they were reluctant to submit to medical treatment.[14] Robinson observed the same: 'They have a great abhorrence of the doctor whom they look on with suspicious horror. They consider he has been instrumental in causing their death'.[15]

Pneumonia is a dreadful way to die, and before the advent of modern medical interventions, victims experienced severe pain and gasping panic as their lungs filled with blood and mucus. Such an end was no less gruelling for the friends and family hovering helplessly by their side. Beyond the loving attention of their kin, the Tasmanians had only their belief in magic to dull the pain and fear. The panacea for all maladies was to cast out the evil spirits that possessed the victim. Alongside the practice of cutting, they did this by holding sacred relics against the afflicted area.

The most notable of these relics was Parperermanener's

skull, which was 'in constant requisition among the aborigines ever since it was first prepared'.[16] When Droomteemetyer fell ill in October 1837, for instance, she wore it 'constantly appended to her back, the seat of [the] pain'.[17] Likewise, in February 1836, a 'man who had sprained his knee at the kangaroo dance had it bandaged with human bones and a skull of a child was fastened on the knee pan. These were intended to charm away the pain. The skull was that of King William's infant'.[18] Even Robinson could see that 'it had a singular effect when appended to the jaw of the living person or to the temple, [as] it was sure to be if pain was experienced in those parts'.[19]

Whatever the power of such relics, they did little to stop the mounting death toll or dampen the searing grief that swept the settlement with crushing regularity. The Tasmanians were not reserved in their mourning. 'When a relative dies', Robinson discovered, 'they give themselves up to grief. They break their spears and necklace, throw away kangaroo skins, cut their baskets, don't red ochre themselves, are quite neglectful and mourn'.[20] He observed of one recently widowed woman, that 'Her grief beggars description'.[21] The settlement's doctor, too, was struck by 'their gentle and kindly feeling towards each other their warm sympathy with the sick and afflicted among them. The poignancy of sorrow expressed by them on the death of their friends (which has been often truly painful to me to witness) cannot be surpassed among any class of people'.[22]

During his lengthy visits to the settlement, James Backhouse took a keen interest in Tasmanian's bereavement rituals. 'One day we noticed a woman arranging several stones that were flat, oval, and about two inches [five centimetres] wide, and marked in various directions with black and red lines. These we learned represented absent friends, and one larger than the rest, a corpulent woman'. Following a cremation: 'The ashes of the dead were collected in a piece of Kangaroo-skin, and every morning, before sunrise, till they were consumed, a portion of them was smeared over the faces of the survivors, and a death song sung, with great emotion, tears clearing away lines among the ashes'.[23] And the process of mourning was not brief. 'For some weeks after the death of any of their relatives they sing a death song, the first thing in the morning … as well as wearing the bones of their friends about them.'[24] Bound up with this ritualised grief was an indefinite prohibition on mentioning the names of the dead.[25]

The experience of exile would have been horrific even if disease hadn't taken hold. Everyone grieved for their country. And whether they had spent the last decade fighting the white men or enslaved by them, the eastern exiles had all experienced extreme psychological trauma. Add to this the spiritual and demographic calamity of epidemic disease, and it is remarkable that any of them managed to resist the slide into despondency. Yet resist it they did. In fact, they handled their situation with incredible fortitude. As a people, they were dying, but as a culture, they were very much alive. Their kindred devotion had not wavered. Laughter still echoed regularly around the settlement;[26] Tongerlongeter was himself famously jocular.[27] What's more, the exiles assumed

Robinson and the government still intended to honour their promise; they believed they would see their country again.

For some, the sight of home was not merely a dream. The captain of the island's supply ship noted that, on days when Tasmania's north-east coast came into view, 'the natives have often pointed it out to me with expressions of the deepest sorrow depicted on their countenances'.[28] Indeed, Robinson, Backhouse and several others all remarked on the heartbreaking scenes that unfolded on clear days.[29] Treasury Office clerk Henry Emmett, who took a strong interest in the exiles, noted that these stories were 'abundantly evidenced by the numerous statements of persons on Flinders Island who on seeing on a clear day the coast of Tasmania and the summit of the snow capped Ben Lomond ... shed tears. "There my home, there my country"'.[30] One north-east woman was asked which she preferred, 'Flinders Island, or Ringarooma, her native place. Her eyes brightened up, her countenance became animated, "Sir, Ringarooma, Ringarooma," she exclaimed, "Oh, Ringarooma, to be sure"'.[31] It was perhaps merciful that Tongerlongeter's country was out of sight.

In the beginning at least, the promise of returning home was foremost in the minds of the exiles. It kept them going despite unthinkable suffering. But as time dragged on, they grew impatient. In July 1835, for instance, Nicholls observed a peculiar change among the Aboriginal men,

> who have since my last communication evinced an ardent
> desire to become scholars like white men, and for that
> purpose have voluntarily come forward and attended

the catechist [school] … their object is to write to their
'Governor Father in Hobart Town' that is the Lieutenant
Governor whom they are anxious to induce to remove
them to their native land. They would be perfectly
wretched were they certain they should die here. They all
ardently wish to be removed.[32]

They even started noting their particular country of origin
when signing their letters.[33] Clearly, the exiles were not ready
to forget Robinson's promises.

Many of the Aborigines at Wybalenna seem to have
assumed that Robinson's arrival in October 1835 would
usher in their long-awaited return home. Even as Robinson
prepared to disembark, a warrior named Pallummuck confronted him 'on the deck of the vessel and said the island
was a bad place and he wanted to go to his own country'.[34]
Robinson was certainly in favour of repatriation, but his advo-
cacy was lukewarm. Indeed, he probably no longer considered
it a serious possibility. Arthur was equally uncommitted to
upholding this promise. While in 1834 he quietly raised
the idea of 'allotting them some tract of land in their own
country', he was told flatly that colonists would not stand for
it, and he left it at that.[35] So as months became years and the
death toll mounted, hope turned to desperation. The exiles
castigated Robinson's envoys 'for persuading them to give
themselves up',[36] and they spent more and more time avoiding
the settlement. One north-east man explained their long
absences in simple terms: 'too much MONATIA [sickness] at
Flinders at Pea Jacket [Wybalenna], too much dead man,

VIBER frightened, [instead we] like to [go] CRACKENNY bush'.[37] But simply avoiding the settlement was not a solution – they wanted to go home.

So was the promise of repatriation just what Nicholls assumed it was – 'a delusion [that] has been practiced upon them I conclude for the purpose of keeping them quiet'?[38] One of Robinson's contemporaries, the surveyor James Calder, believed him guilty of 'making promises to them in the name of the Government, which he should have known could not be kept'.[39] Naïve and unrealistic he may have been, but consciously dishonest he almost certainly was not. Robinson was too pious for that. He maintained until the end that, 'I never deceived them'.[40] At some point though, he realised he could not deliver on his end of the bargain, and one does not have to read too far between the lines of his self-justifying reports to see this. He begins one such report by noting his 'peculiar satisfaction' that, with the exception of 'periodical visits' to their country, the promises made to the Aborigines:

have been most amply and scrupulously fulfilled, and indeed in this respect have far exceeded my most sanguine expectations. The natives are also sensible of the kind intentions of the government towards them and excepting the non-fulfilment of the excursions to the main, and which is an occasional source of complaint, they in every other instance duly appreciate the means bestowed to ameliorate their condition … I confess I have frequently deplored the non-fulfilment of this part of the conditions, the more so as in all my dealings with the natives I have been scrupulously exact in keeping faith and have found it extremely painful and unpleasant to refuse compliance when importuned to carry the original intention into effect. The ... disappointment they have experienced in not being removed to a more eligible locality has also created discontent and occasionally given rise to fits of despondency.[41]

Tongerlongeter and the other exiles were naturally pressuring Robinson to deliver on his promise, though it's clear from his correspondence that he was reluctant even to pass on their requests. Removing the Oyster Bay – Big River people had made him an overnight celebrity, and he knew he would be just as swiftly condemned if he brought them back. Since he felt he couldn't repatriate them, Robinson had to appease them in some other way. His solution was to once again tie their fate to his.

Victoria, then known as Port Phillip or New Holland, had recently been opened up to settlement, and the government was considering Robinson for the illustrious post of Chief Protector of Aborigines. Both in Australia and in Britain, officials had been impressed with his results, and they wondered if his conciliatory model might be expanded to Port Phillip. Robinson welcomed the challenge, not least because he craved the adulation that came with 'success'. For a brief moment, he had been the darling of Tasmania. In addition to the handsome reward he received from the government, local communities banded together to present him with trophies and letters of appreciation. The colonial press, once so sceptical of his mission, had lavished him with praise. By the time he became commandant at Wybalenna, though, Robinson and the Aborigines he had removed were yesterday's news. The Port Phillip appointment promised to deliver the status and adventure he hungered for, and yet he hesitated.

Beneath Robinson's bloated ego was a conscience, and it was growing guiltier by the day. As ambitious as he was, the thought of leaving the Tasmanians to die on Flinders Island sat uneasily with him.[42] So, instead of advocating for their repatriation, he lobbied the government for permission to take them with him to Port Phillip. He pitched the idea to the Aborigines on Flinders Island with equal vigour. While they naturally favoured their homelands, their immediate concern was simply to escape the island. It seems they reasoned that, in the short term, Port Phillip would be an improvement. At least it was a place where people lived, unlike Flinders Island, which seemed fit only for dying.

For better or worse, many of the exiles gave their support to the Port Phillip proposal. In December 1835, following a conversation with them 'relative to a removal to New Holland', Robinson wrote in his journal: 'I do trust the home government will remove the people from this place. The chiefs and other natives are very anxious for the change.'[43] He repeatedly exhorted the government to approve the relocation, but the idea was quashed for fear that the Tasmanians would resume their attacks on colonists, and in all probability inspire local Aborigines to join the resistance. Amid the horrendous epidemic of 1837, Robinson again beseeched the government to 'accede to the removal of the present establishment to the adjacent coast of New Holland'. If not, he warned, 'I have no hesitation in stating that the race in a very short period of time will be extinct'.[44] Yet even this fell on deaf ears.

In August 1836, Tongerlongeter had a most extraordinary discussion with Robinson about the prospect of relocating. Robinson seems to have convinced him that he would never be allowed to return to his own country and that Port Phillip was the only hope for his people. He responded by saying that 'some of the native women who had been with the sealers and had seen it assured him it was a fine country. He [Tongerlongeter] said he was like me, he had put away his country', and that now he 'should like to go to New Holland'.[45] At first glance, it seems incredible that Tongerlongeter could just 'put away' his homeland, but what choice did he have? His people looked to him for solutions, not nostalgia.

Two years later, in 1838, thirty Aboriginal men signed a petition urging the government to allow them to relocate to Port Phillip.[46] The Tasmanians were adamant that they were not prisoners of war, that they were free to leave if they chose.[47] And, technically, they were. There was no legal basis for confining them on Flinders Island against their will. This was not what they had agreed to. Years later, when Robinson had gone and scarcely fifty of them remained, they would take their case to the very top of the British government. Their 1846 petition to Queen Victoria began by reminding Her Majesty that they were the free Aboriginal Inhabitants of V.D.L. now living upon Flinders Island … we were not taken prisoners but freely gave up our Country to Colonel Arthur then the Govr after defending ourselves. Your Petitioners humbly state to Y[our] M[ajesty] that Mr. Robinson made for us & with Col. Arthur an agreement which we have not lost from our minds since & we have made our part of it good …[48]

This time, it worked. The following year, forty-seven survivors were repatriated to Oyster Cove, a site south of Hobart from which some were once again able to visit their country. But for Tongerlongeter and most of the other exiles, it was too late.

Tongerlongeter started to suffer from stomach pain around 15 June 1837. The surgeon prescribed some ointment and showed Droomteemetyer how to apply it. By 6 pm on 19 June, the chief declared he was 'perfectly free from pain … [and] was at this time laughing and playing with his wife and others'. But, according to the surgeon, 'about eleven o'clock pm, I was suddenly called to see him. I found him in the most excruciating agony. On examination I found all the symptoms of inflammation of the intestines'. The surgeon then drained a litre and a half of blood from his arm, after which the chief momentarily lost consciousness. This was followed by an enema of castor oil and other laxatives. All of this was done, unsurprisingly, 'without the slightest alleviation of the symptoms.'[49]

Tongerlongeter remained lucid throughout most of the night. He lay 'before the fire supported by several aboriginal men and women and surrounded by a group of mournful friends and attendants all in tears'.[50] Foremost among them was Droomteemetyer. The couple had weathered inconceivable adversity, and now 'the Queen' did all she could to comfort her fading husband. Delirious with pain, the chief repeatedly called out, 'Minatti, Minatti'.[51] It's not known whether he was crying out for lost friends, lost country, or simply for mercy. By dawn, he was insensible. The surgeon 'applied a large blister to the abdomen and pit of the stomach and, subsequently, bled him to the extent of twenty-four ounces [700 millilitres] more … and directed preparations to be made for administering another enema'.[52] He needn't have bothered.

A storm was lashing the island on the morning Tongerlongeter died. From his quarters, Robinson heard the eruption of 'lamentations' through the howling wind and pelting rain. He too 'was quite overcome'. Once the wailing had subsided, he visited the scene. 'Oh, what a sight', he wrote of the mourners who crowded in and around the hut where the chief's body lay:

All stillness, the tears still trickling down the cheek
but no outward wailing or grief. I conferred with [the]
storekeeper and catechist. I was distressed. It appeared
like a dream. I could scarcely credit or believe it real.
Can it, said I, can it be possible that King William, he
who the other day was jocose, and he dead who scarcely
ever was ill whilst on the settlement, a strong hale and
robust man? Oh yes, it is true, it is too true. And then

the effect, I thought, to be produced on the minds of the other natives! The despondency of feeling it would create, the chief dead and the people without an adviser. Where will they find another? None! They had been long endeared to him by kindred, by blood relationship and acts of friendship. Deeds of bygone days were associated with his history and he is dead, gone for ever. Ah, well do I recollect when I first met him in the wilds. All the associations of that event rush at my mind … Rebecca one of the native women came, on her own account and in the name of three other women, for permission to go to the upper huts. She said they had lost their protector and wished to go to King George. I said I should not interfere, they might go if they thought fit. The death of King William has thrown a halo over the settlement. His loss is deeply deplored by all.[53]

Later that day, Tongerlongeter's body was transferred to the medical station. The carpenter measured up an extra-large coffin, while the surgeon conducted a post-mortem. He concluded that the chief had died of peritonitis – an inflammation of abdominal membranes, which is typically due to bacterial infection, often the result of a ruptured organ or abscess.[54] A review of the evidence suggests his case probably originated with a perforated duodenal ulcer.[55] The chief's death was undoubtedly hastened by the decision to drain more than two litres of blood from him, though he would almost certainly have died regardless of what the surgeon did.

Two days later, under a bright midday sun, Tongerlongeter was laid to rest in the Wybalenna cemetery 'with every mark of distinction'.[56] 'Such a funeral', Robinson noted, 'had not been witnessed at Flinders'.[57] Tongerlongeter's body, he tells us, 'was encased in a strong substantial coffin of gum plank', which was placed on trestles and

> covered with a pall of dark blue cloth edged with
> white. On the top of the coffin flowers were strewed
> … the entire of the aborigines all in new dresses were
> assembled, also the officers of the settlement and military.
> The funeral knell announced the solemn warning … At
> the conclusion of the hymn I addressed the audience
> on the solemnity of the occasion and adverted to the
> history of the departed chieftain … The procession
> [then] moved on in slow and solemn order to the grave.
> The burial service was then read. After the interment the
> whole procession returned in the same order to the gate
> of the paddock and retired. As they passed the mound
> of earth which covered the remains of the deceased they
> threw their flowers upon it … Thus has 'slept the sleep
> that never waketh' one who when in his own districts at
> the head of his powerful tribe spread terror and dismay
> throughout the settlements of the colony. He is no more
> and the white man may now safely revel in luxury on the
> lands of his primeval existence …[58]

Tongerlongeter died in his late forties after five and a half years in exile. He had had a profound impact on everyone at Wybalenna. Writing to a friend in the weeks following, Robinson bemoaned how the chief's passing 'had thrown a gloom over the whole settlement',[59] and not just for the Aborigines. The chief was held in high esteem among the Europeans too. Backhouse considered him 'a man of an intelligent mind, who made rapid advances in civilisation, and was very helpful in the preservation of good order at the Settlement'.[60] Major Ryan, who conducted a review of the settlement in 1836, developed 'a great regard for him',[61] and Robert Clark thought him a man of 'outstanding character and capabilities'.[62] But it was Robinson who knew him best. His heartfelt obituary leaves no doubt as to the impression the chief made:

> We are assembled to pay the last sad office to the remains of our departed brother. This is all we can do and these will soon be over, but then when this scene shall have passed away we can so long as hope lasts cherish a fond remembrance of his character, we can call to recollection his beneficence, his prowess, his sagacious proceedings and his fidelity, his humanity and manly bearing, and in my mind they are already indelibly impressed. No length of days will ever efface them from my mind. By me the recollections will be fondly cherished to the latest hour of my remembrance.

In an astonishing coincidence, King William died on the same day as his namesake in Windsor Castle. Both men were leaders, but that's where the similarities end. One led the largest and most technologically advanced empire the world had ever seen; the other led a small nation of hunters and foragers from the longest-isolated and least technological society on Earth. One devoted himself to dispossessing millions of indigenous peoples; the other devoted himself to determinedly resisting that dispossession. One died in the comfort of a lavish castle; the other succumbed in a draughty hut on an accursed island far from home. 'King William' was just a character Tongerlongeter played so that his people might have a voice. If he had anything in common with the British monarch, it was that his death produced a comparable tide of shock and sorrow, albeit confined to a shrinking settlement on a tiny island at the edge of the known world.

Before Tongerlongeter was even in the ground, Robinson moved to ensure an orderly transition of power, appointing Purngerpar (aka Alfred) as 'an elected King'.[63] Over his protestations, Droomteemetyer returned Tongerlongeter's cherished boat cloak, which he in turn bestowed on 'the next in succession, King Alfred', who 'appears to attach importance to this vesture'.[64] Purngerpar was a steady choice. While he is rarely mentioned in the records, political stability appears to have been maintained in the wake of Tongerlongeter's death. After Rolepa (King George) died in 1841, the alliance led by Purngerpar and two other Oyster Bay – Big River men 'claimed full leadership of the settlement'.[65]

Tongerlongeter's influence among the exiles seems to have outlived him. The doctor appointed to Wybalenna in 1843 recorded a short song 'in honour of a Great Chief'. It contained the words 'Toka mengha leah' in triplicate.[66]

While we cannot be certain it was about Tongerlongeter, the phonetic similarity is striking and there were few other candidates. Since then, however, the name of this incredible man – this war hero and celebrated leader – has been all but forgotten. The timber cross erected above his grave has long since vanished. Today, the graves of Tongerlongeter and the other heroes of the Black War are marked not by wreaths or ornate memorials but by thistles.

Conclusion:
'A brave and patriotic people'

Henry Reynolds

The extraordinary procession of Tongerlongeter and his remaining countrymen and -women down Elizabeth Street on 7 January 1832 made a powerful impression on those who witnessed and heard about it. In Bonwick's words of 1870, 'the whole population assembled to witness the procession' and 'shouts of welcome greeted all'. The tender eyes of women, he declared, were 'swimming with tears as the dark race passed on, and kind looks and smiles fell gently on the war-tossed ones'.[1] The surveyor-turned-historian James Erskine Calder had a much darker view of the same event, writing in 1875 that it was 'an awful day for the natives'.[2]

At the time, the overwhelming sense was relief that the war was over, though few contemporaries would have realised that they were witnessing the opening moments in the final act of a profound human tragedy. The twenty-six 'war tossed' veterans were unwittingly marching into an exile from which few of them would return. When the Flinders Island settlement was abandoned in 1847 and the remnant taken to Oyster Cove, a dozen Oyster Bay – Big River people were among the survivors. But of the twenty-six who had walked down Elizabeth Street to meet the governor fifteen years earlier, only two or three were left. Most of those repatriated to Oyster Cove had either been captured before the armistice or rescued from sealers.[3] They were all who remained of the generation of Oyster Bay – Big River people who had so tenaciously resisted the invasion of their country. They had posed the most serious internal threat white Tasmania has ever faced, yet in 1860, when the last warrior died, contemporaries were oblivious to the significance of his passing. The situation is not much different now.

It was not known in the 19th century, and is little appreciated today, that a number of distinct Tasmanian nations had preserved their independence and sense of identity across vast stretches of time. Despite the small size of the island and the limited population (informed estimates range from 3000 to 5500),[4] the Aborigines had not become one people. The nations had clearly cherished their own languages, customs, songs, dances, traditions and historical memories. And this had been the case for at least 300 and likely more generations since the flooding of Bass Strait and the irreversible moment when the last successful journeys were made between Tasmania and mainland Australia. It is a story of cultural continuity perhaps unique in human history. And it had all been transformed in a little more than a generation. Limited vocabularies and small snatches of ethnographic information were all that were preserved. It was a tragedy in the most literal sense of that word. So much was lost to the world.

The resistance we have documented was, then, about much more than access to hunting grounds and sources of water. An ancient way of living was at stake, a profound sense of identity and belonging. Tongerlongeter and the other Tasmanian warriors were not just resourceful and courageous in the way they conducted their campaigns. There was a grandeur inherent in their warfare, its brutality and bloodshed notwithstanding. There were sympathetic settlers who grasped something of this reality and realised that they were dealing with patriots whose defence of their way of life was fully understandable and, indeed, even admirable.

Even those settlers who lacked understanding of what was fully at stake in the war could not avoid a grudging respect for the intensity and skill of the resistance. Calder was the best informed and most perceptive observer and subsequently historian of the war. What he called the 'ever recurring' attacks kept the colonists 'in a state of constant ferment and excitement', and the 'conversations of every fire-side related in some form or other to these deplorable acts of the natives', who not only 'maintained their ground everywhere (the towns excepted) but had by far the best of the fight'. It was, he insisted, 'beyond all doubt' that the settlers were no match for the blacks 'in bush fighting, either in defensive or offensive operations.'[5]

We have shown how the bush fighting came to dominate the life of the colony for several years, eventually forcing the administration of George Arthur to adopt the extraordinary tactic of the Black Line, an event unique in Australian history. In the end, though, the decisive factor was not that great mobilisation but simply the overwhelming demographic advantage that inexorably tipped the balance in favour of the settlers, whose numbers were augmented every few weeks by new arrivals from Britain. It was a relentless and daunting reality of which the warrior bands would not have been fully aware. Their enemies had behind them a vast and unimaginable reservoir of humanity in a distant, unknown land.

In paying tribute to the Tasmanians, Calder wrote: 'Whatever the future historian of Tasmania may have to say of this ancient people, he will do them an injustice if he fails to record that, as a body, they held their ground bravely for 30 years against the invaders of their beautiful domains'.[6] Since Calder wrote this passage in 1875, many historians, both amateur and professional, have written about Tasmania's Black War. Almost every generation has produced a small crop of relevant books. They vary in quality, intention and seriousness. There was a renewal of interest in the topic following the publication of Clive Turnbull's *Black War* in 1948, which set down many themes taken up by more recent writers. The focus has commonly been on the violence and brutality of the settlers, which was certainly relentless. But it is only part of the story, and the emphasis in many accounts completely ignores Calder's assessment that the Tasmanians held their ground and on many occasions had by far the best of the fight. The common approach has been to express pity for the Tasmanians. And that is unexceptional in so far as it goes, but it sits awkwardly with respect or even admiration for their martial spirit and their achievement as brave and resourceful warriors. Turnbull's study, which was the principal reference book for a generation of readers, made no mention of Tongerlongeter. In some accounts the number of Aborigines killed is grossly exaggerated, which at one and the same time belittles the warriors and overstates the capacity of their enemies. At times the implication seems to be that the Tasmanians were either a simple or a uniquely peaceful people who sat passively around their camp fires unable to resist and waiting to be shot. The fact that they could terrorise settler society for years on end finds no place in accounts distorted by well-meaning partiality.[7]

Interpretations that concentrate on violence done to the Tasmanians, on massacre and genocide and on their fate as victims, do them less than justice and misunderstand the motivation of both the settlers and their government. They simplify the moral complexity of the story. As well, they pay little attention to the continuing conflict among traditional enemies for, as Calder observed, 'they fought one another all the time they were thrashing the whites'.[8] They also fail to pay attention to the fact that most of the men working out on the frontier were convict servants who had not chosen to be part of the invasion force and had little to gain from working in dangerous districts without guns or horses. They were understandably terrified by their adversaries, living with levels of acute anxiety. For them there was often a stark and brutal choice of kill or be killed.

What must not be forgotten about Tasmanian history is that the resistance, principally carried out by the warrior bands of the Oyster Bay – Big River nations, turned what might have been an easy dispossession into what Governor Arthur termed 'lamented and protracted warfare'.[9] And it was the most serious conflict fought anywhere on the Australian frontiers. Tongerlongeter and his war bands killed and wounded far more Europeans than any Indigenous nation on the mainland. None of them had anything like the Tasmanians' impact on colonial society. The cost of mobilising 2200 soldiers, settlers and convicts in the Black Line was equivalent to half the colony's annual revenue, a telling tribute to the vigour of Aboriginal resistance.[10]

The war itself stands out as a landmark in Australian history. The death toll alone overshadows that of any other domestic conflict. The 258 European deaths and the similar toll of wounded is far greater than the numbers killed in convict rebellion, bushranging forays or miners' uprising. The number of Tasmanians killed cannot be determined with any certainty. Calder's estimate of 500 should be seen as a bare minimum, and if we include those who died during the war from the terrible rigours of the time, a figure of 1000 is not unreasonable. But even 750 deaths overall is an imposing figure. The per capita loss of life in Tasmania between 1823 and 1831 was greater than during the First World War and considerably higher than during the Second World War. The death toll overshadows the 340 Australian deaths in the Korean War and the 521 in Vietnam.[11] The magnitude of the Tasmanian war, then, is not often appreciated. For that matter neither is its international impact, which has been little understood.

The vigour and the duration of the resistance ensured

that it became well known in Britain. In 1831, the House of Commons asked for copies of all correspondence between Governor Arthur and the Colonial Office on the subject 'of the military operations lately carried on against the Aboriginal inhabitants of Van Diemen's Land'. It was a comprehensive compendium, eighty-six pages long, including all relevant correspondence between January 1828 and March 1831. Two further papers containing Tasmanian material were printed in 1831 and 1834. It was the clearest evidence of the rapidly growing interest in the fate of indigenous peoples of the Empire among the powerful humanitarian lobby, both inside and outside the Parliament. With the abolition of the slave trade in 1833, key figures like Thomas Buxton redirected their reforming zeal to the consequences of British colonisation. Buxton declared in 1834 that his attention had been 'drawn of late to the wickedness of our proceedings as a nation' towards 'the Empire's native people'. We have, he thundered, 'usurped their land, kidnapped, enslaved and murdered themselves'. Their greatest crime, he observed, was that they 'sometimes trespass into the lands of their forefathers'.[12]

In 1835, Buxton succeeded in bringing a motion to establish a Commons Select Committee to examine every aspect of imperial relations with the Empire's indigenous peoples, which reported two years later. During his speech he expressed his horror at the unfolding fate of the Tasmanians, observing that a correspondent had informed him of how survivors of the war 'complained that the white men had rooted them out of the soil'. He was almost certainly referring to a letter from the prominent Quaker James Backhouse, who was in Hobart at that stage and had spent considerable time talking with Tongerlongeter while visiting Flinders Island. Backhouse informed his influential friend that his experience in Tasmania had convinced him that Britain's method of colonisation had proceeded

> upon principles that cannot be too strongly reprobated, and which want radical reformation. Aborigines have had wholesale robbery of territory committed upon them by the government, and the settlers have become the receivers of stolen property, and have borne the curse of it in the wrath of the Aborigines, who, sooner or later, have become exasperated at being driven off their rightful possessions.[13]

Buxton published the Backhouse letter as an appendix to the 1837 Select Committee Report, which among many other things declared:

> It might be presumed that the native inhabitants of any land have an incontrovertible right to their own soil: a plain and sacred right, however, which seems not to have been understood. Europeans have entered their borders, uninvited, and when there, have not only acted as if they were the undoubted lords of the soil, but have punished the natives as aggressors if they evinced a disposition to live in their own country.[14]

There is no doubt, then, that the resistance of the Tasmanians was a major influence on the dramatic changes in British imperial policy in the 1830s. British humanitarians found the evidence compelling. The war itself highlighted the fundamental problems arising from the way settlement in both Tasmania and New South Wales had progressed without treaties or even a recognition of Aboriginal property rights. The high death toll in Tasmania was symptomatic of profound problems. The other lesson driven home by the Tasmanian experience was the catastrophic decline of the Aboriginal population, already apparent in the mid-1830s. Buxton declared that as a result of events in Tasmania 'an indelible stain had been thrown on the British government.'[15]

The armistice that brought the fighting to an end and Tongerlongeter's meeting with the governor coincided exactly with a slave rebellion in Jamaica, which spanned the last week of 1831 and the first week of 1832. It greatly shocked the British public and was a major influence in driving forward the parliamentary battle to outlaw slavery throughout the Empire. It involved far more insurgents than the bush fighting in Tasmania, though it was over very quickly and resulted in the violent deaths of more than 200 slaves but only fourteen Europeans. The cost of the Black War was far higher both in life and treasure, and it was seen in that way among the influential humanitarian reformers. Tongerlongeter and his warriors had shown that even small groups of insurgents could exact a heavy toll on both the British settlers and the imperial treasury.

What the British humanitarian activists found especially alarming was the prospect of future wars of the kind that had been fought on the island. The death toll from comparable conflicts across the rest of the Australian continent would likely run into tens of thousands. Leaders of the recently founded British Aborigines' Protection Society argued that the Black War indicated what was 'to be expected from the like conduct on the extensive and neighbouring continent of New Holland'.[16] It was impossible to conceive 'how long and fearful will be the struggle between the European and the Australian'.[17] George Arthur was alive to what would happen if the experience of Tasmania were replicated elsewhere. In his dispatch of 7 January 1832, the evening after he had met Tongerlongeter and the rest of his band, he reminded the Colonial Office of the great cost arising from the war, which he correctly presumed was then at an end. It was also a tribute to the warriors he had just met. He explained that 'the continued hostility of the natives has operated most injuriously in many ways – great expense has been incurred, dissatisfaction has been incurred – improvements have been retarded and Immigration has been checked'.[18]

Arthur referred to the colony recently established in Western Australia and offered advice about how to avert the many deplorable consequences of the Tasmanian war. He had obviously given a good deal of thought to the problem. He recommended that negotiations be entered into in order to arrange for the purchase of land. To facilitate the process, official protectors should be appointed who would be charged with learning the local languages. The Colonial Office gave serious attention to Arthur's advice. A second dispatch from Arthur arrived when the office was in negotiations with the South Australian Colonisation Commission to establish a new colony in South Australia. Arthur argued that every effort should be made to reach an understanding with the local Aborigines before the settlers arrived. Otherwise events would unfold as they had done in Tasmania, and it would be 'impossible to prevent a long continued warfare' in which the Europeans as well as the Aborigines 'becoming more and more inflamed as their mutual injuries accumulate, will destroy each other in detail'.[19]

His constant reminders of the disastrous turn of events in Tasmania pushed the Colonial Office towards a return to policies that had been disregarded in the settlement of Australia. A copy of his letter was sent to the company officers and they were advised that they must appoint an official protector to arrange for the purchase of Aboriginal land. Letters Patent were drawn up for the new colony that provided for the local Aboriginal peoples and their descendants to remain in 'actual occupation ... of any lands now actually occupied or enjoyed by such natives'.[20]

Arthur was a highly respected colonial official and he had spent twelve years in Tasmania. When he returned to London in 1836, he was probably even more influential and was in close contact with the Colonial Office when plans were being considered for the settlement of New Zealand. He warned the Secretary of State, Lord Glenelg, that unless some 'enlarged plan of Proceeding' was introduced in future settlements, there would be 'an enormous sacrifice of life'.[21]

Reflecting on the intense war in Tasmania, he concluded that he had learnt from his contact with men like Tongerlongeter that they had been motivated by a deep and enduring sense of injustice, and advised Glenelg that: 'On the first occupation of the colony it was a great oversight that a treaty was not, at that time made with the natives, and such compensation given to the chiefs as they would have deemed a fair equivalent for what they surrendered.'[22] There seems little doubt that Arthur's advice was a significant influence on the decision in the Colonial Office to initiate the settlement of New Zealand with the Treaty of Waitangi. If a small Tasmanian nation could bring a British colony to a standstill and kill more than 250 settlers, what might the Māori do?

There was, then, no uncertainty in the minds of contemporaries that Tasmania had experienced a major war. This was manifestly the case on the island itself and was no doubt uppermost in the minds of the crowds that gathered on the summer morning in January 1832 to watch Tongerlongeter lead the remnant of his warrior bands down Elizabeth Street to meet the governor for peace talks. Hundreds had been killed or wounded. The economic cost had hobbled the colony. The vigour of the Tasmanian resistance had surprised many observers and evoked grudging admiration from a wide variety of writers in both the colonies and in Britain. One of the Empire's most dashing military heroes, General Sir Charles Napier, remarked in 1834 that considering the odds they faced in numbers and firearms, the Tasmanians put up 'a most *courageous* resistance against us'.[23] But above all else, the war was impossible to ignore and it consequently came to have a significant influence on the development of imperial policy in the 1830s and beyond.

The most important lesson driven home by the war was the central importance of the ownership and control of land. Leaders of the humanitarian movement came to appreciate that British policy adopted in 1788 to disregard traditional land ownership was bad in practice, fundamentally immoral and certain to provoke desperate resistance. The Colonial Office attempted to remedy the situation in South Australia in 1837 without much success, but was able to assert the principle in New Zealand in 1840, in part because it accepted the advice of George Arthur to impose a treaty from the very start of official colonisation. The recognition of customary rights over all land held under pastoral lease imposed by the Colonial Office in New South Wales, South Australia and Western Australia in 1848 was a parting gift to the Australian colonies on the verge of the introduction of internal self-government.

It had been impossible for British observers to ignore the fact that the Empire had been engaged in war in Tasmania. For their part, the nations of eastern districts of the island could have had no doubt that they too were at war by the middle years of the 1820s. More and more of their land was being occupied by settlers and their animals. In many cases, the intruders treated the traditional owners as trespassers and were clearly not intending to move on. Access to the best hunting grounds and watercourses was being denied. Women were being assaulted and in many cases kidnapped or killed. Children were also being stolen. As casualties mounted, it must have increasingly appeared to be a battle for the survival of the whole nation. The possibility of extermination must have haunted many Tasmanians, and there did not seem to be any way to avoid that terrible fate.

All this makes it very hard to understand why Tasmania's Black War, along with comparable fighting on mainland frontiers, has never been included in Australia's official catalogue of conflict. It's not, after all, a matter of a lack of interest in martial achievement. As a nation we revere fallen warriors and spent hundreds of millions of dollars commemorating the centenary of the First World War. The graves of our soldiers are well maintained in many parts of the world. We disinter the remains of soldiers killed a century ago on the Western Front and accord them a formal military funeral. War memorials are found in every town and village. 'Lest We Forget' is the pertinent phrase employed everywhere with reverential earnestness, but it is never applied to memories of what Calder called 'bush fighting'. Attempts to do so are frequently rebuffed with disdain. It seems much easier for Australians to remember white soldiers than black warriors; to commemorate wars fought far away than those that ravaged our own continent.

Tasmania's commemoration of war lines up with the rest of the country. Monuments are ubiquitous and can be found in even the smallest towns. During the recent cavalcade of commemoration, old monuments were restored and new ones constructed. Avenues of honour were replanted and given fresh plaques naming the young men who didn't come home. It is a similar story with what is often called, anomalously,

Tasmania's first war – the Boer War in South Africa between 1899 and 1902. In company with the five mainland colonies, Tasmania was an enthusiastic participant in the imperial onslaught on the two Afrikaner republics. Eight hundred and fifty Tasmanians went to the Boer War in units called Imperial Bushmen; twenty-four died in combat or from disease. Monuments commemorate the victims in Hobart, Launceston and several other towns, and rolls of honour were installed in many local halls. In recent years the war has been remembered with official ceremonies attended by representatives of local municipalities and the state government and opposition. All the Tasmanians who fought in South Africa are honoured in the Australian War Memorial. There has never been a ceremony of any kind to commemorate the Black War. Not once in nearly 200 years. Nor are there any official monuments to remember the sacrifice of the hundreds, either black or white, who died between 1823 and 1831.

Australia's pantheon, the highly regarded Australian War Memorial across the lake from Parliament House in Canberra, has refused for many years to deal with the frontier wars, despite several generations of scholarship emphasising their vast extent and duration. So we are faced with the anomalous situation where the memorial now lauds the service of Indigenous Australians overseas, largely in the service of either the British or American empires, but eschews the heroic struggles of their ancestors in defence of their ancient homelands.

Comparable countries have no difficulty in recognising frontier conflict as warfare. The official United States list of wars records all the conflicts with the Indian nations, no matter how small and inconsequential. The Māori Wars have always figured prominently in histories of New Zealand. Throughout Latin America historical figures who, like Tongerlongeter, fought against the invading Europeans, are recognised as national heroes. They are commemorated with statues, their names are found on roads and avenues, on schools and other institutions, their faces grace banknotes. A statue of the Chilean Mapuche leader Caupolicán has commanded an imposing position on the rocky outcrop of Santa Lucía Hill in the centre of Santiago since 1910, and there are streets and parks named after him, as well as a town and a theatre. Samuel Sharpe, the leader of the Jamaican slave rebellion, was declared to be a national hero by the government of the newly independent country in 1975. There is a teachers' college and a city square named in his honour, and his face appears on the $50 banknote.

Australia's ignorance of and lack of interest in our First Nations' warriors is a national peculiarity that must surely astound interested foreign observers. By whatever measure is employed, the frontier wars loom large in our history. They lasted in one form or another for well over a hundred years. They were experienced on the coastlines of the Indian and Pacific Oceans, from the southernmost part of Tasmania to the islands of Torres Strait. The death toll will never be known with any certainty, but it increasingly seems likely to have been higher than that of either the First or the Second World War, particularly when we consider that Australia counts among its fallen heroes those who died of any cause, including accidents and disease. The issues in contention in frontier fighting were by any measure of equal gravity to Australia's many overseas entanglements. Frontiersmen and Indigenous warriors were contending for the ownership and control of land across a vast continent. It was warfare *on* this country *for* this country. The linked series of local wars was a conflict of global significance. It was, arguably, Australia's greatest war.

But when Australians seek war heroes, they invariably look to the men and women who battled, suffered and died overseas. The young men who fought at Gallipoli in 1915 are chosen for special attention as exemplars of admirable national characteristics. It is commonly asserted that the nation was made on those distant shores. Thousands of Australians go there on pilgrimages. As in so many other ventures, it was recognition overseas that mattered. With embarrassed eyes averted from brutal bush fighting, Australia was unable to notice the heroes of the Indigenous resistance. By any fair measure, they stood taller than our servicemen and -women who suffered and died overseas. Australian forces were in many cases better equipped, educated and trained than their assorted enemies. They had access to superior medical services and consequently had a much higher chance of surviving injury. They also had what cannot unfairly be called the luxury of fighting on other peoples' lands. They certainly suffered grievously. But they knew all the while that their own country was safe, that their homes and families were secure, that their own property was sacrosanct, and their way of life inviolate.

None of these certainties was available to the warriors of the First Nations who struggled desperately to hold back the irresistible tide of British colonial expansion. The longer the fighting went on, the more the balance of power tilted in favour of the invader. Vast open plains did not provide the sanctuary of Tasmania's rugged hinterland. European guns improved out of sight during the course of the 19th century. Colonial frontiersmen took to the saddle and stayed there. Irregular cavalry, aided by Aboriginal and mixed-descent trackers, was far more effective than the stumbling infantry of early Tasmania and New South Wales.

Aboriginal warriors faced impossible odds, not just now and then, but always. And yet they went on fighting. In the case of the Oyster Bay – Big River nations, they resisted until there were only twenty-six of them left. It is a heroic story in anyone's language. Tongerlongeter and his people were great patriots fighting as patriots have done over time all across the world to defend their homeland against foreign invaders. Sympathetic contemporaries recognised patriotism when they saw it. Lieutenant William Darling, when talking to the exiles in Bass Strait, found they were 'a *brave and patriotic* people' who considered themselves to have been 'engaged in a justifiable war against the invaders of their country'.[24] Gilbert Robertson came to the conclusion that 'they consider every injury they can inflict upon White Men as an Act of Duty and patriotism'.[25]

JE Calder, another Tasmanian settler who thought deeply about the island's war, wrote to a local newspaper in September 1831:

We are at war with them: they look upon us as enemies
– as invaders – as their oppressors and persecutors –
they resist our invasion. They have never been subdued,
therefore they are not rebellious subjects, but an injured
nation, defending in their own way, their rightful
possessions which have been torn from them by force.[26]

Why is it so hard for today's Australians to see what was
clear to observers almost 200 years ago? Why is Tongerlongeter
virtually unknown? There are no relevant monuments. His
name has never been chiselled in stone, cast in bronze or
placed on an honour board. No tree has been planted in his
honour. No one tends his known place of burial. No official
ceremony has ever been held to commemorate his struggles.
There is nothing in the Tasmanian landscape to remind locals
or visitors that once an island of patriots fought a desperate
war against an invader. Why ever is Tongerlongeter not
one of Australia's national heroes? It is hard to think of any
historical figure more deserving of that honour.

The important role he played in Australia's colonial
history is, as we have shown, beyond dispute. He led the most
significant Aboriginal campaign against the British invasion.
He continued to play a leadership role in the life of the exiled
community on Flinders Island until his premature death. The
campaign that he led had a large impact in Tasmania itself,
and helped bring about major changes in British imperial
policy, not as dramatic as the abolition of slavery, but of real
importance to the indigenous peoples of the Empire. The
Treaty of Waitangi in 1840 and the recognition of Aborigini

rights on land held under pastoral lease right across the Australian colonies were innovations that continue to have relevance today. Although almost unknown, Tongerlongeter was without doubt one of the most influential leaders of Australia's First Nations to have emerged since the British first invaded the continent 233 years ago.

Afterword

Nicholas Clements

In December 1840, fully six years after Robinson had trium-
phantly declared the island free of Aborigines, the incisive
surveyor James Erskine Calder led a survey expedition
from Lake St Clair in the central highlands to Macquarie
Harbour on the west coast. The country between these
remote landmarks is extremely rugged. Even today, only the
most intrepid adventurers brave its treacherous weather,
suffocating scrub and jagged mountains. Yet it was here, on
a small plain in the folds of the Franklin River, that Calder
made an extraordinary discovery:

> In the midst of this plain we found two natives' huts,
> *very recently abandoned*, a circumstance which was
> indicated by several portions of Kangaroo flesh, which
> were found here, being still only half decayed. The
> huts were made of bark, and at the time when we fell
> in with them, were sufficiently compact to afford good
> shelter. On the bark that covered them, were some
> extraordinary charcoal drawings; one representing two
> men spearing an animal ... There was also an outline
> of a dog, and an emu, really not badly done; and some

other designs, the exact meaning of which I was not
able to make out.

Some 20 kilometres further west, in the foothills of
Frenchmans Cap, Calder also 'found an excellent spear'.[1]

Whatever happened to the Aborigines whose camp
Calder stumbled across? The year before, another band had
resumed its attacks in the island's north-west after a five-
year silence. These people too had been hiding far from the
settled districts, but being unable or unwilling to maintain
their isolation, they once again descended on the settlements.
At least twenty attacks were made on farms in the north-
west between September 1839 and February 1842, most
if not all by this mysterious band. What became of them
is unknown. They were probably killed by convict servants
who, in that corner of the island, were notorious for their
cruelty.[2] By contrast, the band Calder nearly encountered was
probably from the east. At least some of them were Oyster
Bay people from the Coal Valley.[3] But in 1842, five years after
Tongerlongeter died, even these people were forced down
from the hills. Now reduced to just two adults and four
children, they were picked up by a boat on the west coast and
removed to Flinders Island.

This last family joined a severely diminished community.
The great chief Tongerlongeter had been dead five years.
Four months after his death, Droomteemetyer had also come
perilously close to dying. Stricken with what appears to have
been influenza, she spent many days lying 'near the fire with
the favourite skull of her infant child appended to her breast'.[4]

Droomteemetyer ultimately recovered and, on 4 November 1837, moved in with the new 'king', Purngerpar. On that same day, Robinson tells us, 'Queen Adelaide gave me the skull of her infant child to keep for her in my office.'[5] She died of influenza on 4 March 1839 and is buried beside her sister, who had succumbed to the same malady the day before.

Droomteemetyer died during one of the many influenza outbreaks that ravaged the settlement. At the time, no one understood what was happening or how to prevent it. It is interesting to speculate about what type of community may have arisen on Flinders Island had disease not done its terrible work. What if the exiles' population had grown? What if, armed with words rather than spears, they had continued to assert their culture and their rights? What might this have meant for them and for Tasmania? In one sense, we will never know. Yet in another sense, something like this scenario has in fact played out.

When the last forty-seven exiles were relocated to Oyster Cove in 1847, they continued to die at an alarming rate. In 1876, the Bruny Island woman Truganini died in Hobart.[6] She was believed to have been the last 'full-descent' Tasmanian. The 'race', according to the purist racial thinking of the day, were now 'extinct'. But on the islands of Bass Strait, and probably in one or two other places, a small number of people of mixed descent – mostly the children of Aboriginal women and sealers – were raising families. Over several generations, unique and robust communities developed, though they went largely unnoticed until the mid-20th century when they began reasserting their cultural and political identity as Aborigines. Since then, Aboriginal pride has been growing, and more and more people are discovering or revealing their ancestry. There are now many more Aboriginal Tasmanians than at any time in the past. In the 2016 census, 23 572 Tasmanian residents identified as Aboriginal or Torres Strait Islander, up from 16 767 in 2006.[7] As in the past, there are divisions among some Aboriginal groups, but collectively they now play a prominent role in contemporary Tasmanian life. Theirs is a story of adaptation, resistance and reinvention. It is an ancient story and a modern one – a story of survival against incredible odds.

Acknowledgments

Nicholas Clements

In any work that requires the cobbling together of thousands of disparate pieces of information from hundreds of different sources, the help of others is essential. Directly and indirectly, we are indebted to many people for their assistance and guidance. These generous humans include: Mary Ramsay of the Bothwell Historical Society and Stephanie Burbury of the Oatlands District Historical Society, both of whom shared important local knowledge; orthopaedic surgeon Adam Watson, who helped us make sense of Tongerlongeter's injury and illness; and, of course, the staff of the various libraries and archives we have frequented in the course of gathering our source material.

We are grateful to Murray Johnson, Ian McFarlane, Tom Dunning, Cherry Parker, Dianne Baldock, Val Clarke, Robert Cox and Barry Brimfield for their valuable feedback on the manuscript. Among these, special mention must go to Robert and Barry. Robert was an invaluable sounding board in my quest to piece together Kickertopoller's role in the story. Barry, whose ethnographic knowledge of the early Tasmanians is unmatched, has generously shared his decades of research (the fruit buns are coming, Old Dog). These two men prove that one does not need a PhD to make serious contributions to history.

The professional and flexible publishing team at New-South could have taken on a less complex project, but they believed in this one, and we are beholden to them. Nicola Young, our meticulous and thoughtful copyeditor, not only polished the text but helped us to see it anew.

Finally, we want to thank our families. Margaret has long kept Henry on a true bearing. She gave her support to this book as fully as to all the others. Kristy knew, when she gave me her blessing to embark on this project, that it would entail many sacrifices. But she gave it without hesitation, because she could see what it meant to me, and I will not forget it. My children, Finn (six) and Liffey (two), have, with their cuddles and smiles, done more than they realise to help us resurrect Tongerlongeter from the amnesia of history.

Notes

Abbreviations

AAPS	Australian Aborigines Protection Society
ANU	The Australian National University
AJCP	Australian Joint Copying Project
FM	*Friendly Mission* (*The Tasmanian Journals and Papers of George Augustus Robinson, 1829–1834*, NJB Plomley [ed.], QVMAG and *Quintus*, Launceston, 2008)
HRA	Historical Records of Australia
n.d.	no date
NLA	National Library of Australia
QVMAG	Queen Victoria Museum and Art Gallery
ML, SLNSW	Mitchell Library, State Library of New South Wales
pers. comm.	personal communication
THRA	Tasmanian Historical Research Association
TAHO	Tasmanian Archives and Heritage Office
UQP	University of Queensland Press
VDL	*Van Diemen's Land* (*Copies of All Correspondence …*, AGL Shaw [ed.], THRA, Hobart, 1971)
WiS	*Weep in Silence* (*A History of the Flinders Island Aboriginal Settlement*, NJB Plomley [ed.], Blubber Head Press, Hobart, 1987)

Introduction: Remembering their sacrifice

1   WEH Stanner, *After the Dreaming: Black and White Australians, an Anthropologist's View*, Boyer lectures, ABC, Sydney, 1968.
2   H Reynolds, *Fate of a Free People*, Penguin, Melbourne, 2004, p. 92.
3   Reynolds, *Fate of a Free People*, p. 111.

Chapter 1: An extraordinary day

1   *Hobart Town Courier*, 7 January 1832, p. 2.
2   *Colonial Times*, 11 January 1832, p. 2.
3   Clements online compendium, <https://dx.doi.org/10.25959/hpxk-5f95>.
4   NJB Plomley (ed.) *Weep in Silence: A History of the Flinders Island Aboriginal Settlement*, Blubber Head Press, Hobart, 1987, p. 454. Hereinafter *WiS*.

5   N Clements, 'Frontier conflict in Van Diemen's Land', PhD thesis, School of
      Humanities, University of Tasmania, 2013, pp. 196, 199–201.
6   *Launceston Advertiser*, 26 September 1831, p. 299.
7   J Bonwick, *The Lost Tasmanian Race*, Sampson Low, London, 1884, p. 149.
8   Arthur to Goderich, 6 April 1833, TAHO, CO280/41.
9   Arthur to Goderich, 7 January 1832, TAHO, CO280/33.
10   Arthur to Goderich, 7 January 1832, TAHO, CO280/33.
11   Reynolds, *Fate of a Free People*, pp. 121–57.
12   JE Calder, *Some Account of the Wars, Extirpation, Habits, etc. of the Native
      Tribes of Tasmania*, Henn & Company, Hobart, 1875, p. 32.
13   J Bonwick, *The Last of the Tasmanians or the Black War of Van Diemen's
      Land*, Sampson Low, London, 1870, p. 230.
14   Bonwick, *The Last of the Tasmanians*, pp. 229–30.
15   J West, *The History of Tasmania*, vol. II, Henry Dowling, Launceston, 1852,
      pp. 66, 64.

Chapter 2: The explorers arrive

1   NJB Plomley (ed.), *Friendly Mission: The Tasmanian Journals and Papers of
      George Augustus Robinson, 1829–1834*, QVMAG and *Quintus*, Launceston,
      2008 (first published 1966), journal, 19 November 1831. Hereinafter *FM*.
2   NJB Plomley (ed.), *The Baudin Expedition and the Tasmanian Aborigines,
      1802*, Blubber Head Press, Hobart, 1992, p. 84.
3   J Reynolds (ed.), *The Discovery of Tasmania*, Tasmanian Government,
      Hobart, 1942, p. 31.
4   HL Roth (ed.), *Crozet's Voyage to Tasmania, New Zealand, the Ladrone
      Islands, and the Philippines in the Years 1771–1772*, Truslove & Shirley,
      London, 1891, p. 18.
5   Roth, *Crozet's Voyage*, p. 20.
6   G Mortimer, *Observations and Remarks Made During a Voyage … in the Brig
      Mercury*, L Israel, Amsterdam, 1975 (first published 1791), pp. 19–20.
7   Plomley, *Baudin Expedition*, p. 82.
8   Plomley, *Baudin Expedition*, p. 89.
9   Plomley, *Baudin Expedition*, p. 87.
10   N Baudin, *The Journal of Post-Captain Nicolas Baudin*, Libraries Board of
      South Australia, Adelaide, 2004, pp. 341, 345, 349–50.
11   Plomley, *Baudin Expedition*, p. 82.
12   H Reynolds, *The Other Side of the Frontier*, 3rd edn, Penguin, Melbourne,
      1992, pp. 30–40.
13   Plomley, *Baudin Expedition*, p. 84.
14   Plomley, *Baudin Expedition*, p. 84.
15   Plomley, *Baudin Expedition*, p. 111.
16   Baudin, *The Journal*, p. 340; Plomley, *Baudin Expedition*, p. 111.
17   MF Péron, *A Voyage of Discovery to the Southern Hemisphere*, Richard
      Phillips, London, 1809, pp. 191–92.

Chapter 3: Confrontation at Risdon
1   Cited in P Tardif, *John Bowen's Hobart: The Beginning of European Settlement in Tasmania*, THRA, Hobart, 2003, p. 142.
2   Cited in Tardif, *John Bowen's Hobart*, p. 142.
3   'Caley's account of the colony', *Historical Records of New South Wales*, vol. V, Sydney, Government Printer, 1897, p. 299.
4   Lieutenant William Moore was in command of the detachment of the NSW Corps at Risdon and second in command to John Bowen, who was away from the settlement at the time.
5   Mountgarrett to Knopwood, 3 May 1804, in Tardif, *John Bowen's Hobart*, p. 220.
6   M Nicholls (ed.), *The Diary of the Reverend Robert Knopwood 1803–1838: First Chaplain of Van Diemen's Land*, THRA, Launceston, 1977, p. 51.
7   Tardif, *John Bowen's Hobart*, p. 214.
8   AGL Shaw (ed.), *Van Diemen's Land: Copies of All Correspondence ...*, THRA, Hobart, 1971, pp. 53–54. Hereinafter *VDL*.
9   Cited in Tardif, *John Bowen's Hobart*, p. 219.
10 Tardif, *John Bowen's Hobart*, p. 218.
11 Tardif, *John Bowen's Hobart*, p. 220.
12 Tardif, *John Bowen's Hobart*, p. 73.
13 Cited in Tardif, *John Bowen's Hobart*, p. 147.
14 WC Wentworth, *Statistical, Historical and Political Description of the Colony of New South Wales*, Griffin Press, Adelaide, 1978 (first published 1819), pp. 116–17.
15 GT Lloyd, *Thirty-three Years in Tasmania and Victoria: Being the Actual Experience of the Author Interspersed with Historic Jottings, Narratives, and Counsel to Emigrants*, Heulston & Wright, London, 1862, p. 55.
16 JP Fawkner, *Reminiscences of Early Hobart Town, 1804–1810*, edited by J Currey, Colony Press for the Banks Society, Melbourne, 2007, p. 25.
17 Cited in G Calder, *Levée, Line and Martial Law: A History of the Dispossession of the Mairremmener People of Van Diemen's Land 1803–1832*, Fullers Bookshop, Hobart, 2010, p. 240.

Chapter 4: Coming of age
1   Plomley, *FM*, journal, 8 April 1834, pp. 908–909; 'Nomad', *Merriam-Webster Dictionary*, <merriam-webster.com/dictionary/nomads>, accessed 2020.
2   C Dyer, *The French Explorers and the Aboriginal Australians 1772–1839*, UQP, Brisbane, 2005, p. 151.
3   For example, Plomley, *FM*, journal, 19 and 30 September 1829, 1 January and 15 November 1830, 1 and 9 August 1831, 27 August 1832, 17 June 1833, 5 and 14 January 1834.
4   Our best source for gauging the health of Tasmanians during Tongerlongeter's youth are the French explorers, especially the Baudin expedition. Baudin visited Maria Island in 1802 when Tongerlongeter's

band was present and he was a boy of about twelve (Plomley, *FM*, journal, 19 November 1831). Notwithstanding their Eurocentric prejudices, these observers were impressed with the health of the Tasmanians (see Dyer, *French Explorers*).

5 For example, Calder, *Levée, Line and Martial Law*, pp. 77–81; Plomley, *FM*, journal, 3 September 1829, 27 August 1832; Arthur to Buxton, 31 January 1835, TAHO, GO52/1/6, p. 248.

6 Robinson and the French explorers provide the best evidence of these attributes. See Plomley, *FM*; Plomley, *WiS*; Dyer's *French Explorers*.

7 For example, Smith to Burnett, 22 November 1830, TAHO, CSO1/320, p. 108; *Hobart Town Courier*, 4 April 1829, pp. 2–3; HS Melville, *The History of Van Diemen's Land from the Year 1824 to 1835 inclusive*, edited by G Mackaness, Libraries Board of South Australia, Adelaide, 1967 (first published 1835), pp. 78–79; G Lehman, 'Regarding the savages: visual representation of Tasmanian Aborigines in the 19th century', PhD thesis, School of Humanities, University of Tasmania, 2016, p. 111.

8 For example, GW Walker, J Backhouse & C Tylor, *The Life and Labours of George Washington Walker*, Bennett & Brady, London, 1862, pp. 101–102; JB Walker, *Early Tasmania: Papers Read Before the Royal Society of Tasmania During the Years 1888 to 1899*, MC Reed, Government Printer, Hobart, 1899, pp. 247–48; West, *History of Tasmania*, vol. II, p. 82; RH Davies, 'On the Aborigines of Van Diemen's Land', *Tasmanian Journal of Natural Science*, 1846, vol. 2, p. 419; Plomley, *FM*, journal, 4 September 1832.

9 R Cosgrove, 'Late Pleistocene behavioural variation and time trends: the case from Tasmania', *Archaeology in Oceania*, 1995, vol. 30, no. 3, p. 97; J Chappell & K Lambeck, 'Sea level change through the last glacial cycle', *Science*, 2001, vol. 292, pp. 684–85.

10 D Bunce & L Leichhardt, *Australasiatic reminiscences of twenty-three years' wanderings in Tasmania and the Australasias*, JT Hendry, London, 1857, p. 54.

11 Plomley, *FM*, journal, 25 October 1830, 11 January 1831; NJB Plomley & QVMAG, *The Tasmanian Tribes and Cicatrices as Tribal Indicators Among the Tasmanian Aborigines*, QVMAG, Launceston, 1992, pp. 25–27.

12 Plomley, *FM*, journal, 15 January 1831.

13 Plomley, *FM*, journal, 12 and 15 December 1831; Clark to Burnett, 29 October 1830, TAHO, CSO1/316, pp. 706–11; A Sagona, *Bruising the Red Earth: Ochre Mining and Ritual in Aboriginal Tasmania*, Melbourne University Press, Melbourne, 1994.

14 C Bowern, 'The riddle of Tasmanian languages', *Proceedings of the Royal Society B*, 2012, vol. 279, pp. 4590–95.

15 Brodribb to Aborigines Committee, 11 March 1830, in Shaw, *VDL*, pp. 105–107; Clark to Aborigines Committee, 15 March 1830, TAHO, CSO1/323, p. 324; B Brimfield, 'Palaeo-Tasmanian roads (foot-tracks)', unpublished essay, 2011, NLA ID 6574576; B Brimfield, 2015, 'Food,

foraging and cooking in palaeo-Tasmanian Aboriginal culture, Section 1,
unpublished essay, NLA ID 6813020.

16 For example, W Parramore, *The Parramore Letters: Letters from William
Thomas Parramore, Sometime Private Secretary to Lieutenant Governor
Arthur of Van Diemen's Land, to Thirza Cropper, His Fiancée in Europe and
England, the Majority from 1823–1825*, edited by DC Shelton, Shelton,
Epping Forest, Tasmania, 1993, pp. 30–31; J Holman, *Travels in China,
New Zealand, New South Wales, Van Diemen's Land*, Smith, Elder & Co.,
London, 1840, pp. 405–406.

17 B Gammage, *The Biggest Estate on Earth: How Aborigines Made Australia*,
Allen & Unwin, Sydney, 2011; B Brimfield, 'Terrestrial fauna, food and the
palaeo-Tasmanian Aborigines', unpublished essay, 2014.

18 Walker, *Early Tasmania*, p. 248; Walker, Backhouse & Tylor, *Life and
Labours*, pp. 105–106.

19 NJB Plomley (ed.), *The Westlake Papers: Records of Interviews in Tasmania
by Ernest Westlake, 1908–1910*, QVMAG, Launceston, 1991, pp. 22–23;
J Bonwick, *The Daily Life and Origins of the Tasmanians*, Sampson Low,
London, 1870, p. 11; Brimfield, 'Food, foraging and cooking', Section 1,
pp. 18–20.

20 R Jones, 'Tasmanian tribes', in NB Tindale, *Aboriginal Tribes of Australia:
Their Terrain, Environmental Controls, Distribution, Limits and Proper
Names*, ANU Press, Canberra, 1974, p. 340; R Jones, 'Hunting forebears',
in M Roe (ed.), *The Flow of Culture: Tasmanian Studies*, Australian
Academy of the Humanities, Canberra, 1987, pp. 27–28; NJB Plomley,
The Tasmanian Aborigines, Plomley Foundation, Launceston, 1993 (first
published 1977), p. 47.

21 Plomley, *FM*, p. 727.

22 Plomley, *FM*, journal, 20 June and 21 July 1831.

23 J Backhouse, *A Narrative of a Visit to the Australian Colonies*, Hamilton,
Adams & Co., London, 1843, pp. 104–105; Brimfield, 'Food, foraging and
cooking', Section 1, pp. 18–20.

24 West, *History of Tasmania*, vol. II, p. 82.

25 Plomley, *FM*, journal, 22 August 1831; Tyrell to Anstey, 15 January 1830,
TAHO, CSO1/320, p. 405.

26 W Crowther, 'Notes on the habits of the extinct Tasmanian race. Number
2', *Papers and Proceedings of the Royal Society of Tasmania*, 1926, p. 165, cited
in Brimfield, 'Food, foraging and cooking', Section 1, p. 19.

27 Plomley, *FM*, journal, 15 July 1834; NJB Plomley (ed.), *Jorgen Jorgenson
and the Aborigines of Van Diemen's Land: Being a Reconstruction of His 'Lost'
Book on Their Customs and Habits*, Blubber Head Press, Hobart, 1991,
p. 68; Brown to Mulgrave, 28 February, TAHO, CSO1/323, pp. 117–51;
Clark to Burnett, 29 October 1830, TAHO, CSO1/316, pp. 706–11.

28 HL Roth, *The Aborigines of Tasmania*, F King & Sons, Halifax, UK, 1899
(first published 1890), p. 54; Brown to Mulgrave, 5 February 1830, TAHO,
CSO1/323, pp. 137–39.

29   P Sims, 'No reprieve for Tasmanian rock art', *Arts*, 2013, vol. 2, pp. 182–
      224; Tyrell to Anstey, 15 January 1830, TAHO, CSO1/320, p. 405;
      Plomley, *FM*, journal, 4 November 1831; Walker, *Early Tasmania*,
      pp. 244–45; Backhouse, *A Narrative*, p. 105; Plomley, *Tasmanian
      Aborigines*, pp. 2, 7, 65.

30   John Lyne, unpublished reminiscences, TAHO, NS854/1/1, p. 25. See
      also Robertson to Aborigines Committee, 4 March 1830, in Shaw, *VDL*,
      p. 84.

31   Brown to Mulgrave, 5 February 1830, TAHO, CSO1/323, pp. 137–38.

32   Lloyd, *Thirty-three Years*, p. 48. See also Roth, *Aborigines of Tasmania*, p. 54.

33   Plomley, *FM*, journal, 16 June and 15 August 1831; Lloyd, *Thirty-three
      Years*, p. 48. See also Roth, *Aborigines of Tasmania*, p. 549; Davies, 'On the
      Aborigines', p. 418; A Schayer, *La Terre Van-Diemen*, publisher unknown,
      Berlin, 1836, pp. 14–15.

34   Lloyd, *Thirty-three Years*, pp. 51–52. Lloyd's 'stinging-rays' were probably
      skates.

35   J Milligan, 'On the dialects and language of the Aboriginal tribes of
      Tasmania, and on their manners and customs', *Papers and Proceedings of the
      Royal Society of Van Diemen's Land*, 1855, vol. 3, p. 274.

36   Plomley, *FM*, journal, 13 March 1834.

37   Plomley, *FM*, journal, 27 June 1831.

38   Plomley, *FM*, journal, 13 March 1834.

39   Plomley, *FM*, journal, 3 November 1831.

40   KM Bowden, *Captain James Kelly of Hobart Town*, Melbourne University
      Press, Melbourne, 1964, pp. 35–44; Plomley, *FM*, journal, 24 March 1830;
      Roth, *Aborigines of Tasmania*, p. 136.

41   Plomley, *FM*, journal, 24 December 1831.

42   Plomley, *FM*, journal, 9 and 28 November 1831.

43   B Brimfield, 'Mystic beliefs of the Tasmanian Aborigines', unpublished
      essay, 2015, NLA ID, 8055225, pp. 52–53; Plomley, *FM*, journal,
      18 August 1831; DR Horton, 'Tasmanian adaptation', *Mankind*, 1979,
      vol. 12, no. 1, p. 31.

44   G Robertson, journal, 13 January 1829, TAHO, CSO1/331, p. 115. See
      also *Hobart Town Courier*, 21 March 1829, p. 3.

45   Plomley, *FM*, journal, 28 April 1832; Plomley, *WiS*, p. 231; Walker, *Early
      Tasmania*, p. 251; Davies, 'On the Aborigines', p. 414; Brimfield, 'Mystic
      beliefs', pp. 114–15.

46   Backhouse, *A Narrative*, p. 171.

47   Roth, *Aborigines of Tasmania*, pp. 61–63; Plomley, *FM*, journal,
      16 December 1831.

48   Plomley, *Jorgenson*, p. 67.

49   B Brimfield, 'Disposing of the dead within Palaeo-Tasmanian Aboriginal
      society', unpublished essay, 2014, NLA ID 6574579.

50   For example, Plomley, *FM*, journal, 12 August 1831, 7 and 9 December
      1831; Backhouse, *A Narrative*, p. 181; Brimfield, 'Mystical beliefs',

pp. 39–41; *Port Phillip Herald*, 21 January 1842; T Dove, 'Moral and
social characteristics of the Aborigines of Tasmania', *Tasmanian Journal of
Natural Science, Agriculture, Statistics, &c.*, 1842, vol. 1, p. 253.

51 Cited in Roth, *Aborigines of Tasmania*, p. 54.
52 Plomley, *FM*, journal, 7 June 1829, 25 and 30 October, 14 November, and
9 and 15 December 1831, 10 May, 24 June and 29 July 1832, 24 July 1834.
See also Brimfield, 'Mystic beliefs'.
53 For example, Plomley, *FM*, journal, 19 November 1831, 24 June 1832.
See also Brimfield, 'Mystic beliefs', pp. 39–41.
54 Plomley, *FM*, journal, 16 August 1831.
55 Walker, Backhouse & Tylor, *Life and Labours*, pp. 106–107.
56 Plomley, *Jorgenson*, pp. 122–23.
57 Plomley, *FM*, journal, 7 July 1831, p. 406.
58 Roth, *Aborigines of Tasmania*, p. 55; Brown to Mulgrave, 5 February 1830,
TAHO, CSO1/323, pp. 129, 137–38; Schayer, *La Terre Van-Diemen*,
pp. 14–15; Davies, 'On the Aborigines', p. 407; J Henderson, *Observations
on the Colonies of New South Wales and Van Diemen's Land*, Baptist
Mission Press, Calcutta, 1832, p. 148; R Hare, *The Voyage of the Caroline
from England to Van Diemen's Land and Batavia in 1827–28*, Longmans,
Green & Co., London, 1927, p. 41; Robertson to Aborigines Committee,
4 March 1830, and Hobbs to Aborigines Committee, 9 March 1830, in
Shaw, *VDL*, pp. 48, 50; C Meredith, 'Verbal remarks on the Aborigines of
Tasmania', *Papers and Proceedings of the Royal Society of Tasmania*, 1873,
p. 28; Plomley, *FM*, journal, 3 August 1831.
59 West, *History of Tasmania*, vol. II, pp. 29–30.
60 Brown to Mulgrave, 5 February 1830, TAHO, CSO1/323, p. 140;
Plomley, *Jorgenson*, p. 67; *Colonial Times*, 19 February 1830, p. 3; Plomley,
FM, journal, 25 October 1831.
61 The evidence for initiation rituals is merely circumstantial. Still, it would
be surprising if these secret rites of passage, well attested throughout the
rest of Australia, were not present in Tasmania. See J Clark, 'Devils and
horses: religious and creative life in Tasmanian Aboriginal society', in Roe,
The Flow of Culture, 1987, pp. 50–72; Lloyd, *Thirty-three Years*, p. 49.
62 Robinson's journals provide ample evidence of these practices (see Plomley,
FM).
63 Plomley & QVMAG, *The Tasmanian Tribes and Cicatrices*. These 'tattoos',
often representations of the sun and moon, were also thought to have
healing powers (Plomley, *FM*, journal, 25 October 1830).
64 Plomley, *FM*, journal, 28 September 1829.
65 Plomley, *WiS*, journal, 19 December 1835.
66 This was apparent towards the end of the war, when the chiefs quickly
remarried, but it was also stated explicitly by Kickertopoller, a Poredareme
man (Plomley, *FM*, journal, 25 October 1830).
67 Lloyd, *Thirty-three Years*, p. 45.

68   Plomley, *FM*, journal, 26 September 1830; Roth, *Aborigines of Tasmania*,
      pp. 68–72. Spears were generally made from *Leptospermum* (tea-tree)
      (Jones, 'Hunting forebears', pp. 27–28).
69   Plomley, *FM*, journal, 27 August 1832; Plomley, *Tasmanian Aborigines*,
      p. 47.
70   For example, Plomley, *FM*, p. 948; West, *History of Tasmania*, vol. II, p. 84.
71   Walker, Backhouse & Tylor, *Life and Labours*, pp. 46–47.
72   Plomley, *FM*, journal, 23 September 1830. See also Tyrell to Anstey,
      15 January 1830, TAHO, CSO1/320, p. 405.
73   Horton to Wesleyan Mission Society (London), 3 June 1823, Bonwick
      transcripts, ML, SLNSW, BT52, pp. 1268–74.
74   For example, Walker, Backhouse & Tylor, *Life and Labours*, pp. 46–47;
      Plomley, *FM*, journal, 1 May 1829, 28 November 1831; Plomley,
      Tasmanian Aborigines, p. 48; Roth, *Aborigines of Tasmania*, pp. 70–72.
75   For example, *Hobart Town Courier*, 24 November 1827, p. 2; Plomley, *FM*,
      journal, 25 September 1830, 25 November 1831.
76   Plomley, *FM*, journal, 15 August 1831.
77   Walker, Backhouse & Tylor, *Life and Labours*, pp. 100–101; Plomley, *FM*,
      journal 31 May 1830, 23 October and 1 November 1831.
78   Lloyd, *Thirty-three Years*, pp. 45–46.
79   Roth, *Aborigines of Tasmania*, pp. 98–101. Women and children were
      sometimes used in these efforts.
80   Plomley, *FM*, journal, 19 December 1831.
81   S Morgan, *Land Settlement in Early Van Diemen's Land: Creating an
      Antipodean England*, Cambridge University Press, Melbourne, 1992,
      p. 114.
82   Plomley, *FM*, journal, 29 March, 18 October and 2 November 1830; DJ
      Mulvaney & J Kamminga, *Prehistory of Australia*, Allen & Unwin, Sydney,
      1999, p. 344.
83   Plomley, *FM*, journal, 2 September 1833; HJ Emmett, 'Reminiscences
      of the Black War. Period 1803. By a Leader', 1873, TAHO, NG1216,
      pp. 1–2.
84   Chappell & Lambeck, 'Sea level change', pp. 684–85. Roughly 14 000 years
      ago was when the rising sea level flooded the Bassian Plain enough to make
      it uncrossable. Today, the treacherous, 250 kilometre wide body of water
      between Tasmania and mainland Australia is known as Bass Strait.
85   Clark to Burnett, 29 October 1830, TAHO, CSO1/316, pp. 706–11;
      Plomley, *FM*, journal, 1 August and 12 December 1831.
86   Plomley, *Tasmanian Aborigines*, p. 67; Plomley, *FM*, journal, 25 October
      1830; Walker, Backhouse & Tylor, *Life and Labours*, pp. 101–102; West,
      History of Tasmania, vol. II, p. 82; Lloyd, *Thirty-three Years*, p. 49.
87   Roth, *Aborigines of Tasmania*, pp. 72–73.
88   Plomley, *FM*, journal, 25 October 1830.
89   Plomley, *FM*, journal, 11 January 1831. See also journal, 25 September
      1830, 9 January and 15 December 1831.

90 J Taylor, *A Study of the Palawa (Tasmanian Aboriginal) Place Names*, University of Tasmania, Launceston, 2006, pp. 55, 65, 73; Milligan, 'On the dialects', p. 281.

91 Plomley, *FM*, journal, 19 June 1834. See also journal, 25 October 1830.

92 For example, Plomley, *FM*, journal, 13 August and 15 December 1831.

93 For example, Plomley, *FM*, journal, 5 September 1831; Bowden, *Captain James Kelly*, p. 43.

94 The north-east chief, Mannalargenna, is a good example of this (Plomley, *FM*, journal, 1, 13 and 30 August 1831).

95 For example, Calder, *Some Account*, p. 33.

96 Plomley, *FM*, journal, 23 October 1831.

97 Plomley, *FM*, journal, 15 December 1831. See also journal, 31 May and 25 October 1830.

98 Plomley, *FM*, journal, 27 October 1831.

99 Roth, *Aborigines of Tasmania*, pp. 139–40.

100 Plomley, *FM*, journal, 1 November 1831, 11 April 1832.

101 For example, West, *History of Tasmania*, vol. II, p. 30; B Thomas, *Henry Hellyer's Observations: Journals of Life in the Tasmanian Bush 1826–1827*, North Down Press, Latrobe, Tasmania, 2011, pp. 23–24; Simpson to Burnett, 4 September 1828, TAHO, CSO1/316, p. 160; Minutes of Executive Council, 23 February 1831, in Shaw, *VDL*, p. 80.

102 Backhouse, *A Narrative*, pp. 105–106. See also Walker, *Early Tasmania*, p. 250.

103 Compare Captain James Cook's observation in 1777 (cited in GW Evans, *A Geographical, Historical, and Topographical Description of Van Diemen's Land*, John Souter, London, 1822, p. 12) to what was seen during the Black War. See also S Junger, *Tribe: On Homecoming and Belonging*, HarperCollins, London, 2016, ch. 6.

104 Davies, 'On the Aborigines', p. 418.

105 Plomley, *FM*, journal, 25 October 1830. See also journal, 3 November 1830; Robertson to Lascelles, 17 November 1828, TAHO, CSO1/331, pp. 173–74.

106 Robinson to Arthur, 20 November 1830, TAHO, CSO1/317, pp. 231–33.

Chapter 5: Zombie invasion

1 G Blainey, *Triumph of the Nomads*, Sun Australia, Sydney, 1983 (first published 1975), p. 253.

2 Plomley, *FM*, p. 489, and journal, 14 August 1831.

3 I Clark & DA Cahir, 'Understanding "Ngamadjidj": Aboriginal perceptions of Europeans in nineteenth century western Victoria', *Journal of Australian Colonial History*, 2011, vol. 13, pp. 105–24. This assumption was in fact made by Aboriginal peoples all over Australia (Reynolds, *Other Side of the Frontier*, pp. 37–42).

4 Plomley, *FM*, journal, 11 July 1831. See also journal, 7 July 1831.

5   Plomley, *FM*, journal, 31 May and 12 August 1829. Even within different language groups, variants of this term appear to have been common. See, for example, Smith to Mulgrave, 26 June 1827, TAHO, CSO1/316, pp. 22–27.

6   Backhouse, *A Narrative*, pp. 181–82; Plomley, *WiS*, p. 267; Roth, *The Aborigines of Tasmania*, p. 56; Walker, Backhouse & Tylor, *Life and Labours*, pp. 106–107; Bonwick, *Last of the Tasmanians*, p. 71.

7   Backhouse, *A Narrative*, pp. 181–82.

8   Walker, *Early Tasmania*, pp. 249–50.

9   For example, Plomley, *FM*, journal, 31 May 1829, 6 April and 21 June 1830, 24 August and 25 October 1831, 13 April 1834.

10 Plomley, *WiS*, p. 1015, appendix I.

11 For example, Plomley, *FM*, journal, 11 July 1831, p. 408; Nicholls, *The Diary*, 19 April 1807, p. 132.

12 Robinson's report, 30 April 1838, in Reynolds, *Fate of a Free People*, p. 41; Plomley, *FM*, journal, 20 March 1830.

13 *Colonial Times*, 1 December 1826, p. 2.

14 *Colonial Times*, 29 September 1826, p. 3.

15 For example, *Hobart Town Gazette*, 6 August 1824, p. 2; *Colonial Times*, 27 August 1830, p. 3; Clark to Vicary, 8 September 1830, TAHO, CSO1/316, p. 618; *Hobart Town Courier*, 13 November 1830, p. 3; *Colonial Times*, 26 November 1830, p. 3; S Kemp, 'John Leake, 1780–1865, an early settler in Tasmania', thesis, St John's College, York, UK, 1969, TAHO, NS242/1/1, pp. 17–18.

16 Plomley, *FM*, journal, 11 July 1831. See also journal, 7 July 1831.

17 Paterson to Windham, 29 August 1808, in F Watson, 1921–23, *HRA*, series III, vol. I, Library Committee of the Commonwealth Parliament, Sydney, pp. 550, 672–763; Nicholls, *The Diary*, p. 117.

18 J Boyce, *Van Diemen's Land*, Black Inc., Melbourne, 2008, p. 63.

19 Boyce, *Van Diemen's Land*, p. 49; Nicholls, *The Diary*, pp. 82–147; 'Calcutta voyage to New South Wales [Port Phillip], Australia in 1803 with 295 passengers', Convict Records, <convictrecords.com.au/ships/calcutta/1803>, accessed 17 January 2020.

20 See, for example, published proclamations and orders on 12 January 1804, 29 January 1810, 25 June 1813, 17 May 1817, 13 March 1819, in C Turnbull, *Black War: The Extermination of the Tasmanian Aborigines*, Lansdowne, Melbourne, 1974 (first published 1948), pp. 45–59.

21 For example, M Fels, 'Culture contact in the County of Buckinghamshire, Van Diemen's Land, 1803–11', *THRA Papers and Proceedings*, 1982, vol. 29, no. 2, pp. 58–59; LL Robson, *A History of Tasmania*, vol. I, *Van Diemen's Land from the Earliest Times to 1855*, Oxford University Press, Melbourne, 1983, pp. 48–49; *HRA*, series III, vol. I, pp. 576, 769; B Hamilton-Arnold, *Letters and Papers of G. P. Harris, 1803–1812: Deputy Surveyor-General of New South Wales at Sullivan Bay, Port Phillip and Hobart Town, Van Diemen's Land*, Arden Press, Sorrento, Victoria,

1994, pp. 99–100; Barnes to Aborigines Committee, 10 March 1830, TAHO, CSO1/323, p. 299; Scott to Aborigines Committee, March 1830, TAHO, CSO1/323, pp. 315–17; *Sydney Gazette*, 10 April 1813, p. 2; *Derwent Star*, 29 January 1810.

22 For example, Macquarie to Geils, 1 June 1812, *HRA*, series III, vol. I, p. 479; G Calder, 'Levée, line and martial law: a history of the dispossession of the Mairremmener people of Van Diemen's Land 1803–1832', PhD thesis, School of History and Classics, University of Tasmania, Launceston, 2009, ch. 4; Fels, 'Culture contact', pp. 47–69.

23 Nicholls, *The Diary*, pp. 1–173.

24 Hobbs to Aborigines Committee, 9 March 1830, in Shaw, *VDL*, p. 49.

25 Fels, 'Culture contact', pp. 61, 70; Hobbs to Aborigines Committee, 9 March 1830, in Shaw, *VDL*, pp. 49–50.

26 Hobbs to Aborigines Committee, 9 March 1830, in Shaw, *VDL*, pp. 49–50.

27 N Clements, *The Black War: Fear, Sex and Resistance in Tasmania*, University of Queensland Press, Brisbane, 2014, pp. 191–96.

28 Calder, 'Levée, line and martial law', pp. 132, 147.

29 R Cox, *Broken Spear: The untold story of Black Tom Birch, the man who sparked Australia's bloodiest war*, Wakefield Press, Adelaide, 2021.

30 Nicholls, *The Diary*, pp. 77–78; Fels, 'Culture contact', p. 65.

31 Stewart to Campbell, 1815, *HRA*, series III, vol. II, pp. 575–76.

32 Clements, *The Black War*, pp. 191–203.

33 Calder, 'Levée, line and martial law', pp. 61, 132–37; NJB Plomley & KA Henley, *The Sealers of Bass Strait and the Cape Barren Island Community*, Blubber Head Press, Hobart, 1990, pp. 71–88.

34 Clements, *The Black War*, pp. 197–203.

35 Backhouse, *A Narrative*, pp. 88–89. See also West, *History of Tasmania*, vol. II, p. 23; Plomley & Henley, *The Sealers*, p. 78.

36 Plomley, *FM*, journal, 6 January 1831.

37 Plomley & Henley, *The Sealers*, pp. 48, 85.

38 Plomley & Henley, *The Sealers*, pp. 39, 84.

39 G Meredith, 1824–26, 'Agreements with the crews of his sealing and whaling boats and associated papers', TAHO, NS123/1/7.

40 Plomley, *WiS*, journal, 26 December 1836, 9 January 1837, pp. 405, 414, 671, 677.

41 Plomley, *WiS*, journal, 9 May 1836; L Nyman, *The East Coasters*, TAS, Regal Publications, Launceston, 1990, p. 178; Plomley & Henley, *The Sealers*, p. 54.

42 *Hobart Town Gazette*, 28 November 1818, p. 1.

43 *Hobart Town Gazette*, 20 March 1819, p. 2.

44 *HRA*, series III, vol. II, p. 75; *HRA*, series III, vol. IV, pp. 635–36; *HRA*, series III, vol. VII, p. 285. This figure includes 2312 in the island's northern settlement and 244 convicts at Macquarie Harbour.

45 J Boyce, 'Surviving in a new land: the early European invasion of Van Diemen's Land 1803–1823', Honours thesis, School of Geography and Environmental Studies, University of Tasmania, Hobart, 1994, p. 8.

46 Nyman, *East Coasters*, pp. 12–37.
47 For example, Parramore to family, 19 November 1823, in Parramore, *Parramore Letters*, pp. 30–31; *HRA*, series III, vol. I, pp. 576, 769; Robson, *History of Tasmania*, p. 49.
48 Robertson to Aborigines Committee, 4 March 1830, in Shaw, *VDL*, p. 48.
49 A rare exception can be found in Nicholls, *The Diary*, 15 November 1818, p. 217.
50 For example, Wood to Aborigines Committee, 7 March 1830; Kelly to Aborigines Committee, 10 March 1830; Brodribb Snr to Aborigines Committee, 11 March 1830; Clark to Aborigines Committee, 15 March 1830; Evans to Aborigines Committee, 16 March 1830; Murray to Aborigines Committee, 16 March 1830; O'Connor to Aborigines Committee, 17 March 1830; Anstey to Aborigines Committee, 18 March 1830, all in Shaw, *VDL*.
51 There are several references to entire bands visiting Hobart, the first of which was in 1814. As with nearly all such visitors, they were treated badly by convicts and others who either hated them or wanted their women, resulting in the worsening of relations. See West, *History of Tasmania*, vol. II, p. 9; Bonwick, *Last of the Tasmanians*, p. 59; Plomley & Henley, *The Sealers*, p. 40.
52 Aborigines Committee Report, 19 March 1830, in Shaw, *VDL*, pp. 36–39.
53 J Boyce, 'Journeying home: a new look at the British invasion of Van Diemen's Land 1803–1823', *Island*, 1996, vol. 66, pp. 48, 51; Boyce, *Van Diemen's Land*, p. 87. See also GW Finlay, 'Always crackne in heaven', PhD thesis, School of Theology, University of Tasmania, 2015, appendix I; Plomley & Henley, *The Sealers*, pp. 25–27; Fels, 'Culture contact', p. 65.
54 Brodribb Snr to Aborigines Committee, 11 March 1830, in Shaw, *VDL*, p. 52.
55 Horton to Wesleyan Mission Society, London, 3 June 1823, Bonwick transcripts, ML, SLNSW, BT52, pp. 1268–74. Other examples include Turner to Wesleyan Mission Society, London, 22 November 1822, Bonwick transcripts, ML, SLNSW, BT52, pp. 1205–206; Parramore to family, 19 November 1823, in Parramore, *Parramore Letters*, pp. 30–31.
56 *Hobart Town Gazette*, 18 April 1818, p. 2.
57 *Sydney Gazette*, 18 July 1818, p. 3.
58 *Hobart Town Gazette*, 14 November 1818, p. 1.
59 *Hobart Town Gazette*, 26 December 1818, supplement, p. 1.
60 Bonwick, *Lost Tasmanian race*, p. 77.
61 Horton to Wesleyan Mission Society, London, 3 June 1823, Bonwick transcripts, ML, SLNSW, BT52, pp. 1268–74.
62 *Hobart Town Gazette*, 28 November 1818, p. 1.

Chapter 6: A wayward brother
1 Plomley, *FM*, journals 25 October 1830, 3 November 1831.
2 Luttrell to Bigge, 26 May 1820, and Sorell to Luttrell, 7 December 1819, *HRA*, series III, vol. III, pp. 501, 748.

3 Sorell to Luttrell, 31 December 1819, *HRA*, series III, vol. II, p. 754. The room was a disused mill hired for 10 shillings per week, which equates to a mere $115 today (D Hutchinson & F Ploeckl, 'Five ways to compute the relative value of Australian amounts, 1828 to the present', <MeasuringWorth.com>, 2019, <measuringworth.com/australiacompare>, accessed 19 December 2019).

4 Robson, *A History of Tasmania*, p. 49.

5 Van Diemen's Land governor William Sorell repeatedly expressed frustration with Luttrell's insolence, incompetence and laziness (see *HRA*, series III, vols II, III).

6 Nicholls, *The Diary*, p. 300.

7 Finlay, 'Always Crackne in Heaven', appendix 1; *HRA*, series III, vol. III, p. 365.

8 Bonwick, *Last of the Tasmanians*, pp. 95–96. Regarding language fluency, see also A Laing, 'The Alexander Laing story 1819–1838', n.d., TAHO, NS1116/1/1, p. 56. Regarding the status of the Birches, see Sorell to Macquarie, 3 May 1817, *HRA*, series III, vol. IV, p. 196.

9 Laing, 'The Alexander Laing story', p. 56.

10 Cox, *Broken Spear*.

11 Cited in Bonwick, *Last of the Tasmanians*, pp. 95–96.

12 Cox, *Broken Spear*.

13 Batman to Aborigines Committee, 1 April 1834, TAHO, CSO1/327, p. 129; O'Connor to Parramore, 11 December 1827, TAHO, CSO1/323, pp. 63–75.

14 Plomley, *FM*, p. 121.

15 For example, *Colonial Times*, 1 December 1826, p. 3.

16 Horton to Wesleyan Mission Society, London, 3 June 1823, Bonwick transcripts, ML, SLNSW, BT52, pp. 1268–74.

17 For example, J Ross, *Dr Ross's Recollections of a Short Excursion to Lake Echo 1823*, Sullivans Cove, Hobart, 1992 (first published 1830), pp. 31–35; Parramore to family, 19 November 1823, in Parramore, *Parramore Letters*, pp. 30–31.

18 Horton to Wesleyan Mission Society, London, 3 June 1823, Bonwick transcripts, ML, SLNSW, BT52, pp. 1268–74. See also evidence presented to the Aborigines Committee, in Shaw, *VDL*, pp. 47–55.

19 For example, Horton to Wesleyan Mission Society, London, 3 June 1823, Bonwick transcripts, ML, SLNSW, BT52, pp. 1268–74; Ross, *Recollections*, pp. 31–32.

20 For example, *Sydney Gazette*, 22 April 1824; *Hobart Town Gazette*, 6 August and 16 July 1824; R Jones to Anstey, 15 March 1830, TAHO, CSO1/323, p. 191; JH Wedge, 'Autobiography', unpublished manuscript, ML, SLNSW, A576, CY2802, p. 7; West, *A History of Tasmania*, vol. II, p. 13.

21 N Parry, '"Hanging no good for blackfellow": looking into the life of Musquito', in I Macfarlane & M Hannah (eds), *Transgressions: Critical*

Australian Indigenous Histories, ANU E-Press and Aboriginal History Inc., Canberra, 2007, p. 159.

22   Plomley, *WiS*, journal, 2 October 1837; West, *A History of Tasmania*, vol. II, pp. 12–13.

23   Bonwick, *Last of the Tasmanians*, p. 95.

24   What's more, in 1823 Musquito twice told colonists he was more sophisticated than the 'local blackfellows'. See Horton to Wesleyan Mission Society, London, 3 June 1823, Bonwick transcripts, ML, SLNSW, BT52, pp. 1268–74; L Meredith, *My Home in Tasmania*, Bunce, New York, 1853, p. 139. Citations from Louisa Meredith's reminiscences used in this book are from a section in which she claimed to be quoting 'either from Mr. [Charles] Meredith's own notes, written at my request, or from my own transcriptions of his narratives as related to me'. Charles Meredith experienced the settlement of Oyster Bay from 1821.

25   *Hobart Town Gazette*, 16 July 1824, p. 2; Robertson to Aborigines Committee, 4 March 1830, in Shaw, *VDL*, pp. 47–49.

26   Morgan, *Land Settlement*, ch. 1.

27   Meredith, *My Home*, p. 138. The other key source for this event is the testimony of the surviving colonist, John Radford (cited in *Hobart Town Gazette*, 3 December 1824, p. 3).

28   Calder, 'Levée, line and martial law', p. 167.

29   Radford told the police about sixty-five (*Hobart Town Gazette*, 3 December 1824, p. 3), but he told his neighbour, George Meredith, about seventy-five (Meredith, *My Home*, p. 139).

30   Calder, *Some Account*, p. 48; *Hobart Town Gazette*, 3 December 1824, p. 3.

31   Statement of Thomas McMinn, 16 March 1830, TAHO, CSO1/323, p. 197.

32   'R. v. Musquito and Black Jack, 1824', Decisions of the Nineteenth Century Tasmanian Superior Courts, Division of Law, Macquarie University and the School of History and Classics, University of Tasmania, 2011, <law.mq.edu. au/research/colonial_case_law/tas/cases/case_index/1824/r_v_musquito_ and_black_jack>, accessed 16 October 2018.

33   Melville, *History of Van Diemen's Land*, p. 40. Italics in original.

34   Plomley, *FM*, journal, 13 January 1831.

35   Calder, *Some Account*, p. 51. See also *Hobart Town Gazette*, 3 December 1824, p. 3.

36   *Hobart Town Gazette*, 4 February 1826, p. 2. See also *Launceston Examiner*, 2 October 1847, pp. 4–5; M Steel to J Steel, 24 May 1826, TAHO, NS1480/1/3; Wentworth, *A Statistical, Historical and Political Survey*, p. 115; Emmett, 'Reminiscences', p. 1.

37   For example, O'Connor to Parramore, 11 December 1827, TAHO, CSO1/323, pp. 63–75; R Cox, 'Black Tom Birch: fact and fiction', *Papers and Proceedings of the Tasmanian Historical Research Association*, 2013, vol. 60, no. 1, p. 9.

38   Diary of Adam Amos, 20 November 1823, TAHO, NS323/1/1; Meredith, *My Home*, pp. 141–42.

39 Diary of Adam Amos, TAHO, NS323/1/1.
40 Diary of Adam Amos, 13–15 December 1823, 10 January, and 9, 21, 25, 28 and 29 March 1824, TAHO, NS323/1/1.
41 Bonwick, *Last of the Tasmanians*, p. 99.
42 Bonwick, *Lost Tasmanian Race*, pp. 79–80.
43 Cox, *Broken Spear*; Bonwick, *Lost Tasmanian Race*, pp. 79–80; O'Connor to Parramore, 11 December 1827, TAHO, CSO1/323, pp. 63–75.
44 Diary of Adam Amos, 24 January 1824, TAHO, NS323/1/1.
45 Diary of Adam Amos, 9 and 15 March 1824, TAHO, NS323/1/1; Hutchinson & Ploeckl, 'Five ways to compute', <measuringworth.com/australiacompare>, accessed 9 June 2020.
46 Clements online compendium, <https://dx.doi.org/10.25959/hpxk-5f95>.
47 Parry, 'Hanging no good for blackfellow'; Cox, 'Black Tom Birch'; M Powell, *Musquito: Brutality and Exile: Aboriginal Resistance in New South Wales and Van Diemen's Land*, Fullers Bookshop, Hobart, 2016, p. 120.
48 *Hobart Town Gazette*, 16 July 1824, p. 2.
49 Cox, *Broken Spear*.
50 *Hobart Town Gazette*, 30 July 1824, p. 2.
51 Cox, *Broken Spear*.
52 West, *A History of Tasmania*, vol. II, p. 14; *Hobart Town Gazette*, 20 August 1824, p. 2.
53 Knopwood, diary entry, 13 August 1824, in Nicholls, *The Diary*, p. 429.
54 While the sources do not state it explicitly, Powell (*Musquito*, p. 164) makes the reasonable inference that the group was an 'entirely male warrior assemblage'.
55 Franks to Aborigines Committee, 10 March 1830, TAHO, CSO1/323, p. 307.
56 Sources recounting the visit include Plomley, *FM*, journal, 3 November 1824; Government and General Order, 4 November 1824, and Arthur to Murray, 20 November 1830, in Shaw, *VDL*, pp. 19, 55–57; Franks to Aborigines Committee, 10 March 1830, TAHO, CSO1/323, p. 307; *Hobart Town Gazette*, 5 November 1824, p. 2; Parramore to Cropper, 2 December 1824, in Parramore, *Parramore Letters*, pp. 60–61; West, *History of Tasmania*, vol. II, pp. 15–16; J George, 'Extracts from a diary belonging to James George'. *Oatlands District Historical Society Chronicle*, 2000–2014.
57 Parramore to Cropper, 2 December 1824, in Parramore, *Parramore Letters*, pp. 60–61; Arthur to Murray, 20 November 1830, in Shaw, *VDL*, pp. 55–57; Powell, *Musquito*, pp. 164–65.
58 Powell, *Musquito*, p. 164.
59 Arthur to Murray, 20 November 1830 in Shaw, *VDL*, pp. 55–57; Arthur to Paton, November 1824, TAHO, GO52/1/2.
60 Bonwick, *Last of the Tasmanians*, pp. 103–104. Bonwick's source appears to have been Dr George Story.

61 Emigration Letter no. 10, 2 December 1824, in Parramore, *Parramore Letters*, pp. 60–61; West, *History of Tasmania*, vol. II, p. 15.

62 Diary of John Hudspeth, Royal Society of Tasmania Archives, University of Tasmania, 8/RS/1901/034, in Cox, *Broken Spear*; *Hobart Town Gazette*, 24 December 1824, p. 2.

63 George,'Extracts from a diary'; Plomley, *Jorgenson*, p. 74. In original, bloody is written as 'b____y'.

64 Bonwick, *Last of the Tasmanians*, p. 103.

65 C Rowcroft, *Tales of the Colonies; Or, the Adventures of an Emigrant*, Smith, Elder & Co., London, 1845, p. 447.

66 See, in particular, the timing and location of attacks between 1823 and 1826 (Clements online compendium, <https://dx.doi.org/10.25959/hpxk-5f95>), the reports describing these attacks (especially TAHO, CSO1/316), and various comments in Robinson's journal (especially late 1831).

67 Robertson to Aborigines Committee, 4 March 1830, in Shaw, *VDL*, pp. 47–49. See also West, *History of Tasmania*, vol. II, p. 19; Plomley, *Jorgenson*, p. 96. Jorgenson said Tongerlongeter's brother was Black Jack, but Robertson was in the better position to specify which of the executed men was the chief's sibling.

68 The stockman in question was Thomas Colley, who had previously flogged Jack with a bullock whip (Plomley, *FM*, journal, 13 January 1831).

69 *Colonial Times*, 5 May 1826, p. 3, 15 September 1826, p. 3.

70 *Colonial Times*, 15 September 1826, p. 3.

71 *Hobart Town Gazette*, 16 September 1826, Supplement, p. 1.

72 JH Wedge,'Autobiography', p. 7. See also *Colonial Times*, 2 June 1826, p. 3.

73 Robertson to Aborigines Committee, 4 March 1830, in Shaw, *VDL*, pp. 47–49. See also *Hobart Town Gazette*, 16 July 1824, p. 2; *Colonial Times*, 19 January 1827, p. 3.

74 For example, Bedford to Aborigines Committee, 11 March 1830, in Shaw, *VDL*, p. 51. Town visits and non-violent frontier contact essentially ceased from this point on.

75 *Hobart Town Gazette*, 16 July 1824, p. 2; *Colonial Times*, 19 January 1827, p. 3.

76 Robertson to Lascelles, 17 November 1828, TAHO, CSO1/331, pp. 168–77.

77 Robertson to Aborigines Committee, 4 March 1830, in Shaw, *VDL*, pp. 47–49. See also *Hobart Town Gazette*, 16 July 1824, p. 2; *Colonial Times*, 19 January 1827, p. 3.

78 Calder, *Some Account*, pp. 45–46. See also Bedford to Aborigines Committee, 11 March 1830, in Shaw, *VDL*, p. 51.

79 *Colonial Times*, 1 December 1826, p. 3.

Chapter 7: Retribution: 1824–27

1 Quotation from Roderick O'Connor, midlands settler and lands commissioner, in West, *History of Tasmania*, vol. II, p. 20.

2   K Windschuttle, *The Fabrication of Aboriginal History*, vol. 1, *Van Diemen's Land 1803–1847*, Macleay Press, Sydney, 2002, ch. 3.
3   Plomley, *FM*, journal, 23 November 1829.
4   For example, Plomley, *Jorgenson*, pp. 63, 114; 'Address from inhabitants of the Clyde', 27 February 1830, TAHO, CSO1/316, pp. 438–43; Pearson to Aborigines Committee, 13 June 1830, TAHO, CSO1/323, pp. 380–81; 'Testimony of John Sherwin', 23 January 1830, TAHO, CSO1/316, pp. 430–33; *Colonial Times*, 10 November 1826, pp. 2–3.
5   For example, Minutes of Executive Council, 23 February 1831, in Shaw, *VDL*, p. 81; O'Connor to Aborigines Committee, 17 March 1830, in Shaw, *VDL*, pp. 54–55; Plomley, *FM*, journal, 23 November 1829; *Colonial Times*, 3 September 1830, p. 3; Evans, *A Geographical, Historical, and Topographical Description*, p. 14; A McKay (ed.), *Journals of the Land Commissioners for Van Diemen's Land, 1826–28*, University of Tasmania and THRA, Hobart, 1962, p. 80.
6   Clements online compendium, <https://dx.doi.org/10.25959/hpxk-5f95>. Most of these captives soon escaped.
7   For a full discussion of the nature of the evidence regarding the Aboriginal death toll, see Clements, 'Frontier conflict', pp. 323–31.
8   *Colonial Times*, 14 April and 2 June 1826; Aubin to Burnett, 17 January 1831, TAHO, CSO1/316, p. 840; Bonwick, *Last of the Tasmanians*, p. 117.
9   *Colonial Times*, 5 May 1826, p. 3; Dumaresq to Burnett, 6 January 1831, TAHO, CSO1/316, p. 792.
10   *Hobart Town Gazette*, 11 November 1826, p. 2.
11   For example, Plomley, *FM*, journal, 7 July and 29 August 1831, pp. 405, 447; Robinson's report, 25 January 1832, in Plomley, *FM*, pp. 602–603; Robinson to Burnett, 11 October 1831, in Plomley, *FM*, p. 504; Robinson to Burnett, 5 January 1832, TAHO, CSO1/318, p. 132; Kelly to Aborigines Committee, 10 March 1830, in Shaw, *VDL*, p. 51; Aborigines Committee Report, 19 March 1830, in Shaw, *VDL*, pp. 35–46; Arthur to Goderich, 10 January 1828, in Shaw, *VDL*, pp. 3–4; Arthur to Murray, 20 November 1830, in Shaw, *VDL*, pp. 57–61; *Colonial Times*, 5 April 1836, p. 5.
12   Clements, 'Frontier conflict', pp. 340–41.
13   P Fenton, *James Fenton of Forth: A Tasmanian Pioneer 1820–1901: A Collection of Essays by and About James Fenton (1820–1901) His Family and Friends*, Educare, Melbourne, 2001, p. 201.
14   Plomley, *FM*, journal, 14 December 1829.
15   Robinson mentions the practice of chaining, beating and raping Aboriginal women in several places (for example, *FM*, journal, 24 December 1829, 28 April 1831). And Robinson was certainly not the only contemporary to discuss such cases. See, for example, *Hobart Town Gazette*, 17 April 1819, 14 and 21 October 1826; Aborigines Committee Report, 19 March 1830, in Shaw, *VDL*, p. 39; J George, 'Extracts from a diary'; TWH Leavitt & J Fenton, *The Jubilee History of Tasmania Illustrated: with Which Is*

Incorporated the Early History of Victoria, Biographical Sketches, & Australian Representative Men, Wells & Leavitt, Melbourne, 1881, pp. 53–54; HW Parker, *The Rise, Progress, and Present State of Van Diemen's Land with Advice to Emigrants*, J Cross, London, 1836, p. 29; Bonwick, *Last of the Tasmanians*, pp. 60–61.

16   Clements, *The Black War*, pp. 197–203.

17   Plomley, *FM*, journal, 13 September 1830.

18   Plomley, *FM*, journal, 22 April 1831. See also journal, 28 April 1831, 29 March 1832.

19   Plomley, *FM*, journal, 7 July 1831, p. 405. See also Simpson to Burnett, 8 March 1831, TAHO, CSO1/316, p. 890; *Hobart Town Courier*, 26 March 1831, p. 3.

20   For example, *Colonial Advocate*, 1 July 1828, pp. 14–18; Dry to Aborigines Committee, 7 March 1830, TAHO, CSO1/323, p. 289; Bonwick, *Last of the Tasmanians*, pp. 60–62.

21   Ross, *Dr Ross's Recollections*, pp. 41–42.

22   Clark to Aborigines Committee, 15 March 1830, TAHO, CSO1/323, p. 320.

23   Plomley, *FM*, journal, 24 September 1830, p. 253.

24   Clements online compendium, <https://dx.doi.org/10.25959/hpxk-5f95>.

25   Clements online compendium, <https://dx.doi.org/10.25959/hpxk-5f95>.

26   *Colonial Times*, 10 November 1826, pp. 2–3.

27   With the exception of the handful of Aborigines who came into colonial custody, the names of individual Aboriginal men and women were never recorded during the war.

28   Clements online compendium, <https://dx.doi.org/10.25959/hpxk-5f95>.

29   Meredith Snr to Arthur, 26 July 1824, CSO1/15, p. 212.

30   Cited in Bonwick, *Last of the Tasmanians*, p. 117. Undeterred, Buxton's house was robbed again twelve months later (Aubin to Burnett, 17 January 1831, TAHO, CSO1/316, p. 840).

31   Clements online compendium, <https://dx.doi.org/10.25959/hpxk-5f95>.

32   Amos to family in Scotland, 20 April 1826, TAHO, NS323/1/1, p. 3. Amos refers to such incidents in his diary (for example, 3 December 1823, 18 January 1824, 12 July 1824, TAHO, NS323/1/1).

33   Nyman, *East Coasters*, p. 58.

34   Clements online compendium, <https://dx.doi.org/10.25959/hpxk-5f95>.

35   Rush to Simpson, 22 June 1828, TAHO, CSO1/316, p. 141.

36   The *Colonial Times* (17 November 1826, p. 3), for instance, reported that one of these attacks comprised 300 warriors.

37   Rush to Simpson, 22 June 1828, TAHO, CSO1/316, p. 141.

38   *Hobart Town Gazette*, 18 November 1826, p. 2. See also *Colonial Times*, 17 November 1826, p. 3.

39   *Colonial Times*, 17 November 1826, p. 3.

40   *Colonial Times*, 17 November 1826, p. 3, 24 November 1826, p. 2; *Hobart Town Gazette*, p. 2, 2 December 1826, p. 4 (the latter article names

Kickertopoller among the attackers); Wells to Parramore, 25 November 1826, TAHO, CSO1/316, pp. 12–14; Dumaresq to Burnett, 6 January 1831, TAHO, CSO1/316, pp. 792–98.

41   M Steel to J Steel, 21 February 1827, in G Dow & H Dow, *Landfall in Van Diemen's Land: Steel's Quest for Greener Pastures*, Footprint, Melbourne, 1990, p. 45. See also Wells to Parramore, 25 November 1826, TAHO, CSO1/316, p. 12.

42   Wells to Parramore, 25 November 1826, TAHO, CSO1/316, p. 12.

43   *Hobart Town Gazette*, 9 December 1826, p. 2.

44   Gordon to Arthur, 9 December 1826, TAHO, CSO1/331, pp. 194–95. See also *Colonial Times*, p. 3, 15 December 1826; *Hobart Town Gazette*, p. 2, 16 December 1826; R Cox, *Baptised in Blood: The Shocking Secret History of Sorell*, Wellington Bridge Press, Hobart, 2010, p. 184.

45   *Colonial Times*, 15 December 1826, p. 3.

46   Laing, 'The Alexander Laing story', p. 56. Laing wrote this years after the fact and has some details incorrect. See also Cox, *Broken Spear*.

47   *Colonial Times*, 17 November 1826, p. 3.

48   Government Notice, 29 November 1826, in Shaw, *VDL*, p. 20. Arthur didn't mention Kickertopoller by name here, but rather the 'one or more leaders who, from their previous intercourse with Europeans, may have acquired sufficient intelligence to draw them into crime and danger'. No one else fitted the description, though, and Arthur surely knew this.

49   Bonwick, *Last of the Tasmanians*, pp. 95–97. Bonwick corresponded directly with the 'aged and very estimable' Mrs Hodgson.

50   Cox, *Broken Spear*.

51   *Colonial Times*, 20 April 1827, supplement, p. 3.

52   Cox, 'Black Tom Birch', p. 9.

53   *Colonial Times*, 29 June 1827, p. 3.

54   *Colonial Times*, 29 June 1827, p. 3.

55   *Hobart Town Courier*, 20 October 1827, p. 3, 27 October 1827, p. 1, 3 November 1827, p. 1; *Tasmanian*, 18 October 1827, p. 2.

56   *Tasmanian*, 16 November 1827, p. 3; *Hobart Town Courier*, 17 November 1827, p. 1.

57   Fereday to Colonial Secretary, 18 July 1828, TAHO, CSO1/170, p. 74.

58   Fereday to Colonial Secretary, 18 July 1828, TAHO, CSO1/170, p. 74.

59   Fereday to Colonial Secretary, 23 July 1828, TAHO, CSO1/170, p. 76.

60   *Colonial Times*, 27 July 1827, p. 3.

61   Nyman, *East Coasters*, pp. 71–72.

62   Memorial from settlers of Elizabeth and Macquarie rivers, 30 November 1827, TAHO, CSO1/316, p. 90.

63   Clements online compendium, <https://dx.doi.org/10.25959/hpxk-5f95>.

64   Plomley, *Jorgenson*, p. 114.

65   Plomley, *FM*, journal, 20 August 1830.

Chapter 8: Resistance: 1828–30

1   Lascelles to Burnett, 10 June 1829, TAHO, CSO1/316, p. 273. See also
    Clements, 'Frontier conflict', pp. 170–72, Jorgenson to Arthur, 5 January
    1828, both in Plomley, *Jorgenson*, pp. 33–37.
2   Meredith, *My Home*, p. 84. Although the author, Louisa Meredith, did not
    move to Oyster Bay until 1840, her husband, Charles, whom she claimed to
    be either quoting or paraphrasing, was one of the district's first settlers.
3   Robertson to Lascelles, 17 November 1828, TAHO, CSO1/331, p. 73.
4   Tongerlongeter was commonly referred to this way, for example, Plomley,
    FM, journal, 27 February and 3 July 1832; Plomley *WiS*, journal,
    19 December 1835, 22 June and 17 July 1837; Darling to Arthur, 4 May
    1832, in *WiS*, appendix IVa.
5   Clements online compendium, <https://dx.doi.org/10.25959/hpxk-5f95>.
6   West, *History of Tasmania*, vol. II, p. 39.
7   *Colonial Times*, 27 July 1827, p. 2.
8   West, *History of Tasmania*, vol. II, p. 22.
9   For example, Plomley, *FM*, journal, 8 and 17 November 1831; *Independent*,
    26 November 1831, p. 3; *Hobart Town Gazette*, 23 July 1824, p. 2; *Hobart
    Town Courier*, 31 January 1829, p. 2, 27 August 1831, p. 3. To this day,
    kangaroo numbers have not recovered. Tasmania's kangaroo population is
    now largely confined to the island's north-east corner and Maria Island.
10 West, *History of Tasmania*, vol. II, p. 21.
11 For example, *Colonial Times*, 15 December 1826, p. 2; *Hobart Town Courier*,
    11 December 1830, p. 2; O'Connor to Parramore, 11 December 1827,
    TAHO, CSO1/323, pp. 73–74; Plomley, *Tasmanian Aborigines*, p. ix.
12 Because a number of settlers emphasised the problem of game shortages in
    their statements, the Aborigines Committee made resolving it one of its top
    recommendations (Shaw, *VDL*, p. 44).
13 West, *History of Tasmania*, vol. II, p. 22.
14 Plomley, *Jorgenson*, p. 63. See also *Tasmanian*, 28 November 1828, p. 2.
15 TJ Maslen, *The Friend of Australia: Or, a Plan for Exploring the Interior
    and for Carrying on a Survey of the Whole Continent of Australia*, Hurst &
    Chance, London, 1830, p. 241. See also *Tasmanian*, 21 December 1827,
    p. 3.
16 *Colonial Times*, 3 September 1830, p. 3. See also Burnett to Arthur,
    15 October 1836, Arthur Papers, ML, SLNSW, A1771, vol. 28, pp. 263–
    64; O'Connor to Aborigines Committee, 17 March 1830, in Shaw, *VDL*,
    p. 55; Plomley, *FM*, journal, 8 November and 10 December 1831.
17 Testimony of Aborigines to Gilbert Robertson, cited in *Hobart Town
    Courier*, 22 November 1828, p. 2.
18 Testimony of John Sherwin, 23 February 1830, TAHO, CSO1/316,
    pp. 430–32. Our italics. 'Bugger', a common epithet at the time, was written
    prudishly in the original as 'b_g_rs'.
19 Clements, 'Frontier conflict', pp. 169–70.
20 Plomley, *FM*, journal, 14 December 1831.

21   Many dozens of references attest to this, for example Arthur memorandum, 20 November 1830, Arthur Papers, vol. 28, ML, SLNSW, A1771, p. 45; Lascelles to Burnett, 10 June 1829, TAHO, CSO1/316, pp. 271–73; J Steele to Arthur, 15 June 1829, TAHO, CSO1/316, pp. 281–84; Williams to Burnett, 2 November 1829, TAHO, CSO1/316, pp. 338–39; *Hobart Town Courier*, 28 August 1830, p. 2; *Hobart Town Courier*, 30 October 1830, p. 2.

22   Clark to Aborigines Committee, 15 March 1830, TAHO, CSO1/323, p. 321. See also Minutes of Executive Council meeting, 27 August 1830, in Shaw, *VDL*, p. 64; *Hobart Town Courier*, 28 November 1829, p. 2.

23   Anstey to Aborigines Committee, 18 March 1830, TAHO, CSO1/323, p. 343. See also Anstey to Burnett, 21 December 1830, TAHO, CSO1/316, p. 771; Hobbs to Aborigines Committee, 9 March 1830, in Shaw, *VDL*, p. 50.

24   *Colonial Times*, 1 December 1826, p. 2.

25   Clements, 'Frontier conflict', pp. 344–45.

26   Some contemporaries worried about this possibility, for example Boyes to sister, 31 October 1830, in P Chapman (ed.), *The Diaries and Letters of G. T. W. B. Boyes*, vol. 1, *1820–1832*, Oxford University Press, Melbourne, 1985, p. 378; *Hobart Town Courier*, 11 September, p. 2, and 13 November, p. 2 and 20 November 1830, p. 2.

27   For example, Arthur to Goderich, 7 January 1832, TAHO, CSO280/33, p. 9; Arthur to Buxton, 31 January 1835, TAHO, GO52/1/6, pp. 247–54.

28   Robinson to Burnett, 11 May 1838, SLNSW, Robinson Papers, A7070, vol. 49; Plomley, *FM*, journal, 1 November 1830. See also Plomley, *FM*, journal, 23 October and 17 November 1831; O'Connor to Aborigines Committee, 17 March 1830, in Shaw, *VDL*, p. 54.

29   Robinson to Burnett, 24 February 1831, TAHO, CSO1/317, pp. 275–82; Robinson's Report, February 1831, in Plomley, *FM*, p. 470; O'Connor to Aborigines Committee, 17 March 1830, in Shaw, *VDL*, p. 55.

30   Kickertopoller told Gilbert Robertson that 'Mrs Gough and her child were murdered by the Oyster Bay tribe' and this was approaching the time when there would have been only a few Oyster Bay bands left (Robertson to Lascelles, 17 November 1828, TAHO, CSO1/331, p. 73).

31   Coroner's inquest into Gough and Geary deaths, 11 October 1828, TAHO, CSO1/316, pp. 166–72.

32   Clements online compendium, <https://dx.doi.org/10.25959/hpxk-5f95>.

33   *Hobart Town Courier*, 26 September 1829, p. 2. Gough was attacked again on 23 August 1830 (Anstey to Burnett, 24 August 1830, TAHO, CSO1/316, p. 592).

34   Clements, 'Frontier conflict', p. 344.

35   Coroner's inquest into Gough and Geary deaths, 11 October 1828, TAHO, CSO1/316, pp. 166–72. According to John West (*History of Tasmania*, vol. II, p. 36), the Gough/Geary attack was revenge for the particularly grisly murder of two Aboriginal women.

36 Plomley, *FM*, journal, 23 November 1829.
37 Plomley, *FM*, journal, 11 July 1829.
38 *Tasmanian*, 12 September 1828, p. 3. See also *Hobart Town Courier*, 27 September 1828, p. 3; *Colonial Advocate*, 1 October 1828, p. 392.
39 Dalrymple to Burnett, 28 October 1828, TAHO, CSO1/316, p. 189. The war party in question appears to have attacked several nearby properties in the same week (Dalrymple to Burnett, 28 October 1828, TAHO, CSO1/316, p. 189; Aubin to Burnett, 17 January 1831, TAHO, CSO1/316, p. 840; *Tasmanian*, 12 September 1828, p. 3; *Hobart Town Courier*, 27 September 1828, p. 3; *Colonial Advocate*, 1 October 1828, p. 392).
40 Meredith, *My Home*, pp. 146–47.
41 Statement of John Rayner, 1 April 1830, TAHO, CSO1/316, pp. 486–89.
42 Meredith, *My Home*, p. 147.
43 Lord to Burnett, 1 April 1830, TAHO, CSO1/316, p. 484; Meredith, *My Home*, p. 147; *Colonial Times*, 9 April 1830, p. 3; *Hobart Town Courier*, 10 April 1830, p. 2. On 17 April, the *Hobart Town Courier* claimed its report of Rayner's death on the 10th had been a mistake, but the claim by his employer (Meredith) that he died of his wounds seems conclusive.
44 For example, Plomley, *FM*, journal, 18 December 1829; Anstey to Burnett, 21 December 1830, TAHO, CSO1/316, p. 771; *Colonial Times*, 12 November 1830, p. 3.
45 *Colonial Times*, 19 November 1830, p. 2.
46 Vicary to Burnett, 9 February 1830, TAHO, CSO1/316, p. 402. See also Plomley, *FM*, journal, 5 November 1831.
47 Coroner's Report on Mary Roberts and Thomas Clark, 4 November 1829, TAHO, CSO1/316, pp. 363–67. 'Bugger' is written 'B_____r' in the original. See also Tyrell to Anstey, 23 November 1829, TAHO, CSO1/320, p. 395. See also Plomley, *Jorgenson*, p. 72.
48 Plomley, *FM*, journal, 24 November 1831. Lest the reader mistake Montpelliatta as invariably chivalrous, it should be pointed out that Robinson attributes to him the deaths of two white women, as well as two Aboriginal women (Plomley, *FM*, journals 25 October, and 20 and 24 November 1831, 16 January 1834).

Chapter 9: Striking terror: 1828–30

1 For example, Smith to Parramore, 22 March 1830, TAHO, CSO1/316, pp. 480–82; Chadwick to Williams, 31 August 1829, TAHO, CSO1/316, pp. 296–300; *Hobart Town Gazette*, 1 April 1825, p. 3.
2 For example, Lloyd, *Thirty-three Years*, p. 45; Roth, *Aborigines of Tasmania*, pp. 68–72, 81, 98; Plomley, *Tasmanian Aborigines*, p. 47; Coroner's Report on Mary Roberts and Thomas Clark, 4 November 1829, TAHO, CSO1/316, p. 363.
3 Unsigned letter, O'Connor Papers, Connorville (private collection), item 7, miscellaneous letters folder.

4   N Clements & A Gregg, '"I am frightened out of my life": Black War, white fear', *Settler Colonial Studies*, 2015, vol. 7, no. 2, pp. 221–40; Reynolds, *Fate of a Free People*, pp. 53–86.

5   Calder, *Some Account*, p. 80.

6   *Hobart Town Courier*, 18 October 1828, pp. 2–3. See also Hudspeth to Aborigines Committee, 16 March 1830, TAHO, CSO1/323, p. 331; Plomley, *Jorgenson*, p. 23.

7   *Colonial Times*, 2 July 1830, p. 2.

8   O'Connor to Aborigines Committee, 17 March 1830, in Shaw, *VDL*, p. 54.

9   Plomley, *Jorgenson*, p. 23.

10 For example, *Hobart Town Courier*, 15 December 1827, 25 October 1828, 13 February and 11 September 1830; *Launceston Advertiser*, 19 July 1830, p. 2; Torlesse to Vicary, 15 February 1830, TAHO, CSO1/316, pp. 422–23; Anstey to Burnett, 21 December 1830, TAHO, CSO1/316, pp. 762–82.

11 For example, *Colonial Times*, 27 July 1827, p. 2; *Colonial Advocate*, 1 April 1828, p. 94; Curtin (40th Regiment) to Burnett, 5 March 1828, TAHO, CSO1/316, p. 113; *Hobart Town Courier*, 22 March 1828, p. 4; *Hobart Town Courier*, 12 April 1828, p. 2; Anstey to Burnett, 24 August 1830, TAHO, CSO1/316, pp. 591–94; Anstey to Burnett, 21 December 1830, TAHO, CSO1/316, p. 774.

12 *Hobart Town Gazette*, 29 October 1824, p. 2.

13 For example, Plomley, *FM*, journal, 8 November 1831; *Colonial Advocate*, 1 May 1828, p. 134; *Tasmanian*, 1 November 1827, p. 3; John Allen file, Glamorgan Spring Bay Historical Society archive.

14 Clements online compendium, <https://dx.doi.org/10.25959/hpxk-5f95>.

15 Young to Dumaresq, 8 June 1831, TAHO, CSO1/316, pp. 928–29.

16 Vicary to Burnett, 9 August 1830, TAHO, CSO1/316, pp. 550–58.

17 Anstey to Burnett, 24 August 1830, TAHO, CSO1/316, pp. 591–94. See also original report, Simpson to Colonial Secretary, 23 August 1830, TAHO, CSO1/316, pp. 581–95.

18 For example, *Colonial Times*, 21 September 1827, p. 3; *Colonial Times*, 6 November 1829, p. 3; *Colonial Times*, 20 November 1829, p. 3; *Hobart Town Courier*, 7 November 1829, p. 2; assorted letters, TAHO, CSO1/316, pp. 335–63, 759–70, 922.

19 Robinson to Burnett, 5 January 1832, TAHO, CSO1/318, pp. 127–33; Plomley, *WiS*, journal, 22 June 1837.

20 Plomley, *FM*, journal, 26 December 1830. See also journal, 14 February 1834.

21 Walker, *Early Tasmania*, p. 248.

22 Plomley, *FM*, journal, 2 November 1830.

23 Clark to Aborigines Committee, 15 March 1830, TAHO, CSO1/323, p. 321.

24 For example, Brown to Mulgrave, 28 February, TAHO, CSO1/323, pp. 136–37; G Hobler, *The Diaries of Pioneer George Hobler, October 6,*

1800 – December 13, 1882, C & H Reproductions Inc., Sydney, 1992, journal, 20 September 1828, p. 104; Pearson to Aborigines Committee, 13 June 1830, TAHO, CSO1/323, pp. 381–82.

25 Robertson's journal, 27 September 1829, TAHO, CSO1/331, p. 84; N Brodie, *The Vandemonian War: The Secret History of Britain's Tasmanian Invasion*, Hardie Grant, Melbourne, 2017.

26 Brown to Mulgrave, 5 February 1830, TAHO, CSO1/323, p. 136. See also *Hobart Town Gazette*, 4 February 1826, p. 2; Plomley, *FM*, journal, 7 December 1831, p. 577; *Colonial Times*, 22 May 1829, p. 3.

27 Scott to Aborigines Committee, March 1830, TAHO, CSO1/323, pp. 3, 15–17.

28 For example, Robertson to Anstey, October 1829, TAHO, CSO1/331, pp. 191–92; O'Connor to Aborigines Committee, 17 March 1830, in Shaw, *VDL*, p. 55; Deposition of James Olding, 19 May 1829, TAHO, CSO1/316, pp. 252–59; Clark to Burnett, 15 February 1830, TAHO, CSO1/316, pp. 414–15.

29 Robertson to Aborigines Committee, 3 March 1830, in Shaw, *VDL*, pp. 47–48.

30 Brown to Mulgrave, 5 February 1830, TAHO, CSO1/323, pp. 117, 135.

31 This practice was also observed by French explorers before settlement. See S Anderson, 'French anthropology in Australia, the first fieldwork report: François Péron's "Maria Island anthropological observations"', *Aboriginal History*, 2001, vol. 25, pp. 236–37. Reconnaissance was sometimes even conducted by women; see, for example, Hobbs to Aborigines Committee, 9 March 1830, in Shaw, *VDL*, p. 50; Morgan, *Land Settlement*, p. 147.

32 O'Connor to Aborigines Committee, 17 March 1830, in Shaw, *VDL*, p. 55.

33 Captain W Clark to Aborigines Committee, 15 March 1830, TAHO, CSO1/323, pp. 319–25. See also Vicary to Burnett, 12 February 1830, TAHO, CSO1/316, pp. 404–405; *Hobart Town Courier*, 13 November 1830, p. 3; *Colonial Times*, 30 April 1830, p. 2; *Tasmanian*, 28 May 1831, p. 167.

34 Robertson to Burnett, 2 September 1829, TAHO, CSO1/331, p. 89.

35 PL Brown, *The Narrative of George Russell of Golf Hill: With Russellania and Selected Papers*, Oxford University Press, London, 1935, p. 58.

36 For example, Simpson to Burnett, 23 August 1830, TAHO, CSO1/316, pp. 581–82; Anstey to Burnett, 21 December 1830, TAHO, CSO1/316, p. 769; Bonwick, *Last of the Tasmanians*, pp. 117–18. Quotation from *Tasmanian*, 11 April 1828, p. 3.

37 Aborigines Committee Report, 19 March 1830, in Shaw, *VDL*, p. 43.

38 For example, Anstey to Burnett, 21 December 1830, TAHO, CSO1/316, p. 765; O'Connor to Aborigines Committee, 17 March 1830, in Shaw, *VDL*, p. 54.

39 *Colonial Times*, 30 January 1829, p. 3.

40 Hooper to Anstey, 19 August 1830, TAHO, CSO1/316, pp. 571–74. See also Batman to Anstey, 1 February 1830, TAHO, CSO1/320, p. 167;

Deposition of James Olding, 19 May 1829, TAHO, CSO1/316, pp. 252–59.

41 For example, *Colonial Times*, 1 June 1831, p. 2; *Hobart Town Courier*, 8 December 1827, p. 1; Harte to Burnett, 20 March 1828, TAHO, CSO1/316, pp. 126–28.

42 Scott to Aborigines Committee, March 1830, TAHO, CSO1/323, pp. 315–17.

43 Minutes of Executive Council, 27 July 1830, in Shaw, *VDL*, p. 63.

44 Plomley, *FM*, journal, 8 November 1831.

45 *Hobart Town Courier*, 8 March 1828, p. 2.

46 For example, Clark to Aborigines Committee, 15 March 1830, TAHO, CSO1/323, p. 321; *Hobart Town Gazette*, 1 April 1825, p. 3; Roth, *Aborigines of Tasmania*, pp. 41–42, 73; West, *History of Tasmania*, vol. II, p. 85.

47 *Hobart Town Gazette*, 1 April 1825, p. 3.

48 *Colonial Advocate*, 1 April 1828, p. 94.

49 Meredith, *My Home*, p. 81.

50 Scott to Major Douglas, 30 September 1830, TAHO, CSO1/316, pp. 652–55.

51 Clements, 'Frontier conflict', pp. 173–75.

52 For example, 'Address from inhabitants of the Clyde', 27 February 1830, TAHO, CSO1/316, pp. 438–43; *Hobart Town Courier*, 13 March 1830, p. 2, and 20 March 1830, p. 2; *Colonial Times*, 25 May 1831, p. 4; Wood to Aborigines Committee, 7 March 1830, TAHO, CSO1/323, p. 98; Meredith, *My Home*, p. 84.

53 For example, *Colonial Times*, 26 November 1830, p. 3. Other examples include Anstey to Burnett, 13 December 1830, TAHO, CSO1/316, p. 762; Clark to Vicary, 8 September 1830, TAHO, CSO1/316, p. 618; Meredith, *My Home*, p. 81.

54 *Colonial Times*, 16 July 1830, p. 3.

55 *Launceston Advertiser*, 15 June 1829, p. 2.

56 J Steele to Arthur, 15 June 1829, TAHO, CSO1/316, pp. 281–84.

57 Lascelles to Burnett, 10 June 1829, TAHO, CSO1/316, pp. 271–73.

58 Robertson to Lascelles, 17 November 1828, TAHO, CSO1/331, pp. 169–70.

59 For example, Story to Arthur, 25 October 1831, TAHO, CSO1/316, pp. 1015–19; Robinson to Burnett, 25 January 1832, TAHO, CSO1/318, p. 127; Plomley, *FM*, journal, 1 and 15 November 1830, 25 and 28 October 1831.

60 Robinson to Arthur, 20 November 1830, TAHO, CSO1/317, p. 228; Plomley, *FM*, journal, 16 June, 25 and 26 October, and 10 November 1831; Vicary to Burnett, 1 June 1830, TAHO, CSO1/316, pp. 517–20; Robinson to Burnett, 5 January 1832, TAHO, CSO1/318, pp. 127–33.

61 For example, Plomley, *FM*, journal, 30 May and 11 August 1829; *Hobart Town Courier*, 20 December 1828, p. 2.

62 Emmett, 'Reminiscences', p. 1.
63 Plomley, *FM*, journal, 2 December 1831.
64 Brown to Mulgrave, 5 February 1830, TAHO, CSO1/323, pp. 137–42. See also Robertson to Aborigines Committee, 3 March 1830, in Shaw, *VDL*, pp. 47–48.
65 Jorgenson to Anstey, 30 November 1830, TAHO, CSO1/320, pp. 396–98. See also Batman to Anstey, 1 February 1830, TAHO, CSO1/320, p. 167.
66 Plomley, *FM*, journal, 30 October 1831.
67 Brown to Mulgrave, 5 February 1830, TAHO, CSO1/323, p. 136.
68 *Hobart Town Courier*, 20 June 1829, p. 2.
69 Lascelles to Arthur, 16 June 1829, TAHO, CSO1/316, p. 275.
70 O'Connor to Aborigines Committee, 17 March 1830, in Shaw, *VDL*, p. 55.

Chapter 10: White devils
1 Clements, 'Frontier conflict', ch. 11. While there is some evidence of them moving under a full moon, there are almost no credible accounts of them attacking at night (see pp. 155–56).
2 Plomley, *WiS*, journal, 22 July 1837.
3 During the second half of the conflict, Aborigines were, with few exceptions, fired at whenever they were seen (for example, *Colonial Times*, 5 January 1827, p. 2, and 2 July 1830, p. 2; Plomley, *FM*, journal, 21 September 1830, 13 January, 26 and 30 October, and 5 November 1831).
4 Plomley, *FM*, journal, 11 September 1831; *Tasmanian*, 22 October 1830, p. 741.
5 Plomley, *Jorgenson*, p. 56. See also Lloyd, *Thirty-three Years*, p. 157.
6 For example, Robertson to Lascelles, 17 November 1828, TAHO, CSO1/331, pp. 170–71; Wilson to Anstey, 15 December 1828, TAHO, CSO1/320, pp. 353–54.
7 For details of colonial firearms as they were used against Aborigines, see D Denholm, *The Colonial Australians*, Penguin, Harmondsworth, UK, 1979, pp. 27–46.
8 Brown to Mulgrave, 5 February 1830, TAHO, CSO1/323, p. 150.
9 *Launceston Advertiser*, 2 August 1830, p. 3; Hobler, *The Diaries*, 16 May 1829; Meredith, *My Home*, p. 81.
10 *Launceston Advertiser*, 2 August 1830, p. 3.
11 West, *History of Tasmania*, vol. II, pp. 31–32.
12 For example, Plomley, *FM*, journal, 25 September 1830, 14 April, and 4 and 5 November 1831; J George, 'Extracts from a diary'. *Oatlands District Historical Society Chronicle*, 2002, vol. 2, p. 13; J Bonwick, *John Batman: The Founder of Victoria*, Wren, Melbourne, 1973 (first published 1867), p. 1; HM Hull, 'Lecture on the Aborigines of Tasmania', Mechanics Institute, Mercury, Hobart, 1870, p. 9; Lloyd, *Thirty-three Years*, p. 110;

Colonial Times, 19 March 1830, p. 3; Jorgenson to Mrs Anstey, 10 March 1830, TAHO, CSO1/323, p. 189.

13   Danvers to Anstey, 9 December 1828, TAHO, CSO1/320, section E.

14   Anstey to Colonial Secretary, 9 December 1828, TAHO, CSO1/329, p. 269. See also *Hobart Town Courier*, 13 December 1828, p. 2; *Tasmanian*, 12 December 1828, p. 2.

15   Deposition of Corporal Ayton, 15 March 1830, TAHO, CSO1/330, p. 109. See also Ayton to Aborigines Committee, 1 March 1830, TAHO, CSO1/323, p. 152.

16   Leavitt & Fenton, *Jubilee History*, pp. 53–54.

17   Plomley, *FM*, journal, 17 November 1831.

18   Plomley, *FM*, journal, 5 December 1830, 24 October, and 7, 15 and 24 December 1831.

19   For example, Walpole to Arthur, 29 October 1830, TAHO, CSO1/324, pp. 118–19; Scott to Douglas, circa 3 October 1830, TAHO, CSO1/316, pp. 652–55; Jorgenson to Mrs Anstey, 10 March 1830, TAHO, CSO1/323, p. 189.

20   *Launceston Advertiser*, 2 August 1830, p. 3.

21   Plomley, *FM*, journal, 14 December 1831. See also Plomley, *Jorgenson*, p. 56; J Lyne, unpublished reminiscences, n.d., TAHO, NS854/1/1, p. 25; Emmett, 'Reminiscences', p. 1.

22   The evidence pertaining to the ways south-east Tasmanians traditionally used skins is confusing. Some sources claim women would occasionally wear a skin draped over their shoulder but that men never wore them. Robinson supports this view (for example, Plomley, *FM*, journal, 24 December 1831), and yet this seems unbelievable in the Tasmanian climate. A couple of early sources mention Aborigines joining skins together in the winter to make capes (Boyce, 'Surviving in a new land', pp. 33–32; Evans, *A Geographical, Historical, and Topographical Description*, p. 21), but such references don't exist for the war period.

23   Plomley, *FM*, journal, 20 October 1831.

24   Lloyd, *Thirty-three Years*, p. 157. See also 'Testimony of Corporal Shiners', 30 June 1827, TAHO, CSO1/316, pp. 34–37; Walpole to Arthur, 29 October 1830, TAHO, CSO1/324, pp. 118–19; Roth, *Aborigines of Tasmania*, p. 107; Brown to Mulgrave, 5 February 1830, TAHO, CSO1/323, pp. 123–24; Meredith, 'Verbal remarks', p. 28.

25   Walpole to Arthur, 29 October 1830, TAHO, CSO1/324, pp. 118–19; *Launceston Advertiser*, 2 August 1830, p. 3; *Hobart Town Courier*, 9 October 1830, p. 2; Plomley, *FM*, journal, 26 March 1830; West, *History of Tasmania*, vol. II, p. 29.

26   Robertson to Aborigines Committee, 3 March 1830, in Shaw, *VDL*, pp. 47–48.

27   *Colonial Times*, 19 March 1830, p. 3.

28   For example, Wilson to Anstey, 15 December 1828, TAHO, CSO1/320, pp. 353–54; Melville, *History of Van Diemen's Land*, pp. 71–72; Leavitt

& Fenton, *Jubilee History of Tasmania*, pp. 53–54; *Colonial Times*, 18 September 1829, p. 3; Robertson to Aborigines Committee, 3 March 1830, in Shaw, *VDL*, pp. 47–48.

29 Brown to Mulgrave, 5 February, TAHO, CSO1/323, pp. 136–37.

30 For example, *Launceston Advertiser*, 2 August 1830, p. 3; 'Testimony of Thomas Williams', 30 June 1827, TAHO, CSO1/316, pp. 28–33; Melville, *History of Van Diemen's Land*, pp. 79–81; *Colonial Times*, 19 March 1830, p. 3.

31 M Steele to J Steele, 21 February 1827, in Dow & Dow, *Landfall*, p. 45.

32 *Hobart Town Gazette*, 4 February 1826, p. 2.

33 *Hobart Town Courier*, 1 November 1828, p. 2.

34 For example, Vicary to Burnett, 25 May, TAHO, CSO1/316, pp. 515–16; Clements online compendium (<https://dx.doi.org/10.25959/hpxk-5f95>), which shows winter movement in the highlands.

35 Cited in Roth, *Aborigines of Tasmania*, p. 110.

36 For example, Emmett, 'Reminiscences', p. 2; *Hobart Town Courier*, 6 November 1830, p. 2.

37 I Gregg, 'A young Englishman's observations of the Aboriginals during five years in Van Diemen's Land: who was Dr John Barnes?', *Tasmanian Ancestry*, 2000, vol. 21, no. 1, p. 22.

38 For example, *Hobart Town Gazette*, 18 November 1826, p. 4; *Colonial Times*, 16 June 1826, p. 3; Buxton to family, 14 September 1821, NLA, MS902, folio 3, p. 2; 'Deposition of Thomas McMinn', 16 March 1830, TAHO, CSO1/323, p. 197; Roth, *Aborigines of Tasmania*, p. 17.

39 Plomley, *FM*, journal, 28 November 1831.

40 Plomley, *FM*, journal, 30 March 1830.

41 Journal of James Backhouse, 12 October 1832, in Plomley, *WiS*, p. 231.

42 For example, Plomley, *FM*, journal, 15 November 1830, 20 October and 4 November 1831; Robinson to Arthur, 20 November 1830, TAHO, CSO1/317, pp. 216–33.

43 The scarcity of Aboriginal children travelling with bands in the latter part of the war is well documented (for example, Roth, *Aborigines of Tasmania*, p. 22; Robinson to Burnett, 5 January 1832, TAHO, CSO1/318, p. 131).

44 Plomley, *FM*, journal, 16 July 1832.

45 The prevalence of sadistic violence is evidenced in scores of primary sources, for example Plomley, *FM*, journal, 23 November 1829, 28 April, 18 September and 6 November 1831, and 29 March 1832; O'Connor to Aborigines Committee, 17 March 1830, in Shaw, *VDL*, p. 54; journal of William Grant, 21 January 1829, TAHO, CSO1/331, p. 119; A Calder, 'F. E. Maning, 1811–1883', *Kōtare*, vol. 7, no. 2, 2008; Melville, *History of Van Diemen's Land*, pp. 71–72; Holman, *Travels*, p. 403; Emmett, 'Reminiscences', p. 8.

46 *Colonial Times*, 2 July 1830, p. 2. See also, for example, *Colonial Times*, 5 April 1836, p. 5; Barnes to Aborigines Committee, 10 March 1830, TAHO, CSO1/323, p. 299.

47   West, *History of Tasmania*, vol. II, p. 18.
48   Roth, *Aborigines of Tasmania*, p. 172.
49   Fenton, *Fenton of Forth*, p. 201.
50   Leavitt & Fenton, *Jubilee History*, pp. 53–54.
51   There are only a handful of counterattacks on record, for example *Hobart Town Courier*, 6 August 1824, p. 2, 21 March 1829, p. 1.
52   Plomley, *WiS*, journal 19 December 1835, pp. 324–25.
53   Drometehenner, the other woman who was abducted in this ambush, seems to have ended up enslaved in Bass Strait by the sealer James Munroe. Incredibly, though, she managed to escape back to her people. Eventually, she somehow ended up in the Hobart hospital, from whence she was exiled back to Bass Strait on 3 March 1831 (Plomley & Henley, *The Sealers*, p. 76).
54   Plomley, *FM*, journal, 29 June 1834.
55   Plomley, *Tasmanian Aborigines*, p. 22.
56   Plomley, *FM*, journal, 28 September 1829.
57   Robinson to Burnett, 11 October 1831, in Plomley, *FM*, p. 504. See also Plomley, *FM*, journal, 29 August 1831.
58   Walpole to Arthur, 29 October 1830, TAHO, CSO1/324, pp. 409–12. See also Plomley, *FM*, journal, 22 October 1831.
59   Walpole to Arthur, 29 October 1830, TAHO, CSO1/324, pp. 409–12.
60   *Hobart Town Courier*, 6 November 1830, p. 2.
61   Arthur to Douglas, 25 October 1830, Arthur Papers, ML, SLNSW, A1771; Plomley, *FM*, journal, 6 December 1831.
62   Jorgenson to Arthur, 9 November 1830, TAHO, CSO1/324, pp. 128–29; C Darwin, *Voyage of the Beagle*, Bantam, New York, 1972 (first published 1839), journal, 30 February 1836, p. 387.
63   *Hobart Town Courier*, 30 October 1830, p. 2.
64   Plomley, *WiS*, journal, 19 December 1835.
65   *Hobart Town Courier*, 30 October 1830, p. 2.
66   Douglas to Arthur, 27 October 1830, TAHO, CSO1/316, pp. 703–704.
67   *Colonial Times*, 5 November 1830, p. 3; Douglas to Arthur, 27 October 1830, TAHO, CSO1/316, pp. 703–704. See also *Hobart Town Courier*, 6 November 1830, p. 2.
68   Plomley, *FM*, journal, 14 January; 22 October 1831.
69   Plomley, *FM*, journal, 24 October 1831.

Chapter 11: Things fall apart

1   A Watson, orthopaedic surgeon, Hobart, pers. comm., 22 May 2020.
2   Plomley, *WiS*, journal, 19 December 1835, pp. 324–25. In 1830, an Aborigine lost his hand in a man-trap planted in a cask of flour at a hut along the Little Swanport River. The colonial press made much of this grisly incident, the *Colonial Times* (30 April 1830, p. 2) reporting: 'The unfortunate creature must have undergone dreadful agony, as we hear that the sinews and tendons of the arm were drawn out by main

force, and to use the expression of our informant, resembled those of the tail of a kangaroo'. Putting two and two together, most people who saw Tongerlongeter assumed he must be the 'unfortunate creature' in question, but Robinson was the only one to actually ask the chief, and his testimony would appear to settle the matter. Moreover, the nature and location of the injury, which is laid out in a detailed autopsy, is difficult to account for if he had lost his arm in a trap, but perfectly consistent with a musket ball wound. NJB Plomley, the editor of Robinson's journals and a qualified anatomist, concluded as we have that 'gunshot wound seems the more likely explanation' (*FM*, pp. 617–18).

3   In addition to the evidence discussed in the text, if Tongerlongeter had lost his arm before October 1831 (very near the end of the war), a one-armed chief would surely have appeared in the thousands of pages of testimony describing frontier encounters with Aborigines.

4   Plomley, *FM*, journal, 5 November 1831.

5   Plomley, *FM*, journal, 24 October 1831; Walpole to Arthur, 29 October 1830, TAHO, CSO1/324, pp. 409–12; *Colonial Times*, 5 November 1830, p. 3.

6   LK Whatley-Brown, 'Traumatic amputation: mechanisms of injury, treatment, and rehabilitation', *American Association of Occupational Health Nurses Journal*, 1990, vol. 38, no. 10, pp. 483–86; Watson, orthopaedic surgeon, pers. comm.

7   Someone clearly returned to the campsite, orelse Tongerlongeter would not have known the murdered women had been burnt (Plomley, *WiS*, journal, 19 December 1835, pp. 324–25). Any knives they had would have been taken by the ambushers, but they routinely carried shards of glass for the same purpose. This or a traditional stone cutting tool is likely what they used.

8   Austin to Robinson, 21 June 1837, in *WiS*, pp. 928–29.

9   Watson, orthopaedic surgeon, pers. comm.

10 Plomley, *FM*, journal, 3 July 1832. See also p. 627.

11 Watson, orthopaedic surgeon, pers. comm.

12 Watson, orthopaedic surgeon, pers. comm.

13 Clements online compendium, <https://dx.doi.org/10.25959/hpxk-5f95>.

14 Plomley, *FM*, journal, 16 January 1834; *Hobart Town Courier*, 5 February 1831, p. 3.

15 Clements online compendium, <https://dx.doi.org/10.25959/hpxk-5f95>.

16 *Colonial Times*, 25 May 1831, p. 4.

17 Clements online compendium, <https://dx.doi.org/10.25959/hpxk-5f95>.

18 'Climate statistics for Australian locations: Liawnee Comparison', Bureau of Meteorology, <bom.gov.au/climate/averages/tables/cw_096065.shtml>.

19   Plomley & QVMAG, *The Tasmanian Tribes and Cicatrices*, p. 12;
     R Cosgrove, quoted in P Sanders, 'Beliefs on Aborigines', *Launceston Examiner*, 28 April 2014; Jones, 'Tasmanian tribes', pp. 319–54;
     B Brimfield, 'Tasmania's Palaeo-Aboriginal Population prior to 1772CE', 2014, NLA ID 6929878.

20   By this time, most bands had been reduced to just a handful of individuals and existed now only in composite with other remnants (for example, the Poredareme). Others had been destroyed altogether. See Calder, 'Levée, line and martial law', appendix 2; Plomley, *FM*, journal, 3 November 1830, 20 November 1831.

21   Robertson's journal, 25 February 1829, TAHO, CSO1/331, p. 142.

22   For example, Plomley, *FM*, journal, 10 and 29 November 1831.

23   West, *History of Tasmania*, vol. II, p. 57.

24   *Farmers Cabinet*, 18 September 1835, p. 1 (the correspondent's letter was dated 31 January 1835).

25   Plomley, *FM*, journal, 14 December 1831.

26   Robertson to Lascelles, 17 November 1828, TAHO, CSO1/331, pp. 171–73.

27   For example, Robertson to Aborigines Committee, 4 March 1830, and Hobbs to Aborigines Committee, 9 March 1830, in Shaw, *VDL*, pp. 48, 50; Plomley, *FM*, journal, 24 October 1831.

28   For example, Plomley, *FM*, journal, 27 October, 4 November and 11 December 1831; Robertson to Aborigines Committee, 4 March 1830, in Shaw, *VDL*, p. 48.

29   For example, O'Connor to Aborigines Committee, 17 March 1830, and Robertson to Aborigines Committee, 4 March 1830, in Shaw, *VDL*, pp. 55, 48; Plomley, *FM*, journal, 11 September 1831; *Tasmanian*, 22 October 1830, p. 741.

30   Robertson to Lascelles, 17 November 1828, TAHO, CSO1/331, pp. 171–72.

31   Robertson to Aborigines Committee, 4 March 1830, in Shaw, *VDL*, p. 48.

32   Robertson to Lascelles, 17 November 1828, TAHO, CSO1/331, pp. 171–73. See also *Tasmanian*, 28 November 1828, p. 2.

33   Plomley, *FM*, journal, 24 August 1831, p. 445.

34   Robertson's report on roving party proceedings, February 1829 – February 1830 (notation for 2 November 1829), TAHO, CSO1/331, pp. 85–86.

35   Clements online compendium, <https://dx.doi.org/10.25959/hpxk-5f95>.

36   Jorgenson to Burnett, 24 February 1830, TAHO, CSO1/320, p. 351. See also Walker, *Early Tasmania*, p. 273; Plomley, *FM*, journal, 25 October 1830, 2 September, 13 November and 14 December 1831; Plomley, *Tasmanian Aborigines*, p. 26.

37   *Hobler, The Diaries*, 6 October 1830, p. 187.

38   While the Oyster Bay and Big River nations operated more or less as one from the late 1820s, the only example of traditional enemies fighting in

concert is that of Oyster Bay, Big River and Port Sorell peoples making attacks along the Ouse River in June 1831 and then at Port Sorell two months later (Plomley, *FM*, journal, 14 December 1831; Plomley, *WiS*, journal, 9 December 1836).

39 Robinson to Arthur, 20 November 1830, TAHO, CSO1/317, pp. 216–33; Plomley, *FM*, journal, 2, 3 and 15 November 1830. Of these three women, two had been 'set at liberty from the Aboriginal Establishment'. Robinson was referring here to his mission, which had absorbed a number of Aborigines who had been languishing in southern gaols and had received permission to send a small delegation of them out to convey the government's 'peaceful intentions' to the 'hostile tribes'.

40 Plomley, *FM*, journal, 2 November 1830.

41 The sources mentioning this battle, which conflict in some details, are: Robinson to Arthur, 20 November 1830, TAHO, CSO1/317, pp. 216–33; Plomley, *FM*, journal, 1, 2, 3 and 15 November 1830, 9 January and 27 October 1831; J Gray to Arthur, 19 October 1830, TAHO, CSO1/316, pp. 684–87; W Gray to Arthur, 23 October 1830, TAHO, CSO1/316, pp. 691–95; Walpole to Arthur, 29 October 1830, TAHO, CSO1/324, pp. 409–12; *Tasmanian*, 22 October 1830, p. 741; *Hobart Town Courier*, 23 October 1830, p. 2, and 13 November 1830, pp. 2–3.

42 Robinson to Arthur, 20 November 1830, TAHO, CSO1/317, pp. 216–33. See also Plomley, *FM*, journal, 1 November 1830, 30 December 1831.

43 Plomley, *FM*, journal, 9 January 1831.

44 Walpole to Arthur, 29 October 1830, TAHO, CSO1/324, pp. 409–12.

45 *Tasmanian*, 22 October 1830, p. 741. See also *Hobart Town Courier*, 23 October 1830, p. 2, and 13 November 1830, pp. 2–3; J Gray to Arthur, 19 October 1830, TAHO, CSO1/316, pp. 684–87; W Gray to Arthur, 23 October 1830, TAHO, CSO1/316, pp. 691–95.

46 *Tasmanian*, 22 October 1830, p. 741.

47 There was no significant break in offensive operations in Oyster Bay country during 1830 (see Clements online compendium, <https://dx.doi.org/10.25959/hpxk-5f95>), so not all of Tongerlongeter's people, if any of them, were there.

48 For example, Plomley, *Jorgenson*, p. 68; Brown to Mulgrave, 5 February 1830, TAHO, CSO1/323, pp. 137–38.

49 Plomley, *FM*, journal, 27 April 1829.

50 Plomley, *FM*, journal, 27 April 1829, 2 February 1830, 17 June 1833.

51 For example, S Pinker, *The Better Angels of Our Nature: Why Violence Has Declined*, Penguin, New York, 2011, chs 1–2; M Brogden, *Geronticide: Killing the Elderly*, Jessica Kingsley Publishers, London, 2001, pp. 59–62.

52 Backhouse, *A Narrative*, pp. 84–85. See also *Hobart Town Gazette*, 4 February 1826, p. 2; West, *History of Tasmania*, vol. II, pp. 30, 90; H Widowson, *The Present State of Van Diemen's Land*, Robinson, Joy & Birdsall, London, 1829, p. 191.

53   Plomley, *Tasmanian Aborigines*, p. 58.
54   Robinson to Arthur, 20 November 1830, TAHO, CSO1/317, pp. 216–33; Plomley, *FM*, journal, 2, 3 and 15 November 1830.
55   Cited in Meredith, *My Home*, p. 143.
56   For example, Hull, 'Lecture on the Aborigines', p. 9; West, *History of Tasmania*, vol. II, pp. 31–32.
57   Robertson to Aborigines Committee, 4 March 1830, in Shaw, *VDL*, p. 48.
58   Plomley, *FM*, journal, 25 October and 25 December 1830, pp. 291–92, 333–34.
59   For example, West, *History of Tasmania*, vol. II, pp. 79–80; JE Calder, 'Some account of the wars of extirpation, and habits of the native tribes of Tasmania', *Journal of the Anthropological Institute*, 1874, vol. 3, pp. 13–14; Davies, 'On the Aborigines', p. 412; Dove, 'Moral and social characteristics', p. 252; *Hobart Town Gazette*, 4 February 1826, p. 2; Thomas, *Hellyer's Observations*, pp. 23–24.
60   Emmett, 'Reminiscences', p. 1.
61   Robinson's journals between 1829 and 1839 provide many instances of powerful men exercising priority access to the diminishing pool of available women (see Plomley's *FM*; *WiS*).
62   For a summary of this incident and the key sources pertaining to it, see Clements, 'Frontier conflict', pp. 236, 246–49.
63   Plomley, *FM*, journal, 25 October 1831.
64   Plomley, *FM*, journal, 3 November 1831.
65   Plomley, *FM*, journal, 12 December 1831.
66   Curr to C Arthur, 19 November 1831, Van Diemen's Land Company Papers, AJCP letterbook, NLA, vol. 12, pp. 483–85. See also Curr to Burnett, 5 September 1831, Van Diemen's Land Company Papers, vol. 12, pp. 408–409.
67   G Lennox, 'The Van Diemen's Land Company and the Tasmanian Aborigines: a re-appraisal', draft paper, Hobart, 1991; Curr to C Arthur, 19 November 1831, AJCP letterbook, NLA, vol. 12, pp. 483–85; Plomley, *FM*, journal, 26 December 1831, pp. 597–98, 615; Robinson to Burnett, 15 March 1832, in Plomley, *FM*, pp. 720–21.
68   Plomley, *WiS*, journal, 9 December 1836.
69   Lyne, unpublished reminiscences, pp. 23–25.
70   For summary of this episode and of the relevant sources, see Clements, 'Frontier conflict', pp. 237–38.
71   The full moon had occurred on 21 October. For historical lunar cycles, see <AstroPixels.com, astropixels.com/ephemeris/phasescat/phases1801.html>, accessed 15 May 2019.
72   Lyne, unpublished reminiscences, pp. 23–25. Lyne's estimate of 200 men appears to be an over-estimate. George Story, who was rationing the men from the commissariat store, claimed there were eighty-four men in the cordon as of 24 October, with forty more on the way (Story to Arthur, 25 October 1831, TAHO, CSO1/316, pp. 1015–22).

73   Plomley, *WiS*, journal, 15 November 1837.
74   Plomley, *FM*, journal, 27 December 1831.

Chapter 12: Armistice
1   Plomley & Henley, *The Sealers*, pp. 76–85.
2   Cox, *Broken Spear*. Quotation from *Colonial Times*, 11 May 1827, pp. 2–3.
3   Fereday to Burnett, 18 July 1828, TAHO, CSO1/170, p. 74.
4   Arthur's draft reply to Fereday, 21 July 1828, TAHO, CSO1/170, p. 75.
5   Fereday to Burnett, 23 July 1828, TAHO, CSO1/170, p. 76.
6   *Colonial Advocate*, 1 October 1828, p. 393.
7   Shaw, *VDL*, p. 27.
8   Cox, *Broken Spear*.
9   The transcript of their conversation was printed in Henry Melville's
     1835 *History of Van Diemen's Land* (pp. 75–76). Melville, the editor
     of the *Colonial Times*, was no fan of Arthur. His source, 'a by-stander',
     probably reconstructed much of it from memory and with a bias against
     the governor, so the exchange must be read with a critical eye. That said,
     Arthur had already imprisoned Melville for libel, so the author would have
     well understood the perils of publishing a fabricated account. What's more,
     the swagger and sarcasm sound exactly like Kickertopoller, whose speech
     and personality are well documented in Robinson's journals (see Plomley,
     FM), Gilbert Robinson's papers (TAHO, CSO1/331) and elsewhere.
10   This was the so-called Demarcation Proclamation of 15 April 1828. It had
     been ineffective, and so Arthur had declared martial law on 1 November,
     just over a week before this encounter.
11   M Godfrey, 'Robertson, Gilbert (1794–1851)', *Australian Dictionary of
     Biography*, National Centre of Biography, ANU, 1967, <adb.anu.edu.au/
     biography/robertson-gilbert-2595/text3563>, accessed 26 July 2020.
12   Robertson to Lascelles, 17 November 1828, TAHO, CSO1/331, p. 170;
     Cox, *Broken Spear*.
13   Jorgenson to Anstey, 29 July 1829, in Plomley, *Jorgenson*, p. 25.
14   Robertson to Lascelles, 17 November 1828, TAHO, CSO1/331, p. 170;
     Cox, *Broken Spear*. The hostile relationship between Kickertopoller and
     Umarrah, which stemmed from tribal animosities, is well documented, for
     example: Melville, *History of Van Diemen's Land*, pp. 78–79; Plomley, *FM*,
     journal, 21 August – 12 September, and 18 December 1831.
15   Robertson to Lascelles, 17 November 1828, TAHO, CSO1/331, p. 169.
16   Robertson to Butcher, 26 October 1829, TAHO, CSO1/1/330, p. 49;
     Robertson to Anstey, 20 October 1829, TAHO, CSO1/331, pp. 190–91.
17   Cox, *Broken Spear*.
18   At Elliott Bay on 8 April 1830, Robinson momentarily considered
     attempting to capture a band, but he immediately abandoned the idea.
     While he concealed four firearms, these were only for emergencies. After
     the war, though, when Robinson attempted to remove Aborigines from the
     west coast, he grew impatient and began using more intimidatory tactics,

the most extreme of which was to bring the last people in at gunpoint (see Plomley, *FM*, journal, 1832–33).

19   Plomley, *FM*, p. 123.

20   Kickertopoller was the only Oyster Bay or Big River envoy on the expedition (Plomley, *FM*, p. 276). Besides him, the most notable envoys were Truganini and Woorrady, a couple from Bruny Island whom Robinson had befriended during his failed attempt to establish a mission there the previous year. Umarrah, Kickertopoller's old enemy, was also among them, though he and two of his comrades abandoned the mission at Macquarie Harbour in May, returning to their country via the rugged south-west mountain ranges. But arguably the most important figure in this first mission was a Port Davey woman, Dray, who was closely familiar with the tribes on the south and west coast.

21   For example, *Colonial Times*, 22 February 1831, p. 2, and 1 March 1831, p. 2; *Launceston Advertiser*, 14 March 1831, p. 2. Success, that is, in the eyes of the colonists.

22   Plomley, *FM*, pp. 159, 483, 495, 722. In his role with the floating chapel in 1828, Kickertopoller would have met Robinson. 'The chapel was', as Robert Cox (*Broken Spear*) points out, 'a project of the Van Diemen's Land Seaman's Friend and Bethel Society whose secretary was George Augustus Robinson'.

23   Plomley, *FM*, journal, 11 January 1830.

24   For example, Plomley, *FM*, journal, 24 December 1830, 6 July, 15 August, 11 September, 26 and 29 October, 7 November and 18 December 1831.

25   Robinson to Burnett, 25 January 1832, in Plomley, *FM*, pp. 601–602.

26   Plomley, *FM*, journal, 29 August 1831. Umarrah's remnant band was contacted near Pipers River in the north-east. Since absconding from the mission in May the previous year, the chief had given himself up just before the Black Line, joined that operation as a guide, and then absconded once more (M Roe, 'Eumarrah (1798–1832)', *Australian Dictionary of Biography*, National Centre of Biography, ANU, 2005, <adb.anu.edu.au/biography/eumarrah-12905/text23313>, accessed 29 July 2020).

27   Robinson to Burnett, 5 January 1832, TAHO, CSO1/318, pp. 127–37.

28   Plomley, *FM*, journal, 6 August 1831.

29   Plomley, *FM*, journal, 27 August 1831. See also Plomley, *FM*, journal, 29 August, and 8 and 11 September 1831.

30   Arthur to Murray, 4 April 1831, in Shaw, *VDL*, pp. 78–79.

31   Colonial Secretary to Robinson, 25 June 1831, in Plomley, *FM*, p. 500.

32   Robinson to Burnett, 6 August 1831, TAHO, CSO1/318, pp. 45–51. The idea of an Aboriginal 'reservation' on mainland Tasmania had been discussed in the late 1820s, and several sites considered, but it was dismissed (for example, Arthur to Goderich, 10 January 1828, and Arthur to Murray, 20 November 1830, in Shaw, *VDL*, pp. 4, 59).

33   Plomley, *FM*, p. 618. Kickertopoller seems to have held considerable sway over Polare (also known as Woolaytoopinneyer) even though she had

just married Umarrah (for example, Plomley, *FM*, journal, 26 October 1831). At first glance, her union with Umarrah, a traditional enemy, seems strange, but by the end of the war, with the extreme scarcity of women, chiefs like Umarrah took virtually any single female they fancied. Likewise, Mannalargenna married Tanlebonyer around the same time. Given the patriarchal nature of their society, women may not have had much scope to resist the advances of such high-status men. Tanlebonyer may also have seen that 'MAN.NER.LE.LAR.GEN.NER had cut TEN.COTE.MAIN.NER [a fellow Poredareme woman] with a knife because she would not stop [sleep] with him. The aboriginal females came to my tent and informed me that several of the men had concealed themselves in the bush and took knives with them, and when night came they meant to cut the women. And why would they do so? Because women no marry them' (Plomley, *FM*, journal, 19 November 1830). Polare's marriage to Umarrah helps to further explain her reluctance to lead Robinson directly to them. Umarrah had had his share of battles with the Oyster Bay – Big River people, and in the process had been speared in the side. They had also killed his previous wife (Plomley, *FM*, journal, 9 January, 10 and 15 November 1831).

34   For example, Surridge to Aborigines Committee, February 1832, TAHO, CSO1/321, pp. 393–400; Plomley, *FM*, journal, 4 December 1831.

35   Clements, 'Frontier conflict', p. 88.

36   For example, Plomley, *FM*, journal, 28 August, and 21, 24 and 25 October 1831.

37   Plomley, *FM*, journal, 28 August 1831.

38   Plomley, *FM*, journal, 23 November 1831.

39   Quotation from Robinson to Burnett, 5 January 1832, TAHO, CSO1/318, pp. 127–37. See also *FM*, journal, 3 November, and 4, 6 and 28 December 1831.

40   Plomley, *FM*, journal, 7 December 1831.

41   Robinson to Burnett, 5 January 1832, TAHO, CSO1/318, pp. 127–37.

42   For example, Plomley, *FM*, journal, 6 July, 15 and 28 August, 11 September, 26 and 29 October, 3 and 4 November, and 18 December 1831.

43   Plomley, *FM*, journal, 10 September 1831.

44   Plomley, *FM*, journal, 7 and 9 November 1831.

45   For example, Plomley, *FM*, journal, 1 and 2 November 1830, 3 September and 23 October 1831.

46   Robinson had the additional incentive of a pay increase to £250 per annum backdated to 1829, a gratuity of £100, and a 2500 acre land grant (I McFarlane, *Beyond Awakening: The Aboriginal Tribes of North West Tasmania: A History*, Fullers Bookshop, Launceston, 2008, p. 147).

47   For example, Polare objected to the killings at Port Sorell and ran off immediately after (see previous chapter).

48   Plomley, *FM*, journal, 13 November 1831.

49   Plomley, *FM*, journal, 14 December 1831.

50 Plomley, *FM*, journal, 21 December 1831.

51 Plomley, *FM*, journal, 30 December 1831.

52 Plomley, *FM*, journal, 3 November 1831. See also journal, 20 October 1831.

53 Plomley, *FM*, journal, 30 December 1831. By the time Robinson met them, the Oyster Bay – Big River people 'were accompanied by about 100 dogs' (Robinson to Burnett, 25 January 1832, in Plomley, *FM*, pp. 601–602). Living in the marginal and mostly open high country, they needed this veritable army of hunting dogs to supply their needs and warm their bodies.

54 Robinson's address to AAPS, 19 October 1838, reproduced in *The Colonist*, 31 October 1838, p. 2.

55 Quotation from Plomley, *FM*, journal, 18 March 1830. This was the name given to Robinson by the Port Davey people when he first encountered them.

56 Plomley, *FM*, journal, 30 December 1831.

57 Plomley, *FM*, journal, 11 December 1831. See also journal, 27 October and 4 November 1831.

58 Plomley, *FM*, journal, 6 December 1831.

59 Robinson to Burnett, 25 January 1832, in Plomley, *FM*, pp. 601–602. See also Robinson's address to AAPS, 19 October 1838, in *The Colonist*, 31 October 1838, p. 2.

60 *Tasmanian*, 21 April 1837, p. 4.

61 Robinson to Burnett, 25 January 1832, in Plomley, *FM*, pp. 601–602.

62 Cited in *Tasmanian*, Friday 21 April 1837, p. 4.

63 Robinson to Montagu, July 1838, in Plomley, *WiS*, pp. 747–48.

64 Plomley, *Jorgenson*, p. 77.

65 West, *History of Tasmania*, vol. II, p. 73.

66 For example, *Tasmanian*, 28 November 1828, p. 2; Wedge to Aborigines Committee, 5 March 1831, TAHO, CSO1/323, pp. 273–78; Clark to Aborigines Committee, 15 March 1830, TAHO, CSO1/323, p. 323; West, *History of Tasmania*, vol. II, pp. 57, 66.

67 Robinson's address to AAPS, 19 October 1838, in *The Colonist*, 31 October 1838, p. 2.

68 Plomley, *WiS*, journal, 2 and 17 July 1837.

69 Royal Museums Greenwich, <collections.rmg.co.uk/collections/objects/71292.html>, accessed 4 August 2020.

70 Plomley, *FM*, journal, 12 October 1831.

71 Plomley, *FM*, journal, 24 October 1831.

72 Together with the fact that Montpelliatta would henceforth virtually disappear from the historical record while Tongerlongeter would become a central figure, Robinson's gesture suggests that the latter had seniority over the former.

73 Plomley, *WiS*, journal, 2 July 1837.

74 Robinson to Burnett, 5 January 1832, TAHO, CSO1/318, pp. 130–33.

75   Robinson to Burnett, 25 January 1832, in Plomley, *FM*, pp. 601–602. There are many references to how freely they recounted their sufferings, such as Robinson to Bedford, 26 July 1830, in Plomley, *FM*, p. 269; Plomley, *FM*, journal, 14 December 1831; Darling to Arthur, 4 May 1832, in Arthur Papers, ML, SLNSW, A2188/A1771, vol. 28, p. 108; Minutes of Executive Council, 23 February 1831, in Shaw, *VDL*, p. 81.

76   Robinson to Burnett, 5 January 1832, TAHO, CSO1/318, pp. 130–33.

Chapter 13: Exile

1   While a separate conflict in the north-west continued sporadically until 1842, this was relatively small-scale, consisting only of clashes between western bands and employees of the Van Diemen's Land Company, which had the only farming operation in western Tasmania. For more on this theatre of conflict, see McFarlane's *Beyond Awakening*.

2   Bonwick, *Last of the Tasmanians*, p. 224.

3   Arthur memorandum, 20 November 1830, Arthur Papers, vol. 28, ML, SLNSW, A1771, p. 54.

4   Arthur to Murray, 20 November 1830, and Arthur's memorandum, 20 November 1830, in Shaw, *VDL*, pp. 60, 73.

5   Bonwick, *Last of the Tasmanians*, pp. 228–30.

6   We can take the oscillating newspaper commentaries as a proxy for the spectrum of opinion among Hobart's citizens.

7   Arthur to Buxton, 31 January 1835, TAHO, GO52/6, p. 248.

8   *Launceston Examiner*, 2 October 1847, p. 4.

9   HC Stoney, *A Residence in Tasmania*, Smith, Elder & Co., London, 1856, p. 33.

10   Plomley, *FM*, journal, 14 January 1831.

11   Clements, 'Frontier conflict', pp. 232–33.

12   Clements, 'Frontier conflict', p. 343. The totals from this 2013 compendium (which catalogues violence across Tasmania, not just in Oyster Bay – Big River territory) have since been adjusted based on subsequent discoveries and corrections, most of which appear in Nicholas Clements's online compendium of violent incidents occurring in Oyster Bay – Big River territory, <https://dx.doi.org/10.25959/hpxk-5f95>.

13   B Gammage, 'Plain facts: Tasmania under Aboriginal management', *Landscape Research*, 2008, vol. 33, no. 2, pp. 241–54.

14   Bonwick, *Daily Life*, p. 180.

15   Plomley, *Jorgenson*, p. 67.

16   Bonwick, *Last of the Tasmanians*, p. 230.

17   JL Stokes, *Discoveries in Australia: With an Account of the Coasts and Rivers Explored and Surveyed During the Voyage of H.M.S. Beagle*, vol. 2, London, T & W Boone, 1846, p. 466. See also Bonwick, *Daily Life*, p. 10.

18   Robinson to Montagu, 28 October 1836, Arthur Papers, ML, SLNSW, vol. 28, A1771, p. 318.

19   Plomley, *FM*, journal, 1 July 1832.

20 For example, Brimfield, 'Mystic beliefs', pp. 47–48; Davies, 'On the Aborigines', p. 417; Plomley, *FM*, journal, 6 April 1830; Plomley, *WiS*, p. 99; NJB Plomley, 'A list of Tasmanian Aboriginal material in collections in Europe', *Records of the Queen Victoria Museum*, 1962, no. 15, pp. 15–18.

21 For example, *Hobart Town Courier*, 18 April 1829, p. 3; *HRA*, series III, vol. I, pp. 576, 769; *Tasmanian*, 21 November 1828, p. 2.

22 Plomley, *FM*, journal, 27 February 1832.

23 Backhouse's journal, 12 October 1832, in Plomley, *WiS*, p. 229. See also Walker, *Early Tasmania*, p. 245.

24 Plomley, *WiS*, pp. 57–63, 66, 79, 92.

25 B Brimfield, 'Reconciling the conundrum of Aboriginal population data at their settlements', unpublished manuscript, 2017, NLA ID, p. 40.

26 Darling's military rank was actually ensign, which the army abolished in 1871 in favour of second lieutenant. Because ensign will be unfamiliar to most readers, the modern term has been used. His role at the settlement was then 'superintendent'. Robinson, when he took charge of the settlement in 1835, was the first to use the title of commandant. For consistency, however, we have used commandant for all.

27 Plomley, *WiS*, p. 224; Walker, Backhouse & Tylor, *Life and Labours*, p. 119.

28 Plomley, *WiS*, p. 58; Walker, *Early Tasmania*, p. 246.

29 Darling to Burnett, 4 May 1832, in Plomley, *WiS*, appendix IVa.

30 Brimfield, 'Reconciling the conundrum', p. 46.

31 Plomley, *WiS*, p. 78.

32 L Stevens, '*Me Write Myself*': The Free Aboriginal inhabitants of Van Diemen's Land at Wybalenna, 1832–47, Monash University Publishing, Melbourne, 2017, p. 72.

33 Nicholls to Montagu, 27 November 1834, in Plomley, *WiS*, pp. 84–85. See also *WiS*, pp. 96, 226, 265; Backhouse, *A Narrative*, pp. 169–70; 'The government's understanding was the same as the Aborigines' (Robinson to Montagu, 8 September 1836, Arthur Papers, ML, SLNSW, vol. 28, A1771, p. 218).

34 Darling to Burnett, 4 May 1832, in Plomley, *WiS*, appendix IVa.

35 Walker, *Early Tasmania*, p. 236.

36 Darling to Arthur, 4 May 1832, in Plomley, *WiS*, journal, appendix IVa.

37 Stevens, '*Me Write Myself*', p. 238.

38 Plomley, *WiS*, pp. 88, 265; Stevens, '*Me Write Myself*', p. 78.

39 Backhouse's journal, 15 October 1832, in Plomley, *WiS*, p. 237. See also Plomley, *WiS*, journal, 21 November 1835.

40 Backhouse's journal, 19 February 1834, in Plomley, *FM*, p. 617. Our italics.

41 Nicholls to Montagu, 9 July 1835, in Plomley, *WiS*, p. 88.

42 While there are many examples of this, one of the most touching occurred following the death of Mannalargenna (Plomley, *WiS*, journal, 4 December 1835).

43 Plomley, *WiS*, pp. 228, 251, 336; Walker, *Early Tasmania*, pp. 246–47; Walker, Backhouse & Tylor, *Life and Labours*, p. 101.

44 Plomley, *WiS*, pp. 78–88.

45 Nicholls to Montagu, 9 July 1835, in Plomley, *WiS*, p. 88.

46 Plomley, *WiS*, journal, 16 October 1835.

47 Robinson to Montagu, 4 July 1836, Arthur Papers, ML, SLNSW, vol. 28, A1771, pp. 208–209.

48 Robinson to Montagu, 8 September 1836, Arthur Papers, ML, SLNSW, vol. 28, A1771, p. 214. See also *Hobart Town Courier*, 4 December 1835, p. 2; Davies, 'On the Aborigines', pp. 410, 416.

49 For an example of how Robinson was able to avert a serious conflict, see Plomley, *WiS*, journal, 21 December 1835.

50 For example, Plomley, *FM*, journal, 23 November 1829, 15 November 1830, 14 March 1831; Plomley, *WiS*, journal, 7 October 1836.

51 TAHO, CSO1/325 contains voluminous correspondence regarding supplies for the settlement. See also Plomley, *WiS*, p. 635; Darling to Arthur, 4 May 1832, in *WiS*, appendix IVa.

52 Nicholls to Montagu, 27 November 1834, in Plomley, *WiS*, p. 85.

53 Plomley, *WiS*, p. 635.

54 Plomley, *WiS*, p. 73; Walker, *Early Tasmania*, p. 240; Robinson to Montagu, 8 September 1836, Arthur Papers, ML, SLNSW, vol. 28, A1771, pp. 250–51.

55 Stevens, '*Me Write Myself*', p. xii.

56 Plomley, *FM*, p. 1015. No other tribal names are recorded for Tongerlongeter, though the Europeans encountering him invariably heard and spelled his name differently.

57 Brimfield, 'Reconciling the conundrum', pp. 37–38; *Hobart Town Courier*, 20 February 1835, p. 2. Seven months later, Robinson returned five children to the Orphan School.

58 Plomley, *WiS*, pp. 74, 82, 96–97, 257, 745; Backhouse, *A Narrative*, p. 93; *Hobart Town Courier*, 20 February 1835, p. 2.

59 Nicholls to Montagu, 18 April 1835, in Plomley, *WiS*, p. 86. See also p. 314.

60 Stevens, '*Me Write Myself*', pp. 55, 81–82.

61 Plomley, *WiS*, journal, 25 February 1837.

62 Plomley, *WiS*, journal, 6 May 1837.

63 Plomley, *WiS*, journal, 29 December 1837.

64 For example, Plomley, *WiS*, pp. 61, 224–25, 267; Walker, *Early Tasmania*, pp. 244–45.

65 Plomley, *WiS*, pp. 84, 264.

66 Stevens, '*Me Write Myself*', p. 78.

67 Plomley, *WiS*, journal, 23 August 1836.

68 Robinson to Montagu, 8 September 1836, Arthur Papers, ML, SLNSW, vol. 28, A1771, p. 222.

69 *Colonial Times*, 20 November 1838, p. 5, referring to Robinson's address to AAPS, 19 October 1838 (*The Colonist*, 31 October 1838, p. 2).

70 Walker, *Early Tasmania*, p. 238; Darling to Arthur, 4 May 1832, in Plomley, *WiS*, journal, appendix IVa.

71 Plomley, *WiS*, pp. 73, 85.
72 Davies, 'On the Aborigines', p. 416.
73 Stevens, *'Me Write Myself'*, p. 71.
74 Plomley, *WiS*, p. 99.
75 Nicholls to Montagu, 18 April and 9 July 1835, in Plomley, *WiS*, p. 84; Robinson to Montagu, 4 July 1836, Arthur Papers, ML, SLNSW, vol. 28, A1771, pp. 208–209; Walker, *Early Tasmania*, p. 244.
76 Walker, *Early Tasmania*, p. 246.
77 Cited in Plomley, *WiS*, p. 288.
78 This point is evidenced by various anecdotes, for example, Plomley, *WiS*, journal, 21 December 1835.
79 Tongerlongeter's relationship with Darling was discussed earlier in this chapter. The mutual respect between him and Robinson is especially evident in the latter's journal for 2 July 1837.
80 Mannalargenna would likely have become Tongerlongeter's main rival, but the savvy north-east chief died just weeks after arriving on the island in October 1835.
81 Plomley, *WiS*, journal, 9 August 1836.
82 Plomley, *WiS*, journal, 16 October 1835.
83 Plomley, *WiS*, journal, 13 December 1835.
84 Plomley, *WiS*, journal, 30 July 1836.
85 Plomley, *WiS*, journal, 5–7 August 1836.
86 Plomley, *WiS*, journal, 20 and 28 December 1835, 15 July 1836; Backhouse, *A Narrative*, pp. 180–81.
87 For example, Plomley, *WiS*, journal, 6 August 1836, 21 March 1837.
88 Plomley, *WiS*, p. 98.
89 *Colonial Times*, 20 November 1838, p. 5, referring to Robinson's address to AAPS, 19 October 1838.
90 Plomley, *WiS*, journal, 6 February 1837. See also Plomley, *WiS*, p. 98.
91 Robinson to Montagu, 8 September 1836, Arthur Papers, ML, SLNSW, vol. 28, A1771, pp. 224–25.
92 Plomley, *WiS*, journal, 6 February 1837.
93 Plomley, *WiS*, journal, 2 February 1837.
94 Robinson to Montagu, 8 September 1836, Arthur Papers, ML, SLNSW, vol. 28, A1771, pp. 225–26.
95 Plomley, *WiS*, journal, 8 February 1837. See also p. 692.

Chapter 14: 'Till all the black men are dead'
1 Plomley, *WiS*, journal, 21 March 1837. See also journal, 17 November 1837, 25 May 1838.
2 Brimfield, 'Reconciling the conundrum'.
3 Plomley, *WiS*, p. 75; Brimfield, 'Mystical beliefs', p. 43.
4 Clements, 'Frontier conflict', p. 327.
5 *Colonial Times*, 27 July 1827, p. 3.
6 Clements, 'Frontier conflict', appendix 3.

7   Plomley, *FM*, journal, 7 and 16 May 1832.

8   Plomley, *WiS*, p. 75.

9   Reynolds, *Fate of a Free People*, pp. 187–88.

10   Calder, 'Levée, line and martial law', p. 237. Bleeding met with less resistance than it otherwise might have, because Tasmanians used a similar technique themselves (Plomley, *FM*, journal, 27 May 1829; Walker, *Early Tasmania*, p. 244).

11   Plomley, *WiS*, pp. 878–81; Stevens, *'Me Write Myself'*, p. 72. In Robinson's report of July 1836 (*WiS*, p. 644), he claimed that around 250 Aborigines had been brought to the settlement, of whom around 120 had died, but even including the twenty or so who died in transport, this was exaggerated.

12   For example, Plomley, *FM*, journal, 27 May 1829, 3 December 1830; Robinson to Arthur, 15 April 1829, in *FM*, p. 58.

13   Plomley, *FM*, journal, 27 May 1829.

14   Plomley, *WiS*, p. 75.

15   Plomley, *FM*, journal, 6 August 1833. See also journal, 31 August 1831.

16   Plomley, *WiS*, journal, 4 November 1837.

17   Plomley, *WiS*, journal, 20 October 1837. See also journal, 28 October 1837.

18   Plomley, *WiS*, journal, 18 February 1836.

19   Plomley, *WiS*, journal, 4 November 1837.

20   Plomley, *FM*, journal, 29 June 1834.

21   Plomley, *WiS*, journal, 12 October 1836.

22   Walsh to Robinson, 28 July 1838, in Plomley, *WiS*, p. 569.

23   Backhouse, *A Narrative*, pp. 104–105.

24   Backhouse's journal, 12 October 1832, in Plomley, *WiS*, p. 229.

25   Backhouse, *A Narrative*, p. 93; Walker, Backhouse & Tylor, *Life and Labours*, p. 108; Plomley, *FM*, journal, 10 August 1832; Roth, *Aborigines of Tasmania*, p. 62.

26   For example, Walker, *Early Tasmania*, pp. 245–46; Darling to Arthur, 4 May 1832, in Plomley, *WiS*, appendix IVa; Plomley, *WiS*, pp. 227–28.

27   For example, Plomley, *FM*, journal, 23 August 1830; Plomley, *WiS*, journal, 19 June 1837; Plomley, *Jorgenson*, p. 72; Walker, *Early Tasmania*, pp. 245–46.

28   Davies, 'On the Aborigines', p. 419.

29   Robinson to Montagu, 4 July 1836, Arthur Papers, ML, SLNSW, vol. 28, A1771, p. 210; Backhouse's journal, 30 October 1832, in Plomley, *WiS*, pp. 240–41; West, *History of Tasmania*, vol. II, p. 74.

30   Emmett, 'Reminiscences', p. 8.

31   *Launceston Examiner*, 2 October 1847, pp. 4–5.

32   Nicholls to Montagu, 9 July 1835, in Plomley, *WiS*, p. 85.

33   Stevens, *'Me Write Myself'*, pp. xiv, xlii.

34   Plomley, *WiS*, journal, 13 October 1835.

35   Darling to Arthur, 24 June 1834, in Plomley, *WiS*, p. 1001. This
     prediction was proved correct when the repatriation of the last forty-
     seven exiles was announced in 1847. The move to resettle the ageing
     remnant on the Tasmanian mainland rekindled decades-old fears. A
     public meeting attracting 200 angry citizens condemned the decision as
     a serious threat to public safety (*Launceston Examiner*, 2 October 1847,
     pp. 4–5).
36   *Tasmanian Tribune*, 9 May 1876, p. 3.
37   Plomley, *WiS*, journal, 3 October 1837.
38   Nicholls to Montagu, 9 July 1835, in Plomley, *WiS*, p. 85.
39   Calder, *Some Account*, p. 23.
40   Plomley, *WiS*, journal, 22 June 1837.
41   Robinson to Montagu, report July 1838, in Plomley, *WiS*, pp. 747–48.
     See also Robinson to Montagu, 4 July 1836, Arthur Papers, ML,
     SLNSW, vol. 28, A1771, pp. 210–11.
42   Robinson pushed repeatedly for the removal of the Tasmanians from
     Flinders Island, even offering his own farm (Plomley, *WiS*, journal,
     11 December 1838).
43   Plomley, *WiS*, journal, 21 December 1835.
44   Robinson to Montagu, 24 June 1837, Robinson letterbook, ML,
     SLNSW, A7044, pp. 218–327.
45   Plomley, *WiS*, journal, 16 August 1836.
46   C Gamboz, 'Australian Indigenous petitions: emergence and negotiations
     of Indigenous authorship and writings', PhD thesis, School of Arts and
     Media, University of New South Wales, 2012, p. 72. The petition failed,
     though the following year, when he took up the position of chief protector
     of Aborigines at Port Phillip, Robinson managed against orders to take
     fifteen Tasmanians with him.
47   Stevens, *'Me Write Myself'*, p. 72.
48   B Attwood & B Markus, *The Struggle for Aboriginal Rights: A
     Documentary History*, Allen & Unwin, Sydney, 1999, pp. 38–39.
49   Austin to Robinson, 21 June 1837, in Plomley, *WiS*, pp. 928–29.
50   Plomley, *WiS*, journal, 20 June 1837.
51   Austin to Robinson, 21 June 1837, in Plomley, *WiS*, pp. 928–29.
52   Austin to Robinson, 21 June 1837, in Plomley, *WiS*, pp. 928–29.
53   Plomley, *WiS*, journal, 20 June 1837.
54   Austin to Robinson, 21 June 1837, in Plomley, *WiS*, pp. 928–29.
55   Austin to Robinson, 21 June 1837, in Plomley, *WiS*, pp. 928–29;
     Watson, Orthopaedic surgeon, pers. comm. Other possibilities include
     appendicitis or cholecystitis (inflammation of the gall bladder).
56   Robinson to Allen, 22 June 1837, in Plomley, *WiS*, pp. 697–98.
57   Plomley, *WiS*, journal, 22 June 1837.
58   Robinson to Allen, 22 June 1837, in Plomley, *WiS*, pp. 697–98.
59   Plomley, *WiS*, p. 697.
60   Backhouse, *A Narrative*, pp. 180–81.

61   Plomley, *WiS*, p. 705.
62   Plomley, *WiS*, p. 729.
63   Plomley, *WiS*, journal, 22 June 1837. Robinson later revealed that he spoke to only two Aboriginal men about who should succeed Tongerlongeter (journal, 2 July 1837).
64   Plomley, *WiS*, journal, 2 and 17 July 1837.
65   Stevens, *'Me Write Myself'*, p. 222.
66   Milligan, 'On the dialects', pp. 239–82. Davies ('On the Aborigines', p. 411) refers to a song that must be the same one (albeit transcribed quite differently). He didn't know who its subject was, but he attributes it to the Ben Lomond Tribe.

Conclusion: 'A brave and patriotic people'

1   Bonwick, *Last of the Tasmanians*, p. 228.
2   Calder, *Some Account*, p. 62.
3   B Brimfield, 'The 47 at Putalina', unpublished manuscript, 2019.
4   Clements, 'Frontier conflict', pp. 324–25.
5   Calder, *Some Account*, pp. 8, 73.
6   Calder, *Some Account*, p. 73.
7   Reynolds, *Fate of a Free People*, pp. 203–206.
8   Calder, *Some Account*, p. 8.
9   Arthur to Goderich, 7 January 1832, TAHO, CO280/33.
10   J Connor, 'British frontier warfare logistics and the "Black Line", Van Diemen's Land (Tasmania), 1830', *War in History*, 2002, vol. 9, no. 2, pp. 143–58.
11   Australian War Memorial, 'Australians at War', n.d., <awm.gov.au/articles/atwar>, accessed 22 March 2020.
12   C Buxton (ed.), *Memoirs of Sir Thomas Fowell Buxton*, John Murray, London, 1848, p. 360.
13   *British Parliamentary Papers*, 1836, vol. 7, no. 538, p. 680.
14   *British Parliamentary Papers*, 1836, vol. 7, no. 538, p. 516.
15   *The Colonist*, 17 October 1838.
16   Aborigines' Protection Society, *Fifth Annual Report*, London, 1842, p. 120.
17   Aborigines' Protection Society, *Fifth Annual Report*, p. 24.
18   Arthur to Goderich, 7 January 1832, TAHO, CO280/33.
19   Cited in H Reynolds, *The Law of the Land*, 3rd edn, Penguin, Melbourne, 2003, p. 121.
20   Cited in Reynolds, *Law of the Land*, p. 136.
21   Arthur to Glenelg, 22 July 1837, TAHO, CO290/84.
22   Cited in Bonwick, *Last of the Tasmanians*, p. 329.
23   CJ Napier, *Colonisation, Particularly in South Australia*, T & W Boone, London, 1835, p. 94. Italics in original.
24   Darling to Burnett, 20 February 1833, in Plomley, *WiS*, p. 999; Darling to Arthur, 4 May 1832, Arthur Papers, ML, SLNSW, vol. 28, A2188/A1771, p. 108. Italics in original.

25   Robertson to Lascelles, 17 November 1828, TAHO, CSO1/331, p. 175.

26   *Launceston Advertiser*, 24 September 1831, p. 299.

Afterword

1   JE Calder, 'Some account of the country between Lake St Clair and Macquarie Harbour', *Tasmanian Journal of Natural Science*, 1849, vol. 3, pp. 419–20. Our italics.

2   Clements, *The Black War*, pp. 180–89.

3   William Lanney was one of the last six Aborigines to be removed from the Tasmanian mainland in 1842. He was probably thirteen at the time. Years later, when Lanney had his photo taken, the photographer wrote on the print that he had been born to the 'Coal Valley Tribe', which is in Oyster Bay territory. See 'Aborigines of Tasmania, William Lanney, Coal River Tribe, 26 years; Lallah Rookh, or Truganini (Seaweed), female, Bruni Island Tribe, 65 years', NLA, PIC/7990 LOC Drawer A52; S Petrow, 'The last man: the mutilation of William Lanne [sic] in 1869 and its aftermath', *Aboriginal History*, 1997, vol. 21, p. 93.

4   Plomley, *WiS*, journal, 28 October 1837. See also journal, 6, 17, 18 and 20 October 1837.

5   Plomley, *WiS*, journal, 4 November 1837.

6   There seem to have been three 'full-descent' Tasmanian women who outlived Truganini on Kangaroo Island, South Australia, where they had been taken by sealers. The last of them died in 1888, twelve years after Truganini. See NB Tindale, *Tasmanian Aborigines on Kangaroo Island South Australia*, South Australian Museum, Adelaide, 1937.

7   Australian Bureau of Statistics, 'Quick stats', 2016, <quickstats. censusdata.abs.gov.au/census_services/getproduct/census/2016/ quickstat/6?opendocument>, accessed 12 August 2020. Some of this number will of course be Aborigines who have travelled to Tasmania from elsewhere.

Index

abduction *see also* rescue of abducted
  Aboriginal women
  of Aboriginal children 89, 173,
    192, 196–97, 214
  of Aboriginal women 67,
    72–73, 83–84, 113–14, 176,
    177, 192–93, 197, 214, 229,
    320n53, 336n6
Aboriginal beliefs 59–65, 164, 169,
  173, 181, 215
  about death 64–65, 77–79,
    230–31, 250–52, 262
Aborigines Committee 41, 43, 50, 82,
  89, 134, 153–54, 155, 163, 311n12
Aboriginal police 244–45
Adventure Bay, Tas 28
Amos, Adam 119
Anstey, Thomas 208–209
Anzac Day 4, 279
Arthur, Governor George 7–8, 13,
  17–20, 105–106, 123, 125, 179,
  204, 206–207, 209, 210, 212–13,
  222, 224–25, 226–27, 228, 231,
  234, 235, 237, 254, 259, 268,
  270–71, 272, 275–77, 278
Arthur, Thomas 205–206
Arthur, Walter George 79
Australian War Memorial 280
Ayton, Corporal Robert 167

Backhouse, James 64, 65, 78, 84, 173,
  195, 232, 234–35, 251–52, 253,
  263, 272–73
Badger Corner, Tas 245
Banks, Sir Joseph 40

Bashan Plains, Tas 157
Bass, George 35–36
Bass Strait 83, 84, 85, 193, 213,
  222–23, 229, 231, 267, 283, 288,
  299n84, 320n53
Bathurst, Henry 7
Bathurst, NSW 6–7
Batman, John 193–94
Baudin expedition 24–25, 28–33,
  294n4
Baudin, Nicolas 23, 28, 30, 32, 294n4
Bedford, Rev. William 106
Ben Lomond, Tas 192, 193, 235, 253
Ben Lomond tribe *see also* Rolepa
  235, 335n66
Big River nation *see also* Oyster Bay
  – Big River nations viii, xi, 3, 38,
    39, 67, 98, 109, 113, 144, 148, 150,
    166, 169, 177, 179, 187–90, 193,
    198, 199, 202, 208, 212, 213–14,
    215, 218, 219–20, 224, 228, 230,
    234
  bands 42, 55, 56, 71, 84, 88, 91,
    107, 116–17, 126, 133, 148,
    158, 160, 169
  chief *see also* Montpelliatta 126,
    127, 144–45, 198–99, 224,
    fig. 3
  territory xi, 96, 101–102, 112,
    115, 186, 192
  war parties 126–27, 134, 137,
    138–39, 142–43, 146, 149,
    150, 158
Birch, Sarah 95–96, 101, 103–104,
  123, 125, 203–204

Birch, Thomas 94–95, 96, 101, 103, 125
Black Jack 104, 106–107, 307n67
Black Kit 125–26
Black Line 14, 16, 179, 182, 200, 201, 211–12, 214, 216–17, 219, 227–28, 268, 271, 326n26, *fig.* 10
Black Lives Matter movement 1–2
Black Marsh, Tas 181, *fig.* 11
Black Tom *see also* Kickertopoller 93, 95, 102–103, 109, 120, 123–25, 203–204, 207–208
Blackman Bay, Tas 25, *fig.* 11
Bligh, William 28
Bock, Thomas 21
Boer War 280
Bonwick, James 91, 97, 172, 226, 229, 266
Bothwell, Tas 131, 143, 150, 181
Bowen, Lieutenant John 34, 36, 38, *fig.* 9
British Aborigines' Protection Society 275
Brown, John 82, 85
Bruny Island, Tas 28, 30, 66, 72, 78, 139, 190, 195, 248, 250, 288, 326n20
Burnie, Tas 249
bushrangers 14, 81–82, 97, 271
Buxton, Thomas 117–19, 272–73, 274

Calder, James Erskine 15–16, 20, 73, 109, 147, 255, 266, 268, 269, 270, 271, 279, 283–84, 286–87
Caley, George 40
Campbell Town, Tas 55, 212, 218, 224, *fig.* 11
Cape Portland, Tas 192
Carlton, Tas 162–63
Carlton River, Tas 159, *fig.* 11
Carrotts, James 82

Central Plateau, Tas xi, 16, 42, 55, 115, 181, 183, 186, 189, 191, 193, 199, 218, *fig.* 11
Clark, Robert 235–36, 238, 263
Clark, Thomas 143–44
Clark, William 154
Clyde River, Tas 133, 142, *fig.* 11
Coal River, Tas 88, 90, 122, 247–48
Coal Valley, Tas 23, 42–43, 45, 55, 205, 287, *fig.* 11
Colley, Thomas 307n68
Collins, Colonel David 38, 39, 40–41, 49–50
Constitution Hill, Tas 154, *fig.* 11
convicts 9–10, 14, 36, 38, 80–81, 82–83, 87, 88, 89, 96, 113–14, 120, 124, 126, 131, 140, 142, 146, 179, 227, 233, 237, 238, 245, 270, 271, 287, 302n44, 303n51
Cook, Captain James 28, 300n103
Crozet, Julien-Marie 26

D'Entrecasteaux Channel, Tas 28, 30, 33
Dairy Plains, Tas 186
Darling, William 232–33, 234–35, 250, 283, 300n26
Davies, Richard 241
death tolls *see also* population size 4, 251, 254, 281
   Aboriginal 10, 112, 247, 249, 271, *fig.* 13
   European 13, 116, 271, *fig.* 13
Deloraine, Tas 186
Demarcation Proclamation 206, 325n10
Den Hill, Tas 182–83, *fig.* 11
Derwent River, Tas 8–9, 11, 16, 20, 21, 22, 23, 32, 33, 34 35–36, 38, 39, 43, 49, 55, 87, 122, 192
Derwent Valley, Tas 38, 80, 81–82
disease 65, 108, 112, 172, 247–49, 252, 280, 281–82, 288

dogs 12, 70, 74, 81, 100, 125, 131,
140–41, 152, 158, 162–63, 168,
171, 172, 180, 181, 218, 237,
286–87
Donaldson, Captain 115
Douglas, Major Sholto 180–81
Drometehenner 175–76, 320n53
Droomteemetyer *see also* Queen
Adelaide 67, 197, 200, 201–202,
229–30, 238, 251, 259, 260, 264,
287–88
Dunalley, Tas 25

East India Company 35
Elizabeth River, Tas 121, 126–27
Emmett, Henry 253
Emu Bay, Tas 249
Evans, Douglas 162–63
executions 107–109, 119

Fawkner, John Pascoe 50
fire, Aboriginal strategic burning 42,
56–57, 228
First World War 6, 150, 271, 279,
281–82
Flinders Island, Tas *see also*
Wybalenna 19, 20, 23, 65, 78,
79, 84, 173, 175, 184, 188, 195,
227, 228, 229, 230, 231, 233, 235,
239–41, 248, 253, 254–55, 257,
258–59, 262, 266–67, 272–73,
284, 287, 288, *fig.* 6
Flinders, Matthew 35–36
Franklin River, Tas 286
French explorers 23, 24–25, 26–34,
35, 36, 294n4
Frenchmans Cap, Tas 287
Freycinet, Louis de 33
Freycinet Line 200–201, 219
Freycinet Peninsula, Tas 200, *fig.* 8
Furneaux Islands, Tas 22, 85
Furneaux, Tobias 28

Gallipoli 282
Gavin, Robin 90
Geary, Anne 137–38
Glenelg, Lord 276–77
Glover, John 21
Goodwin, James 90
Gough, Patrick 137–39
Government House, Hobart 11, 12,
13, 19, 226
Grasstree Hill, Tas 45, *fig.* 11
Great Lake 191, *fig.* 11
Great Swanport *see also* Swanport
fig. 7, *fig.* 11
Grimes, Robert 122–23
Grindstone Bay, Tas 86, 92, 98–99,
100–102, 104, 106, 110, 116, 141,
fig. 11
Guinea, John 120–21
guns 27, 30, 46, 79–80, 102–103,
135–36, 147, 155, 158–59, 283

Hamilton, Tas 113, 121, *fig.* 11
Hawkins, Lieut. 140
Hayes, John 35
The Hazards, Tas 200, *fig.* 8
Hibbens, Douglas *see* Evans, Douglas
Hobart, Tas viii, 4, 7, 10, 11, 12–13,
18, 20–22, 38, 39, 50, 79, 83, 86,
88, 90–91, 92, 94, 95, 99–100, 101,
104–105, 106, 107, 125, 129, 131,
141, 159, 198, 203, 204, 209, 210,
217, 222, 224, 239, 247, 253–54,
259, 272–73, 279, 280, 288,
303n51
Hobart Gaol 203–204
Hobart Town *see* Hobart
Hobbs, James 82
Hodgson, Edmund 96, 103
Hodgson, Sarah *see also* Birch, Sarah
123, 203–204
Hollyoak, William 98–99
Horton, Rev. William 91
Howe, Michael 97

hunting
European practices of 31, 39, 80–81, 86, 140–41
Aboriginal practices of 10, 42, 43, 44, 53, 56–58, 60–61, 63, 68–69, 96, 127, 132, 148, 171–72, 177–78, 190, 194, 212–13, 214, 232, 235, 237–38, 241, 245, 263–64, 268, 278
Huon River, Tas 73
Huon Valley, Tas 247

infanticide 196–97
intertribal alliances xi, 55–56, 145, 189–92, 264, 322n38
intertribal conflict 70–73, 190–94

Jericho, Tas 102, 123–24
Johnson, James 123–24
Jones, Samuel 245
Jordan River, Tas 156
Jorgenson, Jorgen 66, 161, 165, 191, 207–208, 222–23, 228–29

Kallerromter 61, 203
Kemp, John 86–87, 92
Kickertopoller viii, 24, 33, 93–99, 101, 102–106, 107, 109, 110, 111, 113, 115, 117, 119–26, 129, 130, 154, 160, 171, 198–99, 202, 203–11, 213–19, 221, 222, 248–49, 298n66, 312n30, 325n9, 329n14, 326n20, 326n22, 326n33
King, Governor Phillip Gidley 32, 36, 49
King's Orphan School 79, 239
King Alexander 243
King Alfred see also Purngerpar 243, 264
King Alphonso 243
King George see also Rolepa 243, 261, 264
King Tippoo 243

King William see also Tongerlongeter 238, 239, 243, 245–46, 251, 260–61, 263–64
Knopwood, Robert 39, 40–41, 81, 83

Labillardière, Jacques 52
The Lagoons, Flinders Island 231–32, 248–49
Laing, Alexander 122–23
Lake Echo, Tas 157, 216, fig. 11
Lake River, Tas 186, fig. 11
Lake St Clair, Tas 286
Lake Tiberias, Tas 150, fig. 11
Lanney, William 336n3
Laremairremener 55
Launceston, Tas 10, 15, 88, 191, 211, 240, 280
Lemon, Richard 82
Little Pine Lagoon, Tas 218, fig. 11
Little Swanport River, Tas 55, 320n2, fig. 11
Little Swan Port, Tas 140, fig. 11
Lloyd, George 50, 59–61, 69
Looerryminer 84–85
Lovely Banks, Tas 96, 103, 104, fig. 11
Luggermairrerner 71
Luttrell, Edward 94, 304n5
Lyne, John 59, 201

Mabo case 5–6
Macquarie, Governor Lachlan 94
Macquarie Harbour, Tas 101, 286, 302n44, 326n20
Macquarie River, Tas 126–27, fig. 11
Mammoa 98–99
Mannalargenna 214–15, 219–20, 300n94, 326n33, 330n42, 332n80
Māori Wars 281
Maria Island, Tas 23, 24, 28, 29, 30, 35, 83, 142, 294n4
Marion Bay, Tas 28
Marion du Fresne, Marc-Joseph 23, 26
Markaneyerlorepanener 65

martial law, declaration of 7–8, 206, 325n10
Martrolibbenner 176
Mathabelianna 85
May, Samuel 124
Mayfield Bay, Tas 117–18, *fig.* 11
McGeary, Alexander 220–21
McKay, Alexander 199
Meander Valley, Tas 116
Meehan, James 39–40
Melukehedee 72–73
Meredith, Charles 130, 305n24
Meredith, George 85–86, 100, 117, 118, 126, 156, 200, 313n43
Meredith snr, George 85, 130, 140
Meredith, Louisa 311n2
Miles Opening, Tas 183
Milligan, Joseph 65
Milton Farm, Tas *fig.* 7
Montpelliatier 17–18 *see also* Montpelliatta
Montpelliatta *see also* Muntipiliyata 127, 144–45, 146, 177, 178, 179–80, 186, 189, 199, 212, 214, 215, 216–17, 219–20, 221–23, 226, 233, 313n48, 328n72, *fig.* 5
Moore, Lieutenant William 41, 44–47, 294n4
Mountgarrett, Joseph 40–41, 42, 44, 47
Munroe, James 320n53
Muntipiliyata *see also* Montpelliatta *fig.* 3
Murray Islands, Tas 6
Musquito 97–102, 104–107, 205, 305n24

Napier, General Sir Charles 277
New Holland *see also* Port Phillip 256, 257–58, 275
New South Wales 6–7, 39–40, 44, 49, 94, 97, 100, 125, 204, 205, 274, 278, 283

New South Wales Corps 40, 44, 294n4
Newport, Ann 143–44
New Zealand 276–77, 278, 281
Nicholls, Henry 235–36, 239, 253–54, 255
Noemy 244
Norfolk Island 97
North Bay, Tas 26, 39, *fig.* 11

O'Connor, Roderick 148, 154
Oatlands, Tas 55, 114, 124, 135, 136, 150, 167, 208–209, *fig.* 11
Orielton Rivulet, Tas 122, *fig.* 11
Osborne, Mary 102–104, 136
Ouse River, Tas *see also* Big River xi, 186, 202, 322n38, *fig.* 11
Oyster Bay, Tas 55, 82, 83, 85–88, 95, 100, 104, 107, 113, 117, 119, 126, 130, 140, 141, 149, 153, 191, 192, 196, 199, 206, 305n24, 311n2, *fig.* 11
Oyster Bay nation *see also* Oyster Bay – Big River nations viii, xi, 3, 24, 25, 26, 28, 30, 34, 38, 59–60, 61, 65, 84, 88, 91, 98, 105, 107, 112–13, 126, 130, 148, 189–90, 196, 198, 200, 213–14, 224, 287
    chief *see also* Tongerlongeter 10, 224, 240, 243–44
    territory xi, 28, 32, 33, 40, 82, 96, 101–102, 145, 158, 185–86, 187, 323n47, *fig.* 12
    warriors 97, 136–37, 145, 194, 312n30
Oyster Bay – Big River
    nations viii, 8, 10, 12, 13, 35, 38, 41–42, 51, 55–56, 58, 66, 71, 84, 109, 113, 127, 133, 160, 166, 169, 177, 179, 187, 189, 193, 198, 202, 208, 212, 215, 218, 228, 230, 231–32, 234, 242, 248, 256, 264, 266–67, 322n38, 326n20, 328n53

territory 58, 112, 186, 329n12, 336n3, *fig.* 12
war parties 13, 107, 127, 146, 148, 326n33
warriors 48, 117, 134, 137, 138–39, 142, 149, 150, 158–59, 270–71, 283
Oyster Cove, Tas 259, 266–67, 288

Pallummuck 254
Parker, James 198, 199, 214
Parperermanener 202, 203, 229–31, 250–51
Parwarehetar 219, 223
Pea Jacket Point, Tas *see also* Wybalenna 232, 254–55
Pedder, John 22
Péron, François 25, 28–33
Pipers River, Tas 192, 326n26
Pitt Water, Tas 59–60, 91, 102, 159, 162, *fig.* 11
Point Nepean, Vic 85
Polare 213–14, 217–19, 221, 248–49, 326n33, 327n47
population size *see also* death tolls
Aboriginal 10, 187, 192, 196, 202, 258, 267, 274, 288–89
European 16, 87, 302n44
Poredareme *see also* Tongerlongeter 55–59, 61, 63, 67, 70, 71, 73, 75, 82, 84, 85, 86, 87, 88, 91–92, 93, 94, 96–97, 98, 100, 101, 107, 109, 110, 111, 112, 117, 119–20, 130, 151, 171, 203, 248, *fig.* 12
Port Dalrymple tribe 189–90, 218
Port Phillip, Vic 256–58
Port Sorell, Tas 198–99, 203, 214, 322n38, 327n47
Prossers Plains, Tas 192, *fig.* 11
Prosser River, Tas 55, 180, *fig.* 11
Purngerpar *see also* King Alfred 243, 264, 287–88

Queen Adelaide *see also* Droomteemetyer 238, 288

Radford, John 98–101, 106, 305n29
Rayner, John 140–42
Recherche Bay, Tas 210
rescue of abducted Aboriginal women 203, 213–14, 229, 232
Richmond, Tas 181, 205, *fig.* 11
Richmond Gaol 208
Risdon, Tas 23, 34, 36–40, 52, 59, 81, 294n4, *fig.* 9
massacre 9, 40–51
Risdon Cove, Tas
Roberts, Mary 143–44
Robertson, Gilbert 63–64, 88, 109, 130, 154, 160, 171, 187, 189–90, 205–206, 207–209, 283
Robertson snr, Gilbert 207
Robinson, George Augustus ix–x, 11, 12–13, 17, 19, 20–21, 24, 58, 62–63, 65, 66, 67, 68, 69, 71, 72, 73–74, 75, 78–80, 85–86, 96, 99, 114–15, 127–28, 134, 136, 139, 144, 152, 157, 161–62, 164, 169, 170, 172–74, 175, 176, 177, 180, 181, 184, 189, 192, 193, 195, 196, 198, 199, 202, 209, 210–21, 222–25, 226–27, 229, 230, 231, 233, 236–37, 238–41, 242, 243–45, 247–64, 286, 288, *fig.* 4, *fig.* 5
Rolepa *see also* King George 235, 244, 245, 247, 264
Rubicon River, Tas 198
Russell Falls, Tas 125, *fig.* 11
Ryan, Major Thomas 237, 263

Sandspit River, Tas 177, 179, *fig.* 11
Scott, Thomas 156, 158
sealers 82–87, 92, 113, 114, 132, 192, 196, 203, 213–14, 229, 231–32, 238, 245, 258, 267, 288, 320n53, 336n6

Second World War 271, 281–82

Select Committee on Aborigines (British Settlements) (1837) 273

Shannon River, Tas 116

Sharpe, Samuel 281

Sorell, Tas 59–60, 123, 177, 179, *fig.* 11

Sorell Plains, Tas 106

Sorell, Governor William 304n5

South Australia, Colony of 276, 278

sovereignty, Aboriginal 5–6

Stanner, WEH 3

Stanton, James 140

Stephen, Alfred 7–8

Stewart, William 84

Stoney Creek nation 189–90

Sullivans Cove, Tas 38

Surrey Hills, Tas 199

Swan Island, Tas 211–12

Swanport, Tas *see also* Great Swanport *and* Swansea 208, 215

Swansea, Tas *see also* Swanport, Tas *and* Great Swanport 117–18

Sydney, NSW 7, 32, 36, 49, 97, 125

Tamar River, Tas 8–9, 192

Tanlebonyer 85, 213–14, 221, 229, 326n33

Tasman expedition 25, 27

Tasman Peninsula, Tas 55

Tasmanian Museum and Art Gallery 2–3

Tekartee 85, 213–14

terra nullius 5

Thomas, Captain Bartholomew 198–99, 214

Tongerlongeter *see also* King William viii–x, xi, 2–3, 10, 13, 14, 17, 19, 20–21, 23, 48, 55, 56, 60, 62, 63, 64, 97–98, 110, 169, 171, 172, 173, 174, 175, 195, 196, 197, 199–200, 201–202, 203, 204–205, 207, 209, 212, 213–14, 215, 216, 217, 219, 221–22, 223–24, 248, 256, 268, 270, 272–73, 277, 287, *fig.* 1, *fig.* 2

    alliances with other tribes 189–92

    armistice (1832) 14–21, 224, 226, 266, 274, 277, *fig.* 5

    attacks by viii, 13, 107, 109, 113, 116–19, 122, 126, 130–36, 139, 146–63, 164, 177–81, 191–92, 194, 209, 212, 219

    brother 107, 307n67

    childhood and adolescence 23, 35, 45, 52–54, 57–58, 83–84, 294n4

    exile 23, 223, 226–46, 247, 248, 249, 252–53, 256, 258

    illness and death 23, 259–65

    marriages 67–68, 197

    response to arrival of first Europeans 76–78, 86, 111–12

    son's birth 203

    son's death 230, 248

    transition to adulthood 66–70, 93

    warrior chief viii, 10, 50, 74–75, 92, 98, 105, 110–12, 127–28, 129–31, 145, 146–63, 175, 224, 281, 283, 284–85

    wife's abduction 176–77

    wounding of 178–85

Tooms Lake, Tas 166–67, *fig.* 11

Truganini 288, 326n20, 336n6

Tukalunginta *see also* Tongerlongeter *fig.* 1, *fig.* 2

Turnbull, Clive 269–70

Umarrah 208, 209, 212, 214, 325n14, 326n20, 326n26, 326n33

Victoria, Colony of *see* New Holland

Victoria, Queen 258

Waitangi, Treaty of 277, 285

Walker, George 65, 68, 78, 232, 241, 242

Walpole, Edward 178–79, 194

Waterloo Point, Tas 118

Wedge, John Helder 108

Wentworth, William Charles 50

West, John 22, 58, 66, 130, 131, 166, 174, 188, 223

Western Australia, settlement in 18, 275, 278

whalers 82–83

White, Edward 41–45

Wight, Sergeant Alexander 231–32

Williams, Henry 143

Wineglass Bay, Tas 200

Woolaytoopinneyer *see* Polare

Woorrady 72–74, 78, 80, 115, 190, 326n20

Wrageowrapper 78, 164, 250

Wybalenna *see also* Flinders Island 232, 234, 236, 237, 249, 254–55, 257, 262–65, *fig.* 6

Lightning Source UK Ltd.
Milton Keynes UK
UKHW050800021122
411498UK00012B/69